# BURIAL PRACTICE
## IN
# EARLY ENGLAND

*To my parents Ron and Diana Taylor,*
*who are not ready for their obsequies yet*


And to the grave I summon all
*Inscription on a bell in Fulbourn church*

# BURIAL PRACTICE
## IN
# EARLY ENGLAND

ALISON TAYLOR

TEMPUS

First published 2001

PUBLISHED IN THE UNITED KINGDOM BY:

Tempus Publishing Ltd
The Mill, Brimscombe Port
Stroud, Gloucestershire GL5 2QG
www.tempus-publishing.com

PUBLISHED IN THE UNITED STATES OF AMERICA BY:

Tempus Publishing Inc.
2 Cumberland Street
Charleston, SC 29401
1-888-313-2665
www.arcadiapublishing.com

Tempus books are available in France and Germany
from the following addresses:

Tempus Publishing Group          Tempus Publishing Group
21 Avenue de la République        Gustav-Adolf-Straße 3
37300 Joué-lès-Tours             99084 Erfurt
FRANCE                           GERMANY

British Library Cataloguing in Publication Data.
A catalogue record for this book is available from the British Library.

ISBN 0 7524 1487 9

Typesetting and origination by Tempus Publishing.
PRINTED AND BOUND IN GREAT BRITAIN

# Contents

# List of illustrations

## Text figures

## Colour plates

# Acknowledgements

Compiling a wide-ranging work of this kind means using material from a great number of people, and I thank everyone who has helped me. I am tremendously grateful to all who have answered questions, supplied data and illustrations and whose work and ideas I have used. Most of the published sources appear in the reading list but it has not been possible to include them in the text. These include discursive works which have been invaluable for their ideas, interpretation and background material, for which I have used the books of Jon Davies (1999), E.O. James (1960), Jocelyn Toynbee (1971) and Robin Lane Fox (1986) most extensively, and also several gazetteer-style compilations, in addition to excavation reports, the best of which all carry highly informative discussion sections. Gazetteers, notably P.H.W. Bristow (1998) for prehistory, Rowan Whimster (1981) for the Iron Age, Robert Philpott (1991) for the Romans, and Audrey Meaney (1964), Helen Geake (1997) and Elizabeth O'Brien (1999) for the Anglo-Saxons, are essential sources. Particular thanks also go to Ian Stead, Martin Welch and Birthe Kyølbe-Biddle who read and removed the worst errors from the Iron Age, early Anglo-Saxon and late Anglo-Saxon chapters respectively, and to Mark Hassall who was able to answer many questions. Archaeologists who gave information in advance of publication include Bob Carr, Philip Crummy, Jonathan Last, Birthe Kyølbe-Biddle, Christopher Evans, Peter Murphy and John Newman.

Collecting illustrations is another task which needs co-operation from a great many individuals and organisations. Those who very kindly gave photographs or allowed illustrations to be used, again often in advance of publication, include Bedfordshire County Council, John Blair, British Gas Transco, the British Library, Cambridge Antiquarian Society, Cambridge University Museum of Archaeology and Anthropology, Cambridge Archaeological Unit, Cambridgeshire County Council Archaeological Field Unit, Bob Carr, Colchester Archaeological Trust, Cornwall Archaeological Unit, the Dorset Natural History and Archaeological Society, Jo Draper, English Heritage, the Haverfield Bequest, the Heritage Trust of Lincolnshire, Hertfordshire Archaeological Trust, Leg II Aug (reconstruction society), Tim Malim, the Museum of Antiquities at Newcastle upon Tyne, Museum of London Archaeology Service, the Nene Valley Research Committee (Peterborough Museum), Northumberland County Council, Oxford

Archaeological Unit, Oxford University Committee for Archaeology, the Prehistoric Society, Ben Robinson, David Sherlock, Suffolk County Council Archaeological Service, University College Oxford, Winchester Excavation Committee and Peter Woodward.

# 1 Introduction

To make the dead to live . . . is not impertinent to our profession.
*Sir Thomas Browne, 1605-82*

# Introduction

Reverence for a select number of the dead goes back to Palaeolithic times. Human ingenuity being what it is, great variety and limitless ceremony came to be attached to the simple practical task of disposing of dead bodies. For those who merited burial, whether as leaders or priests, members of a ruling family or because they belonged to a cultural group that extended the right more democratically, the trouble the bereaved might go to is truly impressive. From Neolithic tombs to Anglo-Saxon treasure to the great cathedrals built to honour saintly clerics, the monuments associated with death are often the greatest of their age. As such they consumed more resources than could be justified for an individual, but this was just the point: funerals even more than marriage have many social functions, some of them practical (consolation for the bereaved, confirmation of the heir) and some more metaphysical, such as enrolling the leader among gods to ensure fertility and good fortune for the land. At times of stress and change these functions become imperative; thus King David's care for the body of Saul, Mark Antony's hijacking of the funeral of Caesar, the extravagance of Sutton Hoo in the last throes of English paganism, and the sudden flourish of ostentatious funerary ritual immediately before and after the Romans ended the Iron Age in Britain. Religious change, which can be independent of a direct political cause, is particularly likely to be marked by radical shifts in burial practice.

Accustomed to the increasingly individualistic nature of modern funerals it is easy for us to forget that the graves and funerals of the past were rarely private. One theme of this book is how collectively burials were treated, with primary graves usually only one phase in the history of a monument. This reuse applies *within* cultures, where people may actually be joining their ancestral kin in Neolithic long barrow or parish church, and *across* historic periods, as later cultures liked to claim such kinship. The Anglo-Saxons were pre-eminent in this respect but it is a feature of many periods — Bronze Age barrows were built on Neolithic sacred sites, their own mounds were appropriated in later ages, and the Anglo-Saxons took over any monument that spoke to them of past glory. Even when we are looking at a site within a single culture we can see centuries of adaptation and reuse that confuses any archaeologist trying to reconstruct one original design.

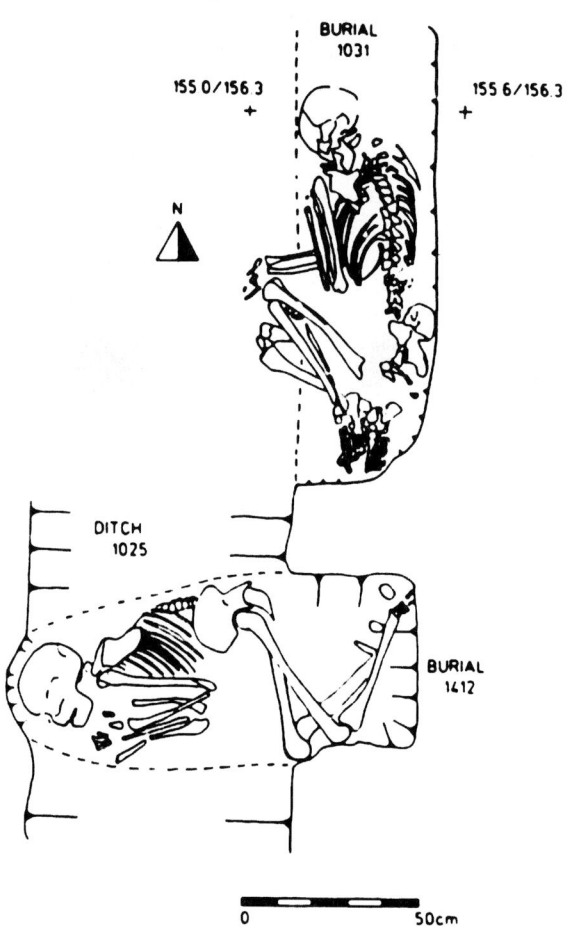

1  *These two Roman skeletons from a field ditch near Godmanchester are part of a very long tradition of burial, usually with legs bent, and hands near the face and without any grave goods. Such burials are found over much of Britain from prehistoric to post-Roman times, irrespective of dominant cultures that affected more prestigious graves. In times and places where fields were not normally ditched, burials of any kind are even harder to find.*
© Cambridge Antiquarian Society

Another contrast with modern times that is easily forgotten is that burials were not actually necessary until communities grew quite large. It was possible to place the dead in forests or in fields near settlements, where dogs, wolves, boars, birds of prey and other wild beasts would efficiently deal with them, a process easily completed by subsequent ploughing. It was not even necessary to leave the body exposed for this to happen, for shallow graves do not remain undisturbed even in a Britain that has lost its most voracious wild animals, as murder enquiries sometimes make evident. Medieval requirements to enclose graveyards to keep animals, especially pigs, from digging up bodies illustrates the ease with which this could happen. In periods when field ditches were common, such as Iron Age and Roman times, we know that it was normal to use these for burials (**1**). Sites in exceptionally undisturbed conditions demonstrate how bodies might be laid on older monuments with minimal covering, and in Roman law a body needed only a handful of earth over it to be legally counted as buried. Work on prehistoric earthworks in Yorkshire, where they had escaped ploughing and other disturbance until attracting antiquarian attentions in the nineteenth century, gives some clues as to why so many burials have not survived in normal vulnerable conditions. For example, on a Bronze Age barrow at Uncleby the bodies were laid *on top of* the mound and then covered with earth, and on an Iron Age bank and ditch at Garton the graves also were just soil over bodies laid in the hollow. In East Anglia and other arable areas not much of such sites would be ever be found today.

Grave goods are scarce with such burials. Often there is nothing at all with the occasional exception of a pot or clothes fastener. This absence of evidence is not evidence of absence, for ordinary clothing, food, drink, wooden or leather vessels, flowers and other likely offerings will leave no trace. Baskets of fruit found in waterlogged conditions with Roman burials at Les Martres-de-Veyre hint at the sort of offerings we have lost. Children in particular had shallow graves, so that even within cemeteries they were vulnerable, and cremations could be lost even more

2 *Urns to contain cremated remains are an important part of the burial tradition, especially in Bronze Age and Anglo-Saxon periods. Motifs on Anglo-Saxon pots, which use decorative techniques to aid identification of the individual within them, can be particularly attractive, such as this example from Millgate, Notts*

easily unless they were deposited in a deep pit within a ceramic or metal vessel. Other forms of burial, such as excarnation on high platforms and deposition in water, are sometimes suggested for lost corpses, but there is scant evidence for these in England and simpler explanations are more likely. It is in fact quite possible for the bodies of whole communities to 'disappear' in archaeological terms, and this is just what happens at several stages. For much of the past therefore it is misleading to talk of élite burials, for any burial deep enough to survive, with grave goods that have withstood millennia of British soil conditions, must be unusual in some way.

Groping for the meaning and significance of Thomas Browne's 'sad sepulchral vessels' (**2**) and the burials they accompany may not be impertinent but it *is* extremely difficult. Hence this book is mostly descriptive, tending to avoid the social analysis well dealt with elsewhere. However, keeping faith with the past involves trying to understand the frameworks of thought-constructs in those times. *Pace* many theoretical studies, this has to be about religion, a notoriously difficult field even with written records. In England such records are virtually absent until the very end of our period (post-AD 600) and so relevant foreign data is brought in, for this at least illuminates possibilities and guides us away from misleading modern materialism. There is also some justification for such references in the widespread and conservative nature of the great religious ideas, resulting in common themes occurring across millennia as well as across continents. Increasing acceptance that Britain actually is part of Europe and has never been cut off from this wider world perhaps makes such use of foreign sources more acceptable today than it has been in recent years.

Amongst these common themes is the close relationship between the meaning of death and the next life and seasonal myths of winter and spring. Thus death cults and fertility became linked throughout the Near East and the Mediterranean world, and a god who dies, descends to the underworld and is reborn (Osiris, Baal, Persephone/Kore, Baldr, Christ), commonly relates to both. Connected to such ideas is the rebirth of the king as a successful member of a happy and active afterlife where he will continue to safeguard the interests of his people. This lies behind widespread early burial rites, for any ruler's death was a threatening time for the kingdom, a time when it was important to placate dangerous spirits and enable the leader to journey to the next life safely and create the right impression when he or she arrived. Amongst the functions of burial therefore we can see the need to dispatch leaders of society to the gods so they can intercede on behalf of the people and land they have left. To do this there were correct procedures to be followed, later democratised to get souls in general to an afterlife where they would at least cause no harm to the living. This theme is seen explicitly in the death cult of Egypt, where increasingly elaborate rites were accorded to pharoahs because their rebirth in the kingdom of the sun god was vital to the well-being of the whole people. Social emulation soon meant that similar procedures were adopted by nobles, and these then extended in a scaled-down form to more ordinary people. This process of democratisation through emulation can be seen in the development of burial rites in many cultures, and in archaeological terms can happen so fast that it is easy to lose sight of its original rationale.

In addition to the death/fertility concepts, the god who dies and rebirth of the king, there are two notions of an afterlife which are evident in many cultures. These notions conflict with each other but both were persistent. In one, probably the earliest, the soul has its home in the tomb which is therefore a sacred place where the dead can be visited, brought food, flowers etc, and their ghostly presence (whether frightening or comforting) can be felt. In the other the spirit moves on, helped by the correct rituals, to another world which is variously placed below ground and in the sky, the sky generally being the most inviting option. Linked to these two ideas and a source of constant concern to spiritual authorities are rival attitudes to dead bodies. The dichotomy between two traditions, with corpses as sacred or polluting, was to be so insistent and cross-cultural that it is often unclear whether we are seeing foreign introductions or the re-emergence of submerged native practices, a particularly intriguing issue in early Christian times. This aspect of burial is discussed more fully in chapter 6.

When we look at these concepts in more detail we see how it is the older tradition which holds that the body itself remains sacred and can continue to be used for the benefit of society. Frequent handling of the bodies and bones of influential members of society and using them for processes of divination and other magic are aspects of this belief. It was dominant in the Neolithic, and undercurrents are detectable in Roman and above all Christian behaviour. The tradition was expressly forbidden in various biblical episodes of Jewish history, in Rome ('Collecting a dead man's bones for later burial is not allowed' — Tenth Table), and in Anglo-Saxon England, prohibitions that are generally a good indicator of what people were actually doing. Still necromancy survived as black magic, a constant popular undercurrent to later authorised religions, tellingly involving women rather than an all-male priesthood. Even Saul, who took severe actions against wizards and familiar spirits, went to the witch of Endor when he was desperate, and she conjured up for him the ghost of Samuel, treachery which led to his downfall. Hebrew prophets who inveighed against such practices are echoed in Christian England but witchcraft, the mistreatment of corpses and the power of ghosts persisted. Christianity however gave a different life to the tradition when its reverence for saintly or martyred bodies led to the cult of relics, an attitude abhorrent to respectable Roman and Jewish thought (and also controversial in the early Christian church). In this way the bones of the most venerated in society were traded throughout Europe and the eastern Mediterranean. Today, heads, individual bones and whole bodies that were transported (as gifts, purchases or theft) sometimes hundreds of miles from their origins can be visited in the greatest shrines of civilised Europe, and are still invoked for their powers of healing and for intercession on behalf of the faithful, both alive and dead. The symbolism of skulls and crossbones became a recurring motif on memorials and the illicit use of bones in pseudo-sacred ways has never quite disappeared.

The other powerful tradition was that, provided the proper rites were followed, the spirit left the body and after a journey which often involved crossing a river arrived at what, at least until the centuries shortly before Christ, was a rather dismal shadowy afterlife, usually below ground (familiar as Hades for Greeks and Romans, Sheol for the Jews). Exceptions were made for the greatest, who joined the gods and continued a life of feasting, hunting and other enjoyment, an idealised version of upper-class life on earth, and for the truly awful, who suffered everlasting physical punishment. In northern and western Europe Celtic and Nordic religions followed similar patterns but emphasised fighting as part of the promised eternal fun. Location of this afterlife in the sky led the Egyptian religion in particular to conflate beliefs associated with Osiris, god of the dead, with the sun god. Incorporation of this Sol Invictus had an important influence on succeeding mystic religions and permanently affected Christian practices thanks to early converts (including the emperor Constantine) muddling Christ and the sun god, leading to Christmas on 25 December and burials facing east, the direction of the rising sun.

From about the sixth century BC various mystery religions developed, through which it was possible for a greater number of people to achieve a meaningful afterlife through initiation ceremonies and other conditions. At the same time ethical dimensions were incorporated, living a decent life being another requirement. At this time, following Babylonian and other eastern traditions, Jewish beliefs also developed concepts of paradise for the especially worthy, and a place too for the damned, beliefs that would pass into Christianity. In Christian thought the old shadowy land between was left to the unbaptised, unburied and other restless spirits and the realms of heaven and hell were extended. Initiation through baptism was required but this was less arduous and more open to an inclusive congregation than those of the mystery religions.

In many cultures, particularly those in which the corpse and everything concerning it was believed polluting, burials were separated not only from settlements but also from religious sites and other civic activities. Specialist classes took over the practical considerations of burial, and disturbance of the body or contact with its spirit was forbidden. This attitude was strong in Roman times, though in Britain it was only really effective near towns and villas. At other times burial had a close relationship with the concept of sacred space, an area of religious ritual and also practical concerns such as law enforcement, oath-taking, unarmed negotiation, royal ceremonial and a general meeting place. Such places might be at the centre of a tribal area or on its boundaries. In either case royal, heroic or saintly burials would sanctify such a place, apparently a deliberate policy with princely burial mounds in the seventh century and no doubt at many times when our knowledge of politics is more blurred. There are problems concerned with disentangling priorities in this respect. Did a site become sacred/an accepted boundary/meeting place/trading centre because there was an important burial there, or did burial follow recognition of activities at the place? In general it seems that burial (a single grave or a cemetery) should be seen as just one of the events, though dominating the archaeological record by its permanence and ease of interpretation. It is perhaps helpful in this respect to think of cathedrals and churches: some of the earliest were sited over the graves of saintly founders or within newly dedicated cemeteries, they were compulsory burial places for almost all in the community until recent times, and some came to be treated almost as mausolea (by landed gentry in their parish church, bishops and royalty in cathedrals and other worthies in centres such as Westminster Abbey), yet we know this is only part of their significance and role. Similar models may apply to mortuary areas of the distant past.

Nor should we forget the role of burial in expressing and consoling private grief. This is easily lost when we study graves as historical processes and pathological case histories but it is a useful reminder when confused by the random nature of the detail attending burials within any cultural framework. It is sometimes claimed that people in the past felt less grief because death was so common, and this is particularly applied to children, for families are said to be large and the mortality rate high. In fact, although more children were born, overall family sizes were not normally large, and in any case it is easily observed today that parents with many children are quite as doting as those with few. We can assume an infant mortality rate of at least 30-50 per cent so the shock of child death might be less than today but individual grief, occasionally found expressed in words such as those of King David, Cicero and touching memorials on Roman gravestones,

3 *Children are under-represented in the burial records of most periods but they could be mourned in the same way as their elders. This memorial to five-year-old Marcus Cocceus, found in Old Penrith, is a life-like representation of the boy in his short tunic, holding a whip and a toy*

was quite as great. There are many child graves where lavish and personal attention is evident (**3**), and it is also worth remembering nineteenth-century England, when horrific infant mortality was common but mourning was intense.

4  *A funeral meal was an important part of the ceremony in many cultures. The Romans
   in particular included the dead in the graveside feast, providing food and drink for their
   journey to the next life whilst imagining their literal presence, as seen on this tombstone
   from Kirkby Thorpe*

Elaborate rites, of which we can see virtually nothing in the archaeological record,
must also be in our minds (**4**). In *The Iliad* Patroclus' funeral rites included cutting
hair, leading horses three times round the body, quenching the pyre with wine,
careful collection of the hero's bones whilst leaving those of the sacrifices (including
human ones), wrapping bones in a double caul of fat, raising a mound but leaving
the urn accessible for Achilles' ashes, the careful selection and felling of trees for a
funeral pyre, human and animal sacrifices, and games. In the archaeology of England
a few rare traces — eyebrow clippings in a Bronze Age urn, a rose and wreath of box
leaves in a Roman barrow, a pillow of bay leaves in a lead coffin, myrrh around the
face of a baby, burnt grain or charcoal beneath a body, flints freshly knapped into a
burial urn, slain horses, ubiquitous food and drink — can be seen to fit with funerary
activities described by Greek, Roman, biblical and Anglo-Saxon writers, but they are
the tip of a vast iceberg. Growing and cutting hair, fasting and feasting, ritual washing
and going unwashed, sexual abstinence or unusual indulgence, dancing, prayer,
wailing, self-laceration, animal and human sacrifice, destruction of property, building
new structures and memorials, eulogy, music, dancing, games, fire, water, lighting
lamps, strewing flowers and herbs, cleaning and arranging the body — these are just
some of the expected accompaniments of a good funeral, the event itself lasting for
many days and the memorial rites perhaps for years.

Sad and Sepulchral Pitchers, which have no joyful voices, silently expressing old mortality. Sir Thomas Browne (**5**)

What do survive in abundance are items that we categorise as grave goods, some incidental to the clothing or coffin of the deceased, some that were part of the ritual, some intended for use in the afterlife and some simply marks of respect, affection or prestige. These categories overlap and may never have been clear-cut — when does a brooch become jewellery rather than a clothes fastener? — but they are important for understanding the ritual.

*5 A typical Bronze Age urn and cremation*

There was general acceptance of the necessity for grave goods in the Near East, source of so much religious inspiration, and throughout the Mediterranean world. This applies even to the early Hebrews, who were taught to abhor cults of the dead and lifelike activity beyond the grave as extreme blasphemy. They, like their contemporaries, deposited food, clothing, pots and other personal objects (women with jewellery, men with weapons), including lamps and amulets, suites of artefacts standard in all this world up to late Roman times. With some Bronze Age exceptions grave goods in England were usually less generous, often just a flint flake, single pot or bronze object, until Roman influences were felt in the late Iron Age. Even clothing is not well represented in prehistoric burial, though traces of Bronze Age fabric are known and Iron Age brooches are found in some areas. Nor are items of dress common in Roman burial, with the exception of hobnails from boots given for the journey to the afterlife, the crucial stage for which we assume pots and other items representing food and drink, as well as coins placed in hands or mouth, were provided. Carefully selected joints of meat in certain graves show how specific and symbolic some requirements for the simple matter of a meal might be. Provision within rich graves for a tribal leader to preside over mass entertainment and sacrificial feasts as in life become another feature of specific tribal areas in the late Iron Age, a custom that recurs occasionally in early Roman Britain and again in the seventh century. The normal Roman tradition was a set of tableware just for personal use. Odd personal items occur in graves of every period, even in strictly

*6  Gib Hill, Arbor Low. A Bronze Age barrow on a Neolithic long barrow, part of a rich ritual landscape in Derbyshire*

Christian times. The most bizarre assortments of these appear in the seventh century as many old rules and traditions collapsed.

Like grave goods individually chosen but within the limits of one culture, other aspects of the grave can be studied for pattern and purpose. The position of the body and the direction it faced were often highly prescribed and full of meaning. Choice of clothing, shroud, coffin, bier, marker, packing and memorial are all likely to be making statements that we only dimly perceive. Today, in the early twenty-first century, we are seeing burial rituals change before our eyes as religious certainties and the infrastructure of Christian funerary arrangements fade and some of the older rites (cremation, clothed burial, flowers, small grave goods, entertainment, the eulogy) reappear, and it is a good time to be looking at how things were done in early times (**6**).

# 2  Neolithic

Abraham buried Sarah his wife in the cave of the field of Machpelah east
of Mamre (that is Hebron) in the land of Canaan. The field and the cave
that is in it were made over to Abraham as a possession for a burying place
by the Hittites.

*Genesis 24, 19-20*

# Neolithic

When Abraham was 'gathered to his people', as his death is significantly phrased, he too was buried in this cave, as were his descendants. These people were classic nomads in a friendly country, rich and owning huge flocks of sheep but no land until the exceptional purchase of a burial place was made, evidently an essential part of founding a new dynasty in a strange land around 2000 BC. The strategy worked well here, for today this tomb is still a place of pilgrimage for his descendants of three great religions, while two, Jews and Muslims, are passionate in their claims to the land Abraham could control in perpetuity simply because his family tomb was here.

Such a concept would long have been familiar in England, for megalithic tombs and long barrows were among the first monuments ever to be built here. Beginning about 4000-3500 BC, a few hundred years after agriculture began, they were memorials to the earliest pastoralists and farmers and, like agriculture and so many later innovations in religion and burial practice, they came to Britain from Europe after original inspiration (in rite though not as structures) from the Near East. Closely related forms are found over a wide area around the fringes of Europe, especially its coastal regions from Spain round to Sweden. Within this distribution there are many distinctive regional styles but common denominators are a walk-in burial chamber, usually at the east end, an elaborate façade in front of an entrance that was generally blocked, and a mound of covering earth. These features were not necessarily contemporary, and at excavated wooden sites there is even evidence that the internal features were destroyed by burning before the mound was built. Such monuments therefore were being used and adapted over centuries, construction phases at West Kennett for example being estimated at a thousand years. While in the tomb bones could be rearranged in many ways, and this rearrangement of bones, along with the elaborate and long drawn-out construction processes, are indicators that the monuments served many more religious and social purposes than the simple disposal of human remains.

The basic construction of mounds covering chambers could be varied in many ways, just the range of natural materials available to the builders forcing diversity. Thus, for example, large stone slabs are found in the long barrows of

7   *An eighteenth-century view of Kits Coty House, Kent*

western Britain, and in the east there are timber chambers. In the Cotswolds-Severn area, particularly between Bristol and Oxford, local limestone was used to build long-lived and elaborate multi-chambered trapezoidal mounds, and this prized limestone was sometimes exported to other areas, for example to West Kennet in Wiltshire. Separate small groups in Kent, best seen at Kit's Coty House (**7**) and in Dorset (**8**), used the large sarsen stones of the area to build chambers in long cairns. In Cornwall, as in Wales and Scotland, huge blocks of the local stone were balanced like houses of playing cards to build the table-like 'portal dolmens', at one stage probably covered in earthen mounds but now often standing dramatically bare, some of England's most romantic monuments (**colour plate 1**). Radiocarbon dates from recent excavations show that many of these regional styles were contemporary. Within them variation in detail at times followed local fashions and at other times was idiosyncratic. Other types of burial site now recognised in this period include flat graves, deposition in other contemporary monuments, and timber mortuary chambers, indicating the complexity and variety of ritual possible within the basic framework of secondary collective burial.

Later on in the Neolithic mounds become oval or even round and they are found over wider areas of England. In Cornwall there were round mounds in which stone was used for long tunnel-like passages, and in Yorkshire barrows covered groups of crouched inhumations buried together in large pits, sometimes with flints or pots as grave goods, an intimation of burials to come in the succeeding Bronze Age. In eastern England excavations are proving

8  *The Hell Stone at Portesham, Dorset. The remains of a stone chamber in a mound at least 30m long. Drawn in 1790, before it was misleadingly rebuilt*

several round barrows and ring-ditches to be Neolithic in origin, for example West Stow, Suffolk, where there was a crouched inhumation with a stone bead and many secondary burials. One round barrow was excavated at Orton Longueville in the valley of the Nene near Peterborough. The low mound covered a mortuary enclosure in which features included postholes, marker stones, a cairn, stone platform, metalled path and internal bank. Three inhumations and parts of several disturbed bodies accompanied by bowls were buried in the first two phases, and there were five inhumations and four pots in the slightly later Food Vessel tradition in the third (**9 & 10**). Norfolk has several oval barrows that are suspected to be Neolithic, and these occur occasionally elsewhere in this region, including counties such as Essex where there are no confirmed long barrows at all. Such oval barrows, usually with continuous ditches, sometimes found in conjunction with round barrows and Neolithic monuments such as cursuses, seem to be a specifically East Anglian type, and even the one standing long barrow in East Anglia, on Therfield Heath, has proved to have a continuous oval ditch that was earlier than the turf core of the mound.

Even amongst those accorded formal burial many would have had no standing monument. A collective grave pit with several partially disarticulated bodies was excavated at Fengate near Peterborough, and at Elton in the same area a multiple

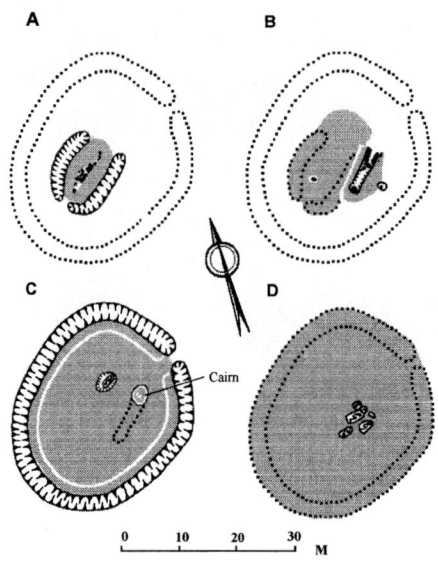

9  *Successive phases of Neolithic round barrow at Orton Longueville.* Plan by Nene Valley Research Committee, redrawn by Linda Meadows

inhumation grave contained the mixed semi-articulated bones of four adults and a child, with two Neolithic flint blades. At Flagstones, Dorchester, an enclosure was dug as a series of pits in the late fourth/ early third millennium, into which were placed child inhumations and an adult cremation. Other pits contained slabs of sarsen, and similar stones were used to cover graves in this and in later periods, suggesting there was perhaps originally a stone monument here in the tradition seen at nearby sites such as the Hell Stone (**8**) and the Grey Mare and her Colts at Long Bredy. The chalk of enclosure ditch walls here were engraved with patterns made with antler picks.

Burials, which are often though not always fragmentary, are common on public monuments of the Neolithic, especially causewayed camps. Hambledon Hill, Dorset, where the remains of over 70 bodies have been excavated, was one ritual site where the dead were left exposed. At Haddenham, Cambridgeshire, there were human remains along with other special deposits in the ditches of a causewayed camp near to an excavated long barrow. Sometimes these are in graves within the enclosure ditches, others being just deposited in the ditch. Quite a few are accompanied by grave goods. At Whitehawk, Sussex, for example, a woman and her newborn child had perforated chalk lumps, two fossils and an ox bone. Although it is never possible to be certain, in many cases it seems likely that the burials were sacrificial rather than natural deaths. A curled up child in a posthole at Whitehawk is one such possibility, as are children at Windmill Hill who were placed in the camp ditch in exactly the same way as young animals. There was also one complete male skeleton, apparently with his feet bound, who had been left to decay before his grave was filled in and covered with the camp bank. The sites of cursuses too attracted Neolithic and Bronze Age burials, and fragments of bone are sometimes found in their ditches.

Less common, but not rare in the few areas where natural sites were available, was the use of caves for burial. About 70 such cave sites are known, comprising some 256 Neolithic burials, only recently recognised after a programme of

*10 One of the Neolithic graves at Orton Longueville in which the structure of the coffin is preserved as iron-pan.* © Nene Valley Research Committee

radiocarbon dating. All are in limestone areas where suitable sites occur naturally, and there is no evidence for deliberate enlargement or refashioning, as found for example in the Near East. One such is Tom Tivey's Hole in Somerset where, just outside the overhang of a cave, there was a woman with a Neolithic (Windmill Hill ware) cup.

## Distribution and siting

Many early Neolithic sites were meant to be very visible, often sited high up. Surviving long barrows are usually found on chalk or limestone uplands, in southern England often clustering around causewayed camps such as Windmill Hill and Salisbury Plain in Wiltshire, the Dorset Ridgeway and Cranborne Chase. In northern England most are on the chalk wolds of Lincolnshire and Yorkshire. East Anglia has few barrows, for mounds of all periods in this arable area have normally been ploughed flat. It had been assumed the cultures here were very different but aerial photography, used to pick up the parallel or (in East Anglia) oval ditches delimiting long barrows, has redressed the balance to some extent. For example, 12 barrows in Suffolk have been recognised from the air. Other clues to the fate of the dead in this region come from the exceptional fenland site of Haddenham (below) and also from an increasing number of round barrows and ring-ditches normally assigned to the Bronze Age which are now being proved by excavation to be Neolithic in origin.

## Treatment of the dead

The deposition of groups of bones within the tombs, often with the bones from several individuals mixed, is usually thought to follow partial or complete decomposition of the bodies elsewhere. Gradations from complete inhumations to single bones can be recognised and sequences of remains were deposited over considerable periods. They were moved around in the tomb with more or less care, the living evidently free to use the dead as they wished. West Kennet included cremated bone laid over complete burials and on stone slabs, some fragmentary bodies, and bones and skulls of others laid against the back wall, showing a succession of rites. In some cases, for example at Pole's Wood, Glos, it is evident that earlier bodies were being pushed aside to make way for others, with the last being left complete and undisturbed, usually in a crouched position. It is possible that some of these undisturbed bodies were Beaker-style burials of the early Bronze Age and so not typical of the Neolithic processes, but the effect on the disposition of remains already in the tombs through rearrangement would be similar at whatever stage this took place. These effects are not unlike those seen in medieval and post-medieval crypts and ossuaria, and so it may not be necessary to invoke the elaborate and unsavoury processes of excarnation in every case where later movement of the decaying body has taken place, but rather a lengthy process of tomb-reuse.

Deposits include disturbed heaps of bone, whole bodies, and bones rearranged and sorted in various ways, with many of them missing. A few examples illustrate the variety of ways they could be arranged. At Chippenham, Wilts, seven skulls had the wrong jaws, while the long bones of several individuals were placed side by side. Later burials were still articulated, the last in a crouched position with a flint flake. At Fussell's Lodge, Wilts, too, nearly 60 disarticulated bodies were heaped together under a common structure, their bones sorted so that skulls and long bones could be arranged separately. They had apparently been thus placed at the same time as the final burial, a crouched young man just inside the enclosure entrance, took place. At Chute, Wilts, an oval barrow had a circle of skulls in its centre, with bundles of long bones within the ring. North Marden, Sussex, another oval barrow, had no burials under the mound but there were deliberate deposits of disarticulated bone, charcoal and pots in the surrounding ditch where decorated chalk blocks also occurred. Within a wooden mortuary house at Wayland's Smithy, some bodies were still articulated but some were moved after they had disintegrated. Sometimes bones were moved about when part-decayed but still with some ligaments in place. At Ascott under Wychwood bodies were interred whole but bits were later removed,

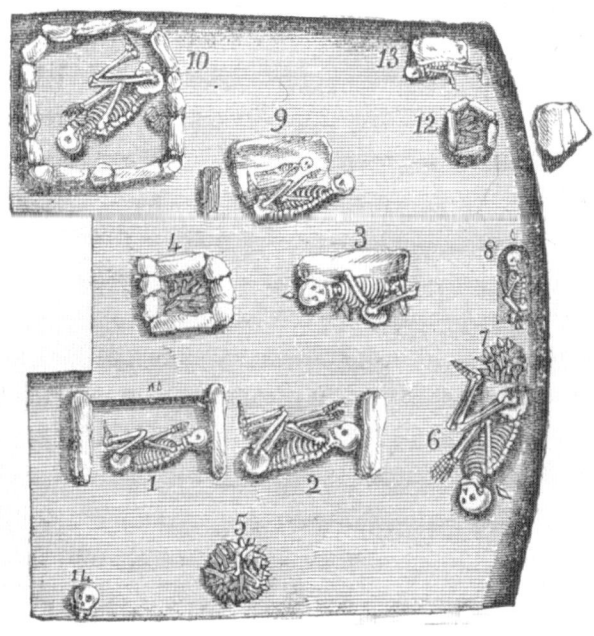

*11 Crouched burials, some in cist-like graves, and cremations at Swinscoe, Yorks (burial 4 is a pig)*

and some disarticulated skeletons were missing only their hands and feet, indicating removal after decay had begun and the extremities had dropped off. At Hazleton, Glos, a long cairn with two chambers had successions of heaped up bones, a few still articulated. Most long bones seem to have been removed for some purpose elsewhere. Skulls were placed in groups around the edge of the chambers. A new style of burial developed towards the end of the period, still collective but with some corpses cremated and others buried complete, as seen beneath an 'elliptical' barrow at Swinscoe, Yorks (**11**).

## Grave goods

Many of the burials had some sort of grave goods, usually personal items or animal parts. These were rarely valuable, might often be broken, and cannot always (for example in the case of flint flakes, pot sherds and animal bones) be distinguished from domestic rubbish. Artefacts include items both of use and of ornament. Useful items are most commonly pots or sherds, flint flakes, and tools such as knives, scrapers, arrowheads, axes and whetstones. Jewellery is nearly always beads, which may be of bone, stone, faience, jet, shale or shell, and there are a few jet rings and other items. Odd decorative objects such as pebbles of red and white quartz and fossils have also been noticed. Animal bones are most commonly from farm animals, cattle (multiple ox skulls are often recorded), sheep or pig, but the hunt is also quite well represented, with several examples of red and roe deer. At Chippenham there was hare as well as ox, sheep and pig, and at Woodchester, Glos, a long barrow had bones of wild boar along with horse, dog and ox accompanying the remains of two men, two women and two children. Hetty Pegler's Tump, Glos, had the lower jaws of several wild boars, and a chambered tomb at Hampnett, Glos, included the jaw of a cat deposited with more than 40 bodies that were also accompanied by flints and pig, ox and sheep bones. A dog was buried with a woman in the chambered tomb at Upper Slaughter, Glos, as well as sheep and pig joints, and there were also dog bones at Nympsfield. Horse was excavated together with ox and pig in the chambered long barrow at Notgrove, Somerset, and at Handley, Dorset, there were horse bones and reindeer horn fragments as well as ox with a central inhumation in a Neolithic round barrow. Other foodstuffs to have survived more than 4000 years of decay are limpets from Winterborne St Martin, Dorset, two perforated whelks with a woman in a cist in a long barrow at Lambourn, Berks, and carbonised hazel shells with cremated bone in a ditch at Carn Brae. Arrows with bodies are sometimes the cause of death rather than a grave good. Examples include one in the throat of a man at West Kennet, three touching the pelvis at Wayland's Smithy, and one lodged in a vertebra at Fengate.

## Social and religious attitudes

These burials imply there were groups of people spread unevenly across Britain who could call upon and organise a co-operative labour force well beyond those who expected to benefit from the results, for the 5-10,000 man-hours estimated construction time for an average long barrow would probably have been beyond the resources of the people buried in them. Within those selected, all age groups and both sexes were represented, if rather unevenly, generally with too many men and too few children, though this pattern was not universal. Those buried in the tombs were presumably family groups, but maintenance and reconstructions over many centuries suggest that the appropriation of ancestors should not always be taken literally and their symbolic role as centres for community veneration perhaps meant more in the long term than family remembrance. In any case, it would have been the *processes* of construction, remodelling and consecration ceremonies that were as useful in social control and consolidation of structured tribal organisations as the actual memorials of mortal remains.

*12West Kennet in the eighteenth century, drawn by William Stukeley. In use for about a thousand years and using far more manpower than the people buried in it supplied, this barrow, like Abraham's cave, gave rights to the land in succeeding generations*

Understanding the beliefs that drove the first farmers to adopt these rites over such a wide geographical area, in landscapes where bodies could quite decently and hygienically have been left to nature to dispose of (as was probably the case for most individuals), can only be attempted in generalised terms. This understanding relates to what we know of contemporary involvement with early agriculture, and hence preoccupation with fertility and with control and division of land — a subtle but important issue in a semi-nomadic society where physical boundaries were not apparent. It was presumably these interests in land rights that developed alongside and then into veneration for ancestors and regard for descendants. Such attitudes, long to be a major feature of rural England, were surely the inspiration for the monuments and fashions of burial adopted at this time.

Clues from a region well outside our area but at a similar economic stage and with historic connections relating to the whole 'origins of agriculture' debate can be found in biblical stories relating to the burial of Abraham and his family with which this chapter opened. Abraham, newly arrived as a nomadic pastoralist in a territory of settled farmers, was offered a burial ground by the local Hittites but insisted on buying his own cave for a family mausoleum. Despite the continued nomadism of the tribe his wives and descendants were also buried there, ownership and use of the site having great significance for a people otherwise rootless. Writers of the Bible left it at that, for later official Jewish practice forbade the handling of polluting corpses and preached against the use of bones as a way of communing with the dead, foretelling the future or seeking intercession with God. However, it is evident from elsewhere in the Bible, and from customs and tradition apparent through much of Europe and the Near East, that older and extremely tenacious beliefs *did* favour

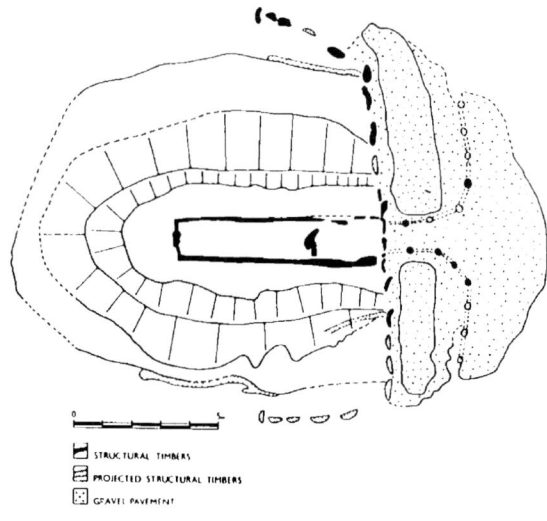

STRUCTURAL TIMBERS
PROJECTED STRUCTURAL TIMBERS
GRAVEL PAVEMENT

*13 A timber chamber within a multi-period long barrow in the Fens at Haddenham, Cambs.*
© Cambridge Archaeological Unit

using ancestral remains in just this way, and the bones of Abraham and his relations would have been handled and re-deposited with great reverence on many occasions. Bones were being treated in this way in the caves of the Near East millennia later. These long drawn-out collective rites, in which the living made use of and communed with the dead — as opposed to permanent individual burial by inhumation or cremation — are the customs we see in the archaeological record in England for most of the Neolithic period (**12**).

## Example

Excavation of the Haddenham long barrow, sited on a small rise in the Cambridgeshire fens near to a causewayed camp, showed that the mound had been covered with alluvial soils and peat until dewatering and late twentieth-century ploughing exposed its upper levels. The mortuary chamber itself, of which parts of the floor, walls and roof survived in a waterlogged state, was flat roofed and rectangular, made of huge oak planks. The chamber was enclosed in banks of clay silt and divided into two by oak posts. In front there was a free-standing façade at right angles to a chamber made of large split oak trunks set close together, and in front of this was a gravelled forecourt crossed by a horned tunnel of post and panel construction that made a false entrance. Deposits of burnt bone were earlier in date than these structures, so the site had already had a history of mortuary customs, and at a subsequent (still Neolithic) date a mound was built over the chamber, 1.2m high and 50m long, with a clay silt core, thick layer of turf, and a capping of gravel. In the inner compartment of the timber chamber were the partially articulated bones of four or five whole bodies, at least one of which was pulled about while in the process of decomposition and whose arm had cuts indicating defleshing. Complete pots were placed in the forecourt but there were very few artefacts of any sort in the burial chamber (**13 & colour plate 2**).

# 3  Bronze Age

High in the midst they heap the swelling bed
Of rising earth, memorial of the dead.
*The Iliad*, trans. Alexander Pope

# Bronze Age

The old monumental tombs were closed either formally or through disuse in the mid-third millennium BC. The new form of round barrow burial overlapped with the Neolithic and in some areas only gradually changed from the old rites, but through sheer numbers and its impact on the landscape, the adoption of barrow burial becomes a defining characteristic for more than a millennium of Bronze Age culture.

Round barrows covering single burials became the norm, built in a more modest way than the great collective monuments of the Neolithic but making up for this in their great quantity. The archetypal rite of Bronze Age warrior burial is one that is found in much of Europe from Scandinavia to Greece. Known as Beaker burials, these are classically burials with weapons, drinking and grooming equipment and dress ornaments, the body prepared for public display before cremation or inhumation. Items making up such a collection were introduced to Britain separately, culminating in a particularly rich group in south-western England, though examples occur in most areas of the country. In this pure form we see customs adopted from abroad, but alongside them more complicated relationships with earlier traditions are evident for, as seen in the previous chapter, customs of round barrows, single burials and limited grave goods had already been developing in the Neolithic period. These developments of native rites seem to be linked to a tradition known as Food Vessel burial (after the pots often found with them, cruder and wider-mouthed than beakers). They are commonly found in northern and eastern England, where the use of timber structures, grave goods limited to the simplest flint tools, the disturbance of corpses, and multiple/family burial all linger into Bronze Age times.

From about 1500 BC cremation became popular, often though not always with the collected bone placed in large and distinctive 'collared' urns. Round barrows continued to be built over these urned cremations and many more urns were inserted in older mounds. Grave goods with cremations are usually few and simple if present at all, but other offerings were probably burnt with the body. Towards the end of the millennium new mound building was abandoned and instead flat urn fields were made or the old mounds reused, the urns being generally larger and cruder than in earlier Bronze Age centuries. Soon after 1000 BC the practice of

*14 The cobbled surface of a barrow at Week Down, Isle of Wight. Bob Carr*

burial seems to disappear. At about this time weapons and other artefacts that can be envisaged as grave goods are found in rivers, lakes and fens, sometimes with wooden structures, animal bones, skulls and other human remains. One theory is that the bodies were being buried in wet areas, though human sacrifice would fit many of these instances just as well.

Burial within a mound of earth or stone has been seen as an heroic ideal in many parts of the world and at many times, though it was never again to be as popular as during the early and middle Bronze Age. Glimpses of what the full ceremony could mean can be found in poetic accounts in *The Iliad* (*c*.2000 BC) or in *Beowulf* (*c*.AD 1000), perhaps the closest we will get to understanding the honours that were given to the dead and the nature of the memorials that were intended to hold mystical powers for all time. Homer's account of the burial of Patroclus, friend of Achilles, with a magnificent cremation accompanied by sacrifices of animals and prisoners of war followed by the raising of a mound (essential even if, being in a foreign land, it had to be a modest structure) over the extinguished pyre, gives a picture of the aspirations behind the low rounded mounds in the English countryside, although the realities of deaths and mourning might be generally more mundane. Three thousand years later *Beowulf*, written down long after barrow burial was even an occasional extravaganza, informs us of magical values and the mixture of terror and treasure still ascribed to ancient mounds, values that folklore records well into the nineteenth century AD and which would have resounded strongly in the milieu of prehistory.

## The monuments

Round barrows typically occur on high ground, often described as being on false crests that were best seen from below, though recent fieldwork has shown that there are more on the middle and lower slopes. They also occurred in great profusion in river valleys though now these examples are rarely visible above ground. Clusters are found around earlier collective monuments, especially henges and cursuses, and also have a relationship to water, many being grouped near springs and the heads of valleys.

Though we now see them as at best low rounded grassy heaps, they would originally have been far more dramatic, many gleaming with white chalk or elegantly cobbled (**14**), and often revetted with timber stakes, turves or blocks of stones or chalk to give a drum-shaped profile. Other deliberate decorative effects include red sandstone over yellow clay as a mound topping at Blackdown, Somerset, red mould scattered with white chalk over a low mound of at Wimborne St Giles, Dorset, and clean gravel in the Fen landscape of Over, Cambs (**colour plate 3**). Experimental work at Overton Down has shown that, unless disturbed, barrows on chalk have only lost about 15 per cent of their height, though weathering has changed their profiles. As upstanding mounds we can now usually only see them in areas that have escaped the effects of ploughing. In much of lowland England barrows generally survive only as ring-ditches, i.e. the mound itself has been destroyed leaving only the quarry ditch that once surrounded it, perhaps with its grave if this was dug deep into the subsoil. This quarry ditch too will have disappeared from the ground surface, but its existence can be detected from the air on most light soils through variation in crop growth over its humus-rich fill, compared to the chalk or gravel of the surrounding subsoil. Natural mounds would also be utilised, and these can fool archaeologists today before excavations begin. One such natural mound at Chippenham, Cambs, was economically used for at least 11 people. They were found with beaker sherds and modest grave goods, but the jumbled bones in recut graves and the family composition they represent (one middle aged, three young and two old women; two younger men; two babies; two older children) recall Neolithic traditions (**15**). Similarly, a crouched body with a flint scraper, buried in a hollowed log within a planked mortuary structure at Feltwell, Norfolk, also belonging to the very early Bronze Age, had been inserted into a 'burnt mound' left by previous activity on the site, which at the time must have looked convincing as a memorial. The mounds themselves take various forms, the most common classified as bowl (mound with

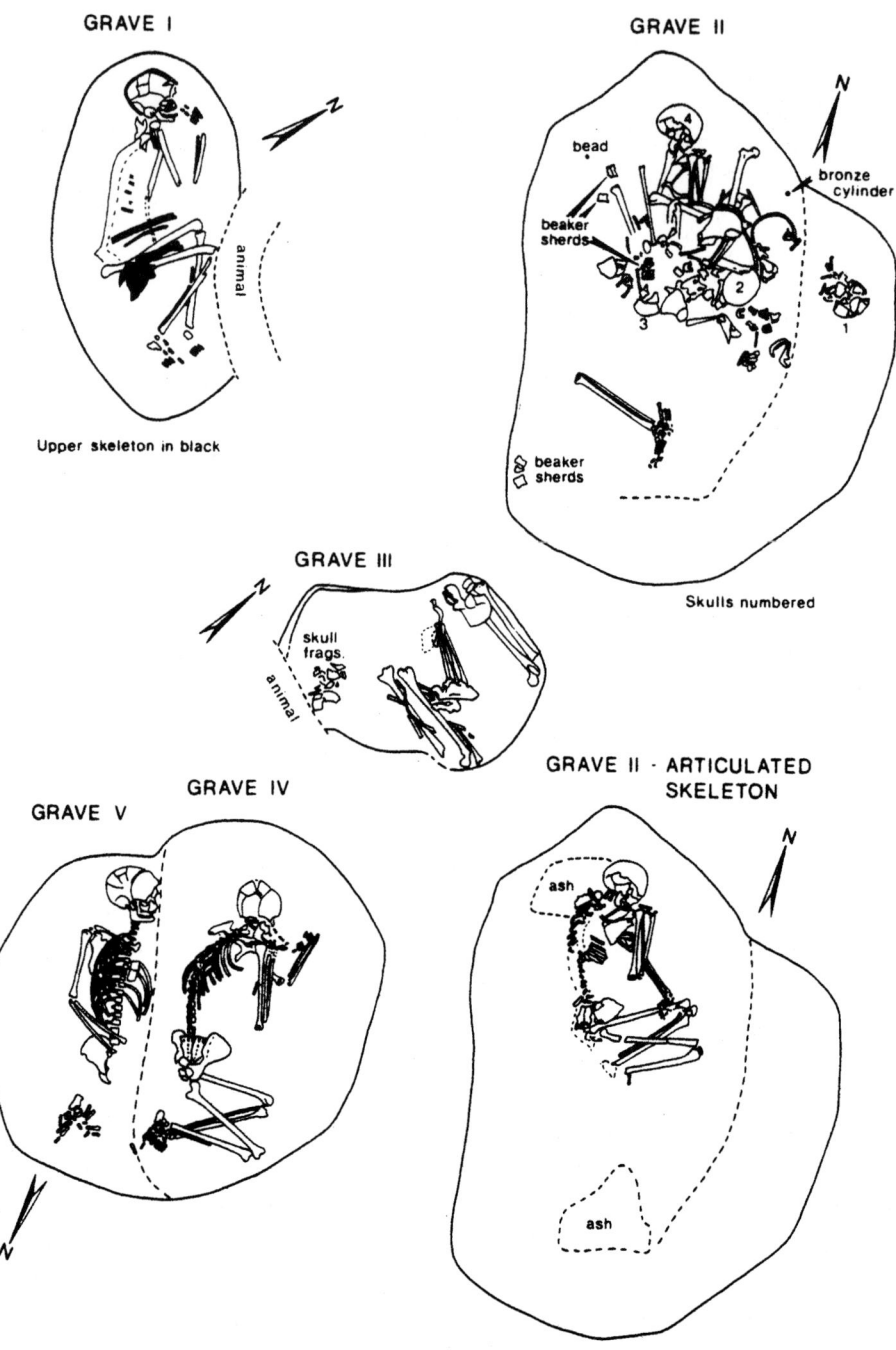

*15 Family burials beneath a natural mound at Chippenham, Cambs*
© Cambridge Antiquarian Society

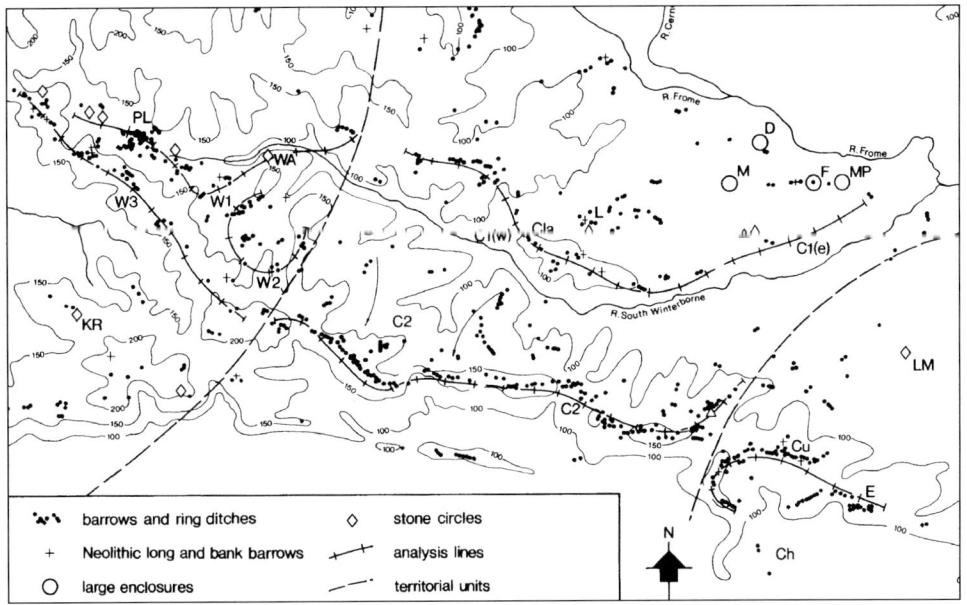

*16 Barrow cemeteries and monuments on the South Dorset Ridgeway: Maumbury (M), Dorchester (D), Flagstones (F), Mount Pleasant (MP), Clandon (Cla), Culliford (Cu), Chalbury (Ch), Little Mayne (LM), Kingston Russell (KR), Poor Lot (PL), Winterborne Abbas (WA).* © Prehistoric Society

ditch immediately around it), bell (gap between mound and ditch), disc (small mound, gap between mound and ditch, outer banks), saucer (low wide mound, outer banks), and pond (no mound, just outer banks). The range of types can sometimes be deduced even when only the ring-ditch survives.

Though a common type of monument, barrows are not to be found evenly spread in the countryside but instead have dramatic concentrations. One of the highest in the country (over 340 barrows) is on the South Dorset Ridgeway, where the barrows can be seen as a continuous cemetery though split into separate groups, all relating to the major Neolithic communal centres of Maiden Castle (a causewayed camp before taking its Iron Age form), Maumbury Rings and Mount Pleasant (both henges) (**16**). In East Anglia their distribution is related to geology, with concentrations in river valleys and on light sand and chalk soils. Upstanding barrows here are generally only found in country used for commons and sheep walks until the nineteenth century, for arable agriculture destroyed all those in more productive areas (**17**). So, though detailed work in Norfolk has concluded that there was a marked preference for poor light land, this may have had more to do with survival than site selection, and in Suffolk and Cambridgeshire standing barrows simply correlate to

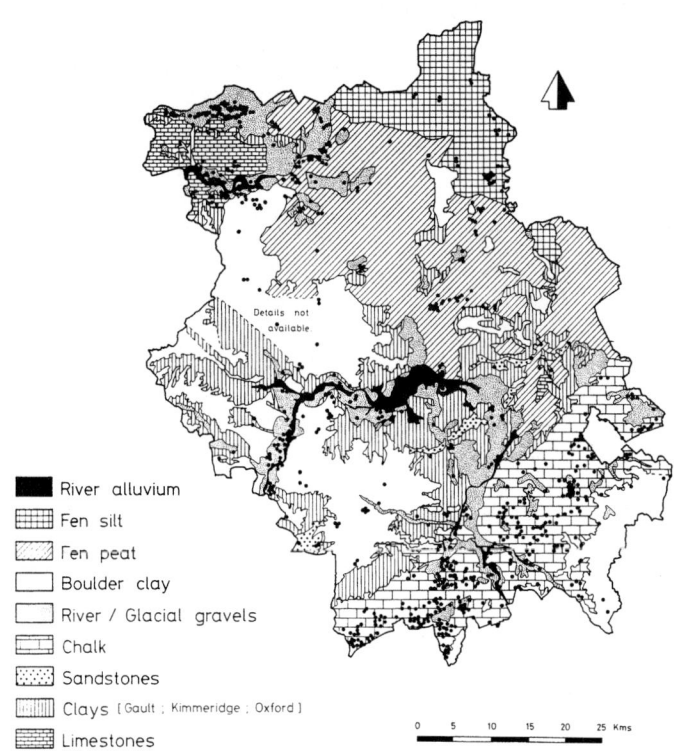

Legend:
- ■ River alluvium
- ▦ Fen silt
- ▨ Fen peat
- ☐ Boulder clay
- ☐ River / Glacial gravels
- ▦ Chalk
- ▦ Sandstones
- ▦ Clays [Gault ; Kimmeridge ; Oxford ]
- ▦ Limestones

Details not available

0  5  10  15  20  25 Kms

*17 Distribution of barrows and ring-ditches related to drift geology in Cambridgeshire*

heaths, commons and sheep walks in the last two centuries. A bias against clay soils, however, does seem to be real.

Structures within mounds show how complex these heaps of earth may be. For example, none of the four barrows excavated at Week Down, overlooking the sea high on the crest of the downs above Ventnor on the Isle of Wight, had a ditch around it, but instead were complicated multi-phase constructions made from clay, loam, gravel, turves and flint nodules. Three of the four barrows excavated here had kerbs of flint surrounding and revetting mounds of earth (**colour plate 3**), two were covered in a flint capping, and in two the mounds sealed cairns over burials. One of these, probably the earliest on the site, had a complete capping of flint nodules, a kerb round the edge and a wall of large nodules within the mound, the gap between being filled with turves. In the centre a large cairn covered a deep pit containing a beaker, jet button and toggle and a flint knife, but the body had been removed. The other three barrows all had secondary cremations in collared urns. Most had been disturbed before the excavation in 1968 but in one there was an off-centre cairn

*18 Urns from Week Down.* Bob Carr

covering a cremation in a pot from Cornwall covered with a collared urn (**18**), contemporary or perhaps even earlier than the robbed primary burial. Domestic Neolithic and Beaker period material, including the base of a pot packed around with charcoal, was quite common in and around these mounds, indicating unusual (most likely ritual) activity in the area as the site was too inhospitable for normal settlement. The mound fills also contained contemporary flint and pottery debris, some no doubt from disturbed graves and from occupations necessary for construction of the mounds and to ceremonies linked with them. The site is just one example of how apparently simple round mounds might include a variety of architectural features, only a few of which were meant for public show, and how they were formed by centuries of use and rededication. As they lack surrounding ditches and only one had a grave-pit, their very existence would probably have gone unnoticed in a lowland landscape.

What is becoming increasingly obvious is that primary burial and actual round barrow construction are only phases in the long history of these sites, and that even these two activities are not necessarily contemporary. Intensive Neolithic use, often with campfires, pits and tree clearance, is regularly noted below the mounds. Rings or horseshoe arrangements of posts or stakes, many of which can be shown to pre-date mound construction, are also very common (for example

Tallington (Lincs), Arreton Down and Week Down (Isle of Wight), Over and Whittlesey in Cambridgeshire, Roxton and Deeping St Nicholas (below)), and it may well have been these features which attracted the burials, rather than being just markers for the burials. In a few cases it has been concluded that stake circles and a later mound could exist without any primary burial at all. This was reckoned to be the case at Buckskin barrow near Basingstoke where excavation and analysis of soils and weathered animal bones proved that structures, including at a later stage the mound, were erected as a site of feasting and ceremony, only being used for 'secondary' burial in the later Bronze Age. In Cornwall, too, excavations have shown that many rituals apart from burial were associated with round barrows and cairns, and in some there were never burials at all. In any case it would often have been impracticable for mound building to happen soon after death, and at a Beaker burial in Pyecombe, Sussex, for example, there must have been a long gap between placing the body in the grave and erecting a mound, for a vole, a shrew and snails had collected in the grave, which could only occur before there was a barrow. The extraordinary wooden monument known as 'Seahenge' recently found on the Norfolk coast without any burial may be a similar sort of structure, except that it never happened to attract mortuary use.

Recent (1999-2000) excavations in Fenland locations in eastern England are now showing how these long, drawn-out processes, away from the initial regions of round barrow burial, saw the transmutation of Neolithic-style rites into Bronze Age traditions. At Whittlesey, for example, a large ring-ditch and small henge found side by side were quite similar in size, and both originated as post circles. The primary grave within the post circle of the ring-ditch was tightly crouched in a log coffin, accompanied by a late Neolithic flint knife, and only later was a Bronze Age burial placed on top of this inhumation. Another smaller barrow had the same sort of central burial in a pit, tightly curled up and with its hand near the mouth, a common Beaker posture. Between the two barrows there then developed a cremation cemetery, two shafts were dug and in the fullness of time a late Bronze Age village was attracted to the sacred area (**19**). At Over the Neolithic/Bronze Age changeover included a partial cremation within a pit on an open site, the same spot being reused for another cremation that was covered, along with several small pits made in the Neolithic tradition, with turves and a ditchless mound. After this a ditch was dug around the whole site and more turves were used to make a revetted mound. Later still the ring-ditch was made deeper and the mound was covered with clean yellow gravel, a contrast to its dark Fenland setting. Other burials on this site included a tightly crouched man with jet toggles around his chin, also noted at Deeping St Nicholas where the fabric of the shroud they fastened survived, and many cremations, some in urns and others just in pits, often marked by a post. By about 1400 BC, the last phase of burial use, agriculture came to the site, fields were laid out, and ritual became part of the settlement pattern.

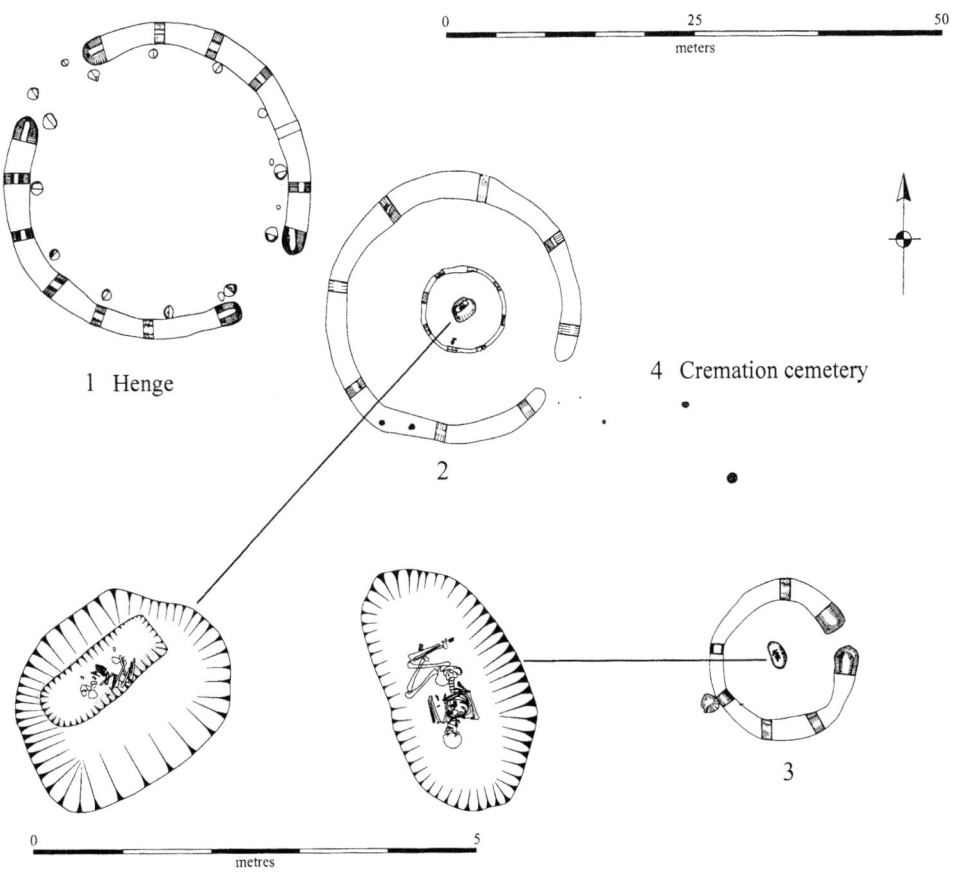

*19 Changing monuments at Whittlesey, Cambs. A small henge (1) was succeeded by a large ring-ditch (2), both of them originating as post circles. The grave within the ring-ditch was in a log coffin, with a late Neolithic flint knife. A Bronze Age burial was placed on top of this inhumation. A smaller barrow also had a central crouched burial (3). A later flat cremation cemetery and two shafts were found between the barrows (4). © Cambridge Archaeological Unit*

Frequent references to beaker sherds within mounds and grave fills imply that on more sites than are easily recognised the first use was for burial without a barrow. Roxton, Beds, was a site where a modest flat grave of this period was recognised as the foundation for a barrow cemetery and many more are coming to light. At Monkton on the Isle of Thanet a rich burial with a beaker, bronze bracelet and a necklace of 217 jet beads was the focus of a row of timber posts, and there were four other flat graves with crouched bodies and complete

*20   Ballidon Moor (Derbys) shows one sort of complication in a particularly well-preserved mound*

beakers before a substantial mortuary landscape of barrows, ring-ditches and satellite middle Bronze Age cremations developed. Similarly at Gallowtree Close, Lockington, Leics, an exceptionally rich and rare group of artefacts (two gold armlets, a long bronze dagger, a collared urn and beaker) were excavated in a pit connected with a circular palisade gully immediately *outside* a round barrow, one of a larger group of monuments. This again indicates that barrow building was only the most visible stage of religious processes linked with the proprietorial veneration of hero ancestors, and that although the link between burial and round barrow construction may be close it was not automatic.

Structural features within mounds include chalk block walls at Little Cressingham and Old Hunstanton and flint walls in Bircham, all in Norfolk, and cairns within mounds at Great Bromley and East Tilbury (Essex), Risby (Suffolk), and Balsham (Cambs). Central post-holes (for markers) are quite normal, as at Martlesham and Eriswell in Suffolk, and Mount Bures and Great Bromley, Essex. A barrow excavated at Ballidon Moor (Derbys) shows one sort of complication in a particularly well-preserved mound (**20**). The urn on the top level of this site contained part of an animal jaw, a bone pin and an arrowhead as well as cremated bone. Fully excavated sites in fact, whether barrows or ring-ditches, nearly always turn out to have more than one phase of construction and usually a mixture of burial rites. At Barnack for example there were at least 22 inhumations and a cremation, and Roxton and Deeping St Nicholas (below) are particularly good examples of complexity and multiple use.

Isolated unmarked burial sites are not uncommon in the East Anglian Fens and human remains are occasionally found on settlement sites, this becoming a more common phenomenon in the late Bronze Age. These are usually fragmentary remains mixed with domestic refuse, presaging a common feature of the Iron Age. Along with deposition in watery locations they indicate that society, now inhabiting more substantial settlements, had other ways to express group loyalty, territoriality, and honour and affection for their leaders and family.

## Wooden coffins and mortuary houses

Burials in which wooden structures survived were quite often encountered in nineteenth-century excavations when the states of preservation, if not the records, were generally better. Where independent dating is available these burials mostly belong in the early years, generally with Beaker or Food Vessel burials, but all too often good evidence is lacking. They are most common as small clusters on the Yorkshire Wolds, due to the damp conditions in that area and the energetic excavations of two antiquarians, John Mortimer and William Greenwell, who between them found over 30 examples.

Thirteen of these Yorkshire sites had substantial pits lined with wooden planks. Where grave goods were present they were of Food Vessel cultures, like the great majority of graves with timber in Yorkshire. These grave goods were mostly simple, though including some bronze earrings and a jet necklace. Another 12 of the Yorkshire sites had wooden planks below and occasionally above the body, most of these too with food vessels and stone tools. Other timber structures have a wider geographical spread but are similarly early in date. At Sutton Veny in Wiltshire a central grave containing a food vessel, dagger and miniature pot was in a coffin made of planks resting on a bier with four handles, and biers have also been found at Flempton, Suffolk, and West Meon, Hants. Coffins, usually made from hollowed tree trunks but sometimes from planks, are widely distributed, and could be used for both inhumations and cremations. Another of the inhumations at Flempton was in a coffin, probably a tree trunk, and others were excavated beneath barrows at Tallington (Lincs), Overton Hill (Wilts), Bowthorpe (Norwich), Hanging Grimston, Towthorpe and Driffield in Yorkshire, and Maiden Bower and Streatley in Bedfordshire. At Milton Lilbourne (Wilts) a hollowed-out log contained a sheet of bark covered by a cremation, and there was also a cremation in an oak

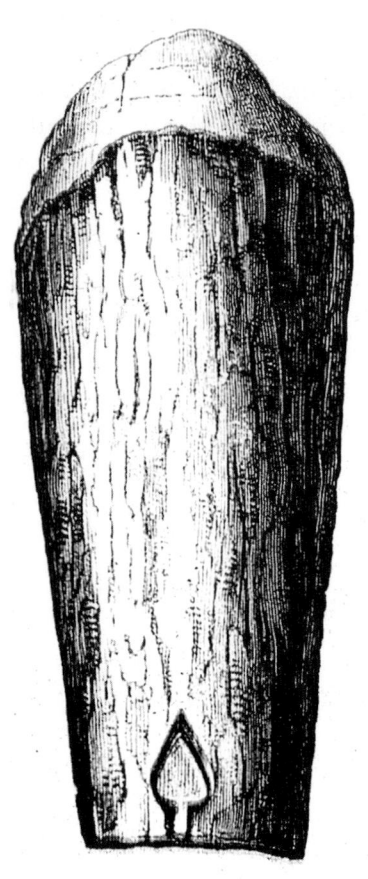 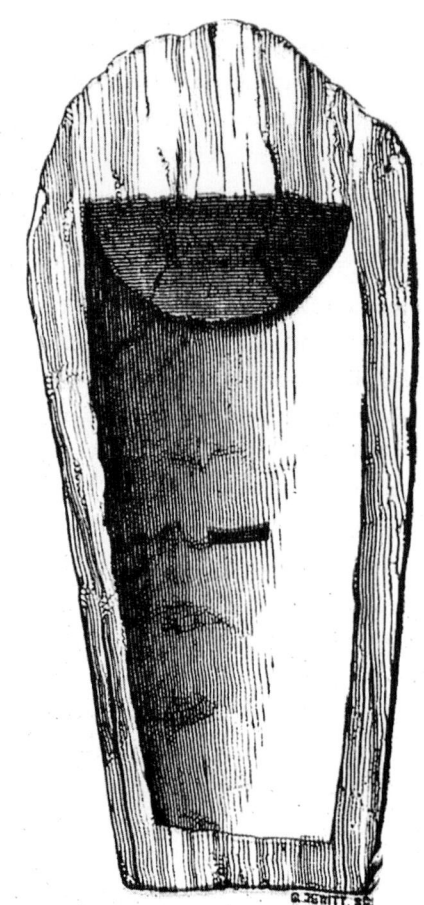

*21 A wooden coffin from Gristhorpe, Yorks, found in the nineteenth century*

coffin from Christchurch, Hants. A ring-ditch at Ravenstone (Bucks), carbon-dated to about 1810 BC, held an empty wooden coffin with red deer antler spatula, and a secondary Beaker burial on an oak plank seemed to be with a small bag holding three flints and a shale button. The coffin in a shaft grave under a bell barrow at Basingstoke appeared to be made of wickerwork. In it was a bag containing the cremation and a carved bone belt hook.

Actual mortuary houses reminiscent of Neolithic structures are rarer. An interesting one was at Calbourne, Isle of Wight, where an elaborate barrow had four burials in this sort of structure, one of these also in a wooden cist and another in a log coffin in a shaft. A second phase of this barrow involved a flint cairn and a burial in another wooden cist, and in a final phase a miniature tree trunk coffin was sunk through the mound. In nearby Hampshire there were mortuary houses at Beaulieu and Chilbolton, the latter example being a Beaker burial with two pairs of gold earrings amongst its grave goods; West Overton had one with plank sides containing a Beaker burial with a trepanned skull and a pile of leather, thought to be a folded hide. Not far away, at Fordington Farm, Dorchester, the first of five phases of barrow construction had disarticulated but carefully arranged bodies in large grave pits with timber lining, as if rearranged within a mortuary house before a mound was built.

Conditions favourable to the survival of wood in graves meant that other organic remains might be found, providing information that is rarely available for the burial ritual though the materials must originally have been commonplace. Damp conditions meant that at Gristhorpe, Yorks, not only the coffin (a small split oak) but pieces of woven woollen cloth in which the body was loosely wrapped from head to foot were recovered (21). At Scale House, also in Yorkshire, an oak tree split into two held a body 'wrapped in the skin of some animal having soft hair', and grave goods included a basket made of bark stitched with animal sinews that contained decomposed remains thought to be food, as well as objects of bone and flint and a small bronze dagger. Vegetable substances in the coffin were mixed with leaves 'supposed to be that of mistletoe'. Amesbury 85 had a bronze dagger and flint scraper packed in moss and yew leaves. In Dorset, the Kings Barrow had a body wrapped in a sewn deer skin in a hollowed trunk of oak, and two bodies in a barrow on Bincombe Hill seemed to be wrapped in cloth shrouds, one fastened with a bronze pin. A Beaker burial in a wicker coffin at Bishops Cannings included the whole head and four hooves of an ox, interpreted as an oxhide, and probable hides were noted at Amesbury and West Overton. A dagger in its sheath and wrapped in cloth was found at Collingbourne Ducis with a cremation in a wooden tree trunk chest, and a cremation in a grave lined with planks at Charlton Down, Oxon, had an awl with a wooden handle and a dagger wrapped in cloth and encased in sheets of bark. At Bishops Waltham a tree trunk coffin had pounded charcoal scattered on its floor, and then a layer of cereal stalks or leaves, while at Aylesford, Kent, a thin layer of burnt willow and a few grains of wheat lay below a skeleton in a flat grave. Traces of a bier at Site XII at Dorchester on Thames were covered with hide.

Burials in areas where suitable stone is plentiful might be in cists, part of a long tradition that occurs sporadically from Neolithic through into post-Roman times. An example found in a barrow at Hitter Hill in Derbyshire had a series of cists accompanied by food vessels and an axe hammer. In Northumberland two cists were found on the beach beneath cairns in the sand dunes at Low Hauxley, one with a crouched inhumation, the other with a cremation and both with beakers (22). On the moors of Cornwall too, where the local stone easily split into manageable slabs, stone burial cists are found, sometimes containing urned cremations.

*22 One of two cists found on the Northumberland coast beneath cairns in the sand dunes at Low Hauxley.*
© Northumberland County Council

Cremated remains too were carefully protected. In some cases the urn is inverted over them, in some another, usually smaller urn is upside down over the cremation urn, as at Roxton (below) and Week Down. An inverted urn at Radwell, Beds, had a thin dark layer beneath it as if it was covered with something organic to stop the contents falling out. At Cataclews, Cornwall, the urn was plugged with clay and granite. Coverings of stone are also quite common and wooden lids are occasionally recognised (for example at Tarrant Launceston, Dorset). Cremated bones in an urn at Balsham, Cambs, appeared to be wrapped in cloth fastened with a bronze pin. When Richard Neville excavated Mutlow Hill, Cambs, in 1850 he recorded how cremations had been wrapped in cloth before being placed in urns, described as 'a yellow gauze veil' which dissolved into powder when touched (though possibly Neville was over-inspired by Homer's 'The urn a veil of linen covered o'er'). The impression of a coarse cloth lining a hole for a cremation remained at Milston, Wilts, and there was linen cloth in an urn at Wimborne St Giles. At Tarrant Launceston a cremated child was wrapped in a bag of woven grass in an urn, at Winterborne Steepleton a cremation was in a woven birch basket, and in a mound at Barrow Hills, Radley, the cremated bones were in a bag fastened with a bronze awl on some sort of wooden tray decorated with gold foil. At West Overton two cremations were in a bag stiffened with withies, while another in an urn had been lowered into its pit in a wicker sling when still hot.

## Grave goods

Translating symbolism from grave goods beyond the obvious links with power, wealth and practical provisions is a dangerous business, though we can assume that the deposition of non-utilitarian objects like jewellery, over-sized weapons and tools, and materials such as gold, amber and jet was part of the process of demonstrating and acquiring prestige. This is at a time when the desire for access to new materials through trade, warfare, tribute, gift exchange and such-like mechanisms was driving social change, and when technological improvements (metal working and better pottery skills in particular) meant there were more novel possessions worth displaying. For a time this created the conditions for an élite which combined economic and military power with claims to moral/mystical rights, abstractions expressed potently in the grave. Soon some goods became more widely available or else changed with fickle fashion, either way losing their iconic status — though some were retained through that other great social force, tradition. Therefore, whether we explain the Bronze Age choice of grave goods as desire for prestige gained through graveside display, a statement of esteem, or as providing useful items intended for the next life, the effect was the same. Lavish and exotic grave goods following tightly prescribed rites were for the few, soon followed by more mundane provision on a wider scale, according to the broad traditions deriving from the élite but with variety in detail and room for improvisation. It is however well to remember that we are looking at about 1000 years of burial, and that Bronze Age barrows are among our most widely studied types of grave because of their ease of identification. We should therefore not be over-impressed with what might appear a surprising level of wealth and sophistication.

So we find, around 2000 BC, an impressive array of Beaker burials, defined by their grave goods of a beaker (a decorative pot apparently designed for a not-insubstantial supply of alcohol), arrows, archers' wrist guards, ornaments and small copper or bronze items, especially daggers. Within a few hundred years similar but richer graves defined what is known as the Wessex culture, though single graves of this type are found in small numbers in most areas of England.

*23 Jet necklace. Especially fine examples were found in Yorkshire, such as this elaborate concoction from Middleton Moor*

Their burials are quintessential graves of warriors and their consorts, with gold playing a noticeable part and grooming and ornament important for both sexes. Weapons are found only with men, women generally having somewhat fewer grave goods, though their necklaces are impressive. It is fair to assume that such burials were the rich and powerful, for only they would have access to the exotic items, and that obvious connections can be made between weapons and warriors, and decorative/symbolic objects and some sort of royalty.

Even though all graves within mounds should be classed as higher than normal status there was much differentiation in the grave goods deposited with them. By no means all had grave goods at all, secondaries in particular often have few if any, and most items are actually rather ordinary — flint tools, stone axes, bone points or pins. East Anglian graves are generally rather poor, with metal objects mostly restricted to bronze awls, with sometimes an axe or occasionally a dagger but a few rich Wessex-style graves do occur. In contrast, the greatest wealth, with a profusion of gold, amber, jet and weapons, is found in the counties of Wessex: at this time Cornwall seems to be included, the only period when such buried wealth occurs there.

Jewellery, occasionally with men and children but most often with women, was the excuse for some of the most dramatic displays. Perhaps the most ornamental grave goods are necklaces made of jet beads, sometimes with amber and bone. Especially fine examples were found in Yorkshire, such as an elaborate concoction from Middleton Moor ( **23**). Wessex-style grave goods in a group of ring-ditches at Radwell, Beds included a jet and amber necklace, an amber button, and a toiletry implement with a double (male and female) cremation. At Stonea, Cambs, there were amber and jet beads accompanying the central cremation of an elderly woman. One necklace at Shrewton was of lignite, amber, sea shell and incised wooden toggles, and another had faience, chalk, shale and periwinkle shell. An inhumation in a bell barrow on Snail Down (Wilts) also had a native sea shell, a perforated cockle shell lying beneath the chin together with three tiny amber beads. Knackyboy cairn on Scilly perhaps had the most exotic beads, including one of Egyptian faience dating to 1320-1200 BC, with eight blue glass beads and bronze earrings. Elsewhere rich graves could have earrings made of gold, and buttons might be of amber, jet or be covered in gold.

Pottery vessels, whether containing food, drink or the cremated bones of the deceased, are so common and follow such well-defined traditions that they are used as the defining characteristics of the cultures of the various types of grave. There is also evidence for containers made from organic materials which would have been far more common than we can now recognise, and occasionally, within the Wessex culture, small vessels were made of the most extravagant materials. Two gold cups are known from Cornwall, one from Rillaton in a cist that was a secondary burial within a mound, together with an urn, dagger and beads, the other from Linkinhorne, St Cleer, also in a secondary cist with a dagger, some ivory, and faience beads. Amber cups come from the Clandon barrow at Winterborne St Martin and from Hove, where a cremation in an oak coffin also had a battle axe, whetstone and a dagger with a bone handle.

The principal weapons in the early Bronze Age, as already noted in many graves, were daggers. The great majority were small and plain and made of bronze. On a few their sheaths and handles of bone or wood are apparent, and very occasionally they have exotic touches, most famously at the Bush Barrow near Stonehenge, where a wooden handle had a pattern made with gold pins. Though by far the commonest in south-western England these wealthy weapon-and-jewellery graves occur in most regions. Little Cressingham, Norfolk, for example, had daggers, gold ornaments and an amber necklace. Barnack near Peterborough had the classic attributes of a Beaker warrior grave, with a wrist-guard studded with gold, a dagger, bone pendant and a beaker (**colour plates 5 & 6**) even though, like other rich graves in this area, the original mound was probably no more than 1m high.

Sometimes there seem convincing indications that an individual's occupation in life is being represented by more than martial attributes. It has been noted above that bronze awls (for cloth and leather working) are the most common metal grave goods in East Anglia. Flint flakes, long thought to be a by-

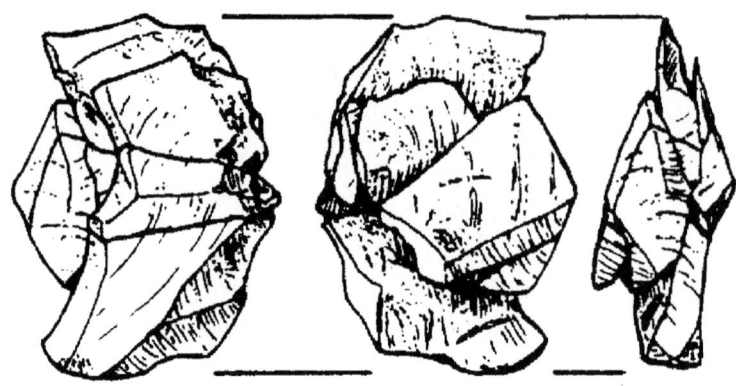

*24 Flints knapped into a woman's grave at Roxton were so fresh they could be pieced back together*

product of casual occupation perhaps associated with workers constructing the mounds, now seem a definite part of the offerings to people, both men and women, whom one might assume had special responsibility for this important aspect of life even after bronze was available. Practical attributes accompanying a mid-Bronze Age cremation at Milston, Wilts, included a whetstone, chipped flints prepared for arrows, and iron pyrites (for fire lighting). At Roxton flint flakes consisting of 10 conjoining flakes (**24**) were in the central woman's grave and there can be no doubt that part of the burial ritual involved knapping a prepared lump of flint into the top of the urn that held her cremated remains. At Chippenham, Cambs, it was also noted that flint had been knapped on the spot, for joining flakes were found in a grave-pit, and at Balsham the cremation urn held several freshly-flaked blades of imported black flint. Flint debris, regularly described as 'fresh', is commonly noted on round barrows and in material washed down into their ditches. It is usually thought that flint knappers used the mounds as convenient sitting places or that there was some other coincidence, which is no doubt often true, but the more deliberate aspect is probably present in a considerable number of cases. Other offerings were less practical. At Winterslow a cremation in a cairn was wrapped in linen and buried with an awl, a razor, amber beads and human eyebrow hair from more than one person, and a Beaker burial at West Overton had a *bos* horn core between his legs, suggested by the excavator to be a penis sheath.

Grave goods throughout the Bronze Age sometimes reveal tendencies to appreciate older values. In a Bronze Age barrow on Salisbury Plain one burial was clutching a Neolithic arrowhead, already several hundred years old. At Mildenhall,

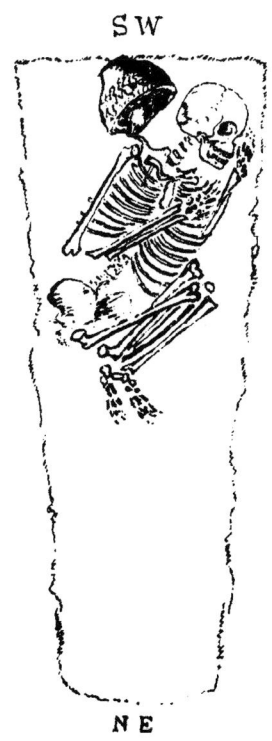

*25 At Mildenhall, Suffolk, 18 huge red deer antlers covered a woman's grave, recorded in 1874*

Suffolk, 18 huge red deer antlers covered a woman's grave (**25**), at Icklingham an inhumation had its feet resting on a deer's skull, recalling Danish mesolithic sites, and at Fovant Down there was a red deer antler in an oak coffin. Barrow 15 at Amesbury contained a man lying on a plank of elm, with stag horns at his head and feet. Polished pig's tusks are another older attribute, found for example at Roxton and Deeping St Nicholas (below), and Duggleby Howe and Liff's Low, Biggin, Yorks. At Naunton, Glos, the cremation of a woman and child in a cist within a round barrow had a layer of charcoal and decomposed animal matter mixed with a boar tusk, horse's tooth and dog's jaw.

## Relationship to earlier and later sites

It was 1000 years after Neolithic burials in a circular enclosure at Flagstones near Dorchester that a Bronze Age barrow used the same site, its central grave containing a young man under a large sarsen. The mound at Stonea sealed an intensive layer of Neolithic settlement debris, Week Down barrows were built over Neolithic pits, and at Melbourn, Cambs, a barrow was surrounded by many prehistoric pits containing flint debitage, animal bone and hazelnuts. Mounds at Roxton covered numerous earlier stake-hole features and the tools and waste products of a Neolithic industry. At Kalis Corner, Hants, a late Neolithic ritual monument was used for early Bronze Age burials, before becoming an urn cemetery, and eventually the focus for late Bronze Age burials in cairns. The same areas were used for pyres and similar techniques for pulverising bone etc were observed in different phases of use on this site. The elaborate series of burials at West Overton started with dismembered parts of a body in the late Neolithic, followed by a small then a larger mound and a cremation cemetery. Here, two free-standing sarsens were thought to be cemetery markers, a function that elsewhere perhaps belonged to less enduring indicators that nonetheless were unmistakable at the time. These are just a random selection of sites where Neolithic use for burial, industry, ritual or occupation can be spotted and it is reasonable to assume the pattern followed a common custom of reuse, itself not surprising given the frequent clustering of Bronze Age barrows around Neolithic monuments. As noted above, subsequent Bronze Age use of the mound areas for flint knapping also seems to be common.

In later periods reuse of the mounds for burial is a still better-attested feature of their history. The greatest number belong to the early Anglo-Saxon period when both rich and poor were attracted to their historical connotations and general romance, but ordinary Roman graves too are not uncommon, and there are a great number that have not been dated. On the other hand, great respect was not always shown to the mounds, especially those in river valleys where arable agriculture was practised and where it was normal to incorporate them into ploughed fields or even

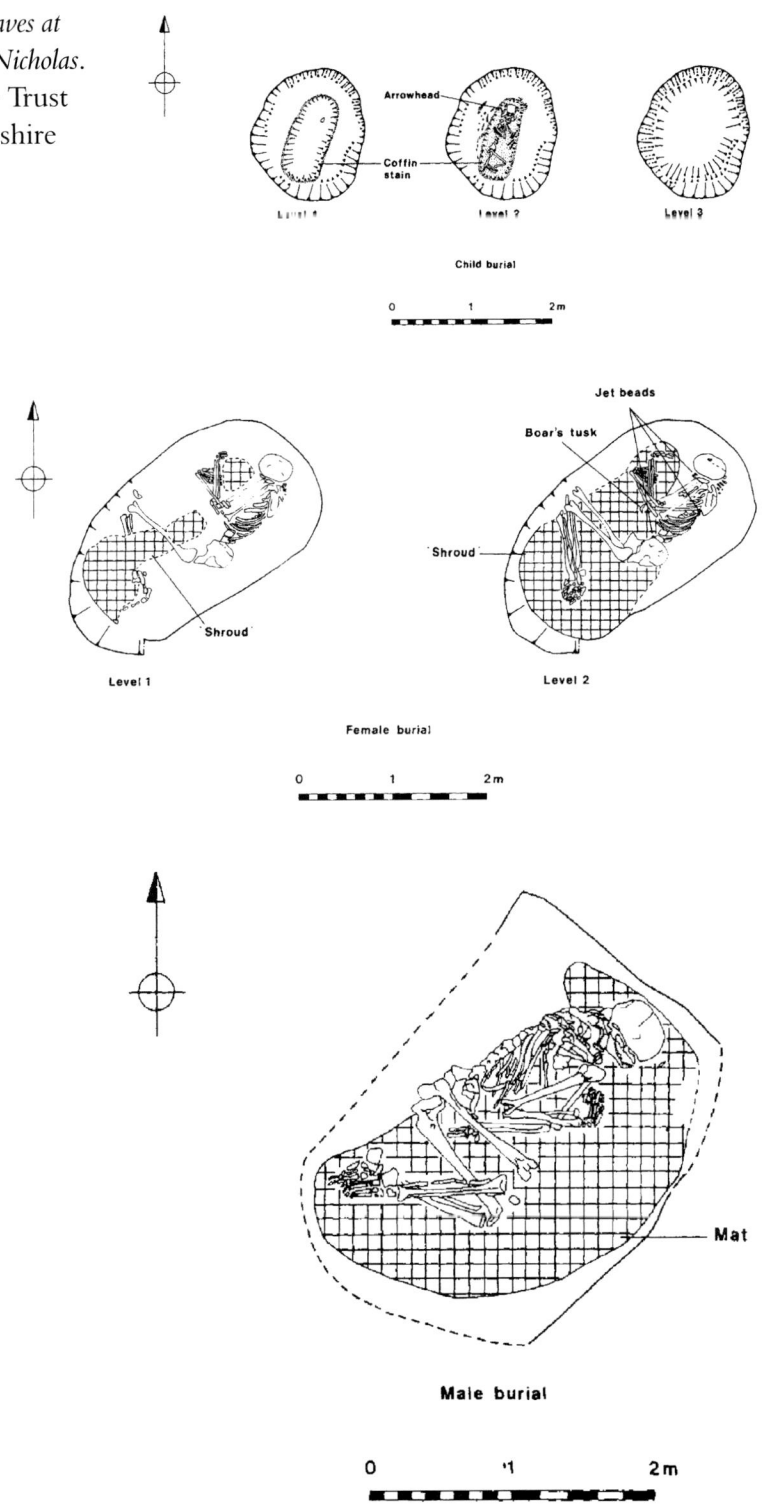

*26 A series of graves at Deeping St Nicholas. © Heritage Trust for Lincolnshire*

Arrowhead

Coffin stain

Level 1   Level 2   Level 3

Child burial

0   1   2 m

Jet beads

Boar's tusk

Shroud

Shroud

Level 1   Level 2

Female burial

0   1   2 m

Mat

Male burial

0   1   2 m

27 *Excavation in progress on one of five ring-ditches at Roxton, Beds, beside the River Ouse.* © Bedfordshire County Council

to use the raised area for a dwelling. People's response to sites of mystery was as variable as it is today.

## Examples

### *Deeping St Nicholas, Lincs* (**26**)

An example of a Bronze Age barrow where, thanks to wet conditions, preservation was good enough for the organic remains of coffins and wrappings to be identified, was excavated in Deeping St Nicholas near the edge of the Fenlands. The first burial on the site, *c*.2000 BC, was a child between three and five years old with an arrowhead, lying in a coffin made either from a hollowed log or rolled bark, the grave pit being surrounded by several concentric rings of stakes. Later, after these stakes had rotted, a barrow was constructed, its appearance soon changed by a circle of posts

*28 Cremation urn and accessory vessel from the centre of a ring-ditch at Roxton, Beds.* © Bedfordshire County Council

set in a ditch around the mound, and a woman wrapped in a shroud, with a string of jet beads and a pig's tusk, was buried in a pit. Afterwards the posts were moved and a man was placed in another pit before the circuit was closed again with smaller posts. He too had either a shroud or a mat. Later on another mound was built, this time over two cists containing cremations, with an urned cremation outside each of them, and further cremations were placed in six pits in the berm between the mound and its surrounding ditch. Oyster shells near one of the cists were probably a food offering for the deceased. These successive activities were spread over nearly three centuries, after which the site was left to be covered by deepening peat levels later in the Bronze Age. By 1000 BC the barrows would have been submerged, only reappearing in the twentieth century as the dried out peat retreated.

## Roxton, Beds (27)

Excavations at Roxton showed that sites surviving only as ring-ditches in arable fields had once been standing round barrows with as much structural variety as those found in upland zones, with bowl, saucer and bell/disc types and stone cairns all represented. This site, situated in a floodplain where the rivers Ouse and Ivel meet, is an interesting one for seeing the development of a prehistoric mortuary landscape within a workaday world.

It had already been used for a late Neolithic flint industry and several early Bronze Age post structures when a tall young man was buried in the same early Bronze Age phase without a mound but in a pit surrounded by a ring of posts, perhaps a small hut. Soon afterwards two barrows were built over urned cremations, and in the middle Bronze Age three more barrows were added. Occasional burials were incorporated in the mounds in late Bronze Age, Roman and Anglo-Saxon times and there was a Roman shrine here. There was a significant amount of flint knapping centred on the mounds during the Bronze Age, and in the Iron Age and Roman periods field systems were laid out over them and they were denuded by several seasons of ploughing.

The initial burial was accompanied only by a flint flake, but urned cremations included a woman with a bone bead, bronze awl, pig tusk, an accessory vessel (**28**) and freshly flaked flints in a central pit surrounded by a post structure. Middle Bronze Age secondaries had a pair of bone toggles, and ploughed-out late Bronze Age secondaries had long bronze pins. The mounds during these years were probably never more than about 1m high, just enough to stand above winter floodwaters. Perhaps it is not surprising that for years their sacred nature could be ignored though not really forgotten, inspiring apparently random mortuary use for more than two millennia.

# 4  Iron Age

They burn and bury their dead with the things they had owned
while they were alive.
*Pomponius Mela, first century AD*

# Iron Age

In every period a great many dead are invisible to archaeology but in the first half of the Iron Age this characteristic is taken to extremes, and in much of England non-burial remains the normal pattern in the whole of this period. The problem of what happened to the population was long considered a conundrum, especially in comparison to the Bronze Age, for even in areas where there are distinctive rites these are limited to specific times and those selective groups exposed to foreign influences. Now we are more willing to accept some apparently very casual dispositions of bones as normal burial. If there were any general native rite it would appear to be crouched inhumation in disused pits or field ditches with the grave goods limited to an occasional brooch that would have been part of normal clothing. Already in the late Bronze Age there had been less use of the ancestral dead to display power and define boundaries, and with the increase in longer-established settlements and hill forts the visibility of the dead became less important and graves ceased to be communal focal points. This situation is reversed at specific times and places for upper-class burials, most notably in middle Iron Age Yorkshire, late Iron Age Dorset and Cornwall, and parts of south-eastern England in the very late Iron Age.

Burials in casual situations, usually disused storage pits, are commonly found within hill forts and other permanent settlements. Modern excavations, notably at Danebury where there were 300 deposits of human bone including whole, incomplete, and mixed disarticulated remains, some with signs of binding or unnatural compression, showed how such human remains found their way into contexts generally described as rubbish, but which on close analysis proved to have a deliberate and even ritual character. Some mixed groups were partially decayed before burial, and others could be corpses brought in after exposure elsewhere. Single bones and disarticulated remains are sometimes explained as the results of excarnation, with exposure of bodies on special towers, though normal shallow graves in densely settled environments with plenty of hungry dogs, pigs and wild animals would lead to similar results. Innumerable other forts (such as Hod Hill, Figsbury Rings, Lidbury, Kingsdown Camp, Winklebury and Wandlebury) had human remains in rubbish pits and defensive ditches in similar conditions, as did settlements such as Gussage All Saints, Portway near Andover, Loxton in Somerset and Gravelly Guy in Oxfordshire. At Glastonbury there was

*29 A sprawled body in the ditch of a fort at Stonea, Cambs.* © Cambridgeshire County Council Archaeological Field Unit

skeletal material inside and just outside the palisaded enclosure, mostly mixed with brushwood that raised mounds for settlement above the fens. At Harston, Cambs, human burials seemed to be treated in ways directly comparable with animals in the same pits, some complete and others in various stages of disarticulation, and one with its head on an animal skull, rather like the cow skulls placed over dogs on the same site and in neighbouring Barrington.

Other burials too appear sacrificial or at least propitiatory. It was repeated discoveries of parts of bodies, especially heads, beneath hill fort ramparts or in post-holes at or near the fort entrances that led to conclusions that human sacrifice played a part in the organisation of society at this time. Examples include Bredon Hill, Glos, with an infant in a post-hole and a woman covered by flint blocks immediately before a rampart was built, Hod Hill, which had the squashed and tightly bound body of a woman in a pit covered with stone just before the bank was thrown up, and burials in different phases of rampart construction at Maiden Castle. Shrines such as Uley and Maiden Castle also have infants in features such as post-holes, where a likely explanation is a foundation or later sacrifice.

*30 Wounded bodies, one flung face down, at Wandlebury hill fort*

War cemeteries are also common in or just outside hill forts, for example at Maiden Castle, Spettisbury and Hod Hill, where mass graves included some with weapon wounds. At Maiden Castle the living were left to bury their dead in the proper local style, some with pots, joints of meat and occasional jewellery, apparently after defeat and massacres at the hands of the Romans. Sprawled bodies on hill forts such as Stonea and Wandlebury (**29, 30**) in Cambridgeshire look more like casual burials of enemy war dead. Whatever the explanations it is clear that treatment after death was for many a ruthless part of the social construct, with little room for sentiment.

In contrast are selective groups with decisively different rites. The first of these begins in the fourth century BC, but is mostly concentrated in the second. This is the Arras culture, found predominantly in Yorkshire, influenced by the Champagne area of France where similar but generally richer burials are common. This rite involved crouched inhumations, mostly in low barrows, furnished with jewellery, pots and meat, and occasional rich graves with carts and horses. A subgroup of these has extended bodies with coffins and weapons. In general, though, a crouched position with the head to the north seems significant: the same position is noted in a scatter of sites in southern England. None of the sites in these areas is directly parallel to the Yorkshire Arras type of grave but they share characteristics such as barrows, swords and other military equipment with men, and mirrors with women, luxury items and horse equipment, though not complete carts.

The coastal strip of southern Dorset was the principal area for another distinctive regional rite influenced from abroad, that of the Durotrigian tradition. This began in the late first century BC and was to continue into the Roman second century AD. In this culture there were formal cemeteries and some of the graves were lined with stones, with a common layout and alignment of body and standardised grave goods, most commonly pots and meat. Burials seem to have included most of the community, sometimes with one wealthy 'warrior' grave as at Whitcombe but the rest without obvious distinctions of wealth. Cist graves, mostly found in Cornwall and Devon, are a parallel variation found in areas with stone, beginning earlier on, in the third to second century BC and continuing to the end of the first century AD. These sites are so scarce it seems most of the population must have used different undetectable rites, though the communities represented had the expected cross-section of ages and sex.

Then, from about 50 BC in south-eastern England, comes a quite separate rite, part of a culture known as Aylesford/Swarling after two type sites excavated in Kent. This tradition saw the reintroduction of cremation along with specific sets of grave goods (mainly food and tableware), some of the graves very simple and some extremely ostentatious to reflect a stratified society, the rites closely paralleled in Europe in the area covering the middle Rhine, northern France and Belgium. Welwyn burials are rich late variants of this culture, found in deep graves, furnished with amphorae, luxury tableware and fire dogs for spit roasting (that is, items devoted to ceremonial feasting). The tradition was to carry on and become more widespread and highly developed in the early Roman period. Its distribution included a few sites in Dorset and Somerset and a denser pattern in Kent and Essex, extending up into south Cambridgeshire. Within this area various zones are recognisable, reflecting the political and trading relationships of tribal groups with each other and with the Roman world.

Side by side with imported practices a native tradition of inhumation in a crouched position without grave goods can be detected even in the areas where rich cremation graves overwhelm the archaeological record. Small numbers for example occur within the large cremation cemeteries of King Harry Lane (Verulamium) and Baldock, on sites such as Mucking near the Thames, and at Clothall Common, Herts, where more than 200 late Iron Age/Roman bodies have been excavated adjacent to the Icknield Way. Some pit burials, as at Flagstones near Dorchester, are part of a normal cemetery, simply making use of disused pits instead of digging new graves, and are best seen as one stage in the development of the Durotrigian tradition.

# Religious beliefs

Useful literary sources for the culture and religious beliefs behind Iron Age burial rites come from Irish literary traditions such as the *Táin bó Cúailnge*, or 'Cattle Raid of Cooley'. These were written down at a much later date but were never interrupted by the Roman conquest and derived from an ancient storytelling culture. It is thus possible to extrapolate data relating to the classes in society, the importance of personal combat (including cattle raiding when nothing more exciting was happening) and personal appearance, the role of the feast in uniting, motivating and structuring a chieftain's fighting band, and the significance of elements such as the hero's portion of best pork, head-hunting, and the artistic embellishment of weapons and horse and chariot equipment. Items that we become familiar with in graves resonate in Irish mythology — for example blood money demanded by the hero Lugh included a spear, a chariot with two horses, pigs, a dog and a cooking-spit, all items appearing in aristocratic graves. We are also able to see in this literature how it was assumed that these important aspects of life would carry on in the life after death. It is therefore no surprise to find time and time again archaeological evidence for the leaders of society being buried with regalia that would enable them to maintain idealised but similar lifestyles.

Classical authors too, some such as Julius Caesar writing contemporarily with the late Iron Age, wrote of their impressions of Iron Age life. They were observing their enemies and so we should expect bias, they were inevitably most struck by things that were strange and unusual, and they were describing a culture they did not understand, but these are not reasons why the comments they make should be ignored. In addition to invaluable if incomplete allusions to religious beliefs their comments help us understand Iron Age attitudes and aspects of behaviour which would be incomprehensible from archaeology alone. Diodorus Siculus for example describes how Celts cut off their enemies' heads and nailed them up in their houses, preserving those of the most important people in oil for display, and he talks of 'hearths blazing with fire with cauldrons and spits containing large pieces of meat. Brave warriors they honour with the finest pieces of meat'; useful background for interpreting graves and loose skulls. Tacitus tells how in Germany bodies of famous men were burned with 'particular kinds of wood' but 'they do not throw garments or spices on the pyre. Only the dead man's arms and sometimes his horse are put into the flames.' Caesar says that food was not eaten as part of the cremation ceremony, unlike Roman customs, so there is a subtle difference between vessels left in Iron Age graves as gifts for the next life, and the place-settings with Roman burials which represent the funeral feast.

The strong belief in an afterlife was regularly affirmed by classical authors and the picture they give is consistent with the Irish myths, which told of a next world where the important things in life, that is fighting and feasting, could continue.

Five banqueting halls would each have a massive cauldron constantly full of whatever food was wanted, with pork the preferred cut for the warrior élite. Classical authors bear out beliefs that the afterlife should be better than what went before for those who deserved it, full of enjoyable laddish action, mostly drinking, fighting and eating large meals, the tone being slightly raised by storytelling and music: pretty much the world of the Valhalla of Viking belief. It is some relief to note that weapons are not common, that women are generally as richly provisioned as men, and that apart from a few double graves for which there could be many explanations there is scant suggestion of human sacrifice in burials. Reality, therefore, seems to have been more sensible than the drama of literature suggests, though Caesar's description of funerals in Gaul — 'splendid and costly. Everything the dead man is thought to have been fond of is put on the pyre, including even animals' — sounds remarkably like some of the finer Aylesford/Swarling graves.

There also seems to have been a parallel belief in reincarnation. Druids, Caesar says, taught that souls passed to other beings, and he claims that it was this belief that made warriors have so little fear of death. Diodorus Siculus said that the Celts believed souls would eventually pass to another person for a new life. This trust in rebirth is echoed in some of the Irish tales. Another variant in Irish tales is the darker side of the afterlife, to which mortals might be enticed and from where spirits might wander at the autumn feast of Samain, our All Souls, the shadowy underworld so many cultures had for the masses. As far as we know no particular Celtic god was associated with this underworld but several had some role in the next life in addition to other attributes. In general, judging by the common occurrence of ritual pits and shafts, the location of gods and the afterlife seems to be chthonic, that is underground rather than over.

## Monuments and memorials

The Arras culture of east Yorkshire has the most consistent evidence for mounds over graves, generally with distinctively rectangular or square ditches. Their low barrows were still visible in the nineteenth century although now only the ditches appear as cropmarks. Cemeteries of these barrows vary from single graves to groups of several hundred at Danes Grave, Wetwang Slack and Burton Fleming. The barrows were placed in a deliberate and coherent way in a densely settled area of the landscape, in association with linear boundary banks and ditches and with the fast-flowing winter streams, and they evidently played a significant part in the division of farmland. The cropmarks of small square barrows with central pits are occasionally noticed elsewhere in England, especially in Essex, Suffolk and Cambridgeshire. At Bromfield, Shropshire, a fifth-fourth-century BC inhumation was surrounded by a small ring-ditch and accompanied by an iron brooch, bracelet and a bronze pendant.

Small, low mounds also seem to be a feature of some Aylesford/Swarling graves, though the evidence is mostly circumstantial. Iron Age burials other than those in rubbish pits or vaults are not deep, even those in mounds often being on the old ground surface. Thus for burials to survive to the present day it is likely they once had a mound; this may also explain why the graves could be respected by those who followed in the same cemetery and how the sites could attract further graves centuries later. Recent excavations where mounds are assumed include a modestly furnished cemetery at Hinxton, Cambs, which had eight cremations in pits, five of them surrounded by miniature ring-ditches (**31**), and Westhampnett, West Sussex, where 161 cremations were excavated, the focal graves being surrounded by empty space then an arc of burials, again as if marked by mounds. Here there were also rows of post-holes apparently associated with mortuary practices, and also rectangular shrines. The one imposing mound of this period is the Lexden tumulus in Colchester (below). This grave was accompanied by many Roman luxury goods, and the concept was inspired by the same Roman world. Augustus, harking back to the glorious memory of archaic Etruscan and republican Roman traditions, built a round barrow for himself and his family in Rome on a monumental scale and thus initiated a new generation of barrow building in impressionable parts of the Roman world.

## Care of the body

A feature of Westhampnett was the presence of pyre sites containing burnt animal and human bone, dress fittings and jewellery. The dead here were cremated in full costume, a ceremony in line with Caesar's description of Gallic cremations. These pyres were built over shallow pits with 'arms' designed to catch the prevailing wind. The woods used were mostly oak and ash, with some maple, cherry and small quantities of yew. Nails from the pyres were probably from biers. A sample only of the remains had been hand-collected from the cooled pyre. In a few cases there were dual burials, usually an adult and child. At Hinxton too the bone was cremated to a high temperature and then picked clean and broken up. Metal (and probably other less durable items) also went through the fire but pots and meat were placed separately. The cart burials of Yorkshire had corpses placed over the wheels and axle of the vehicle, with the body of cart inverted above. In one, Kirkburn, the corpse was covered with a complete mail tunic.

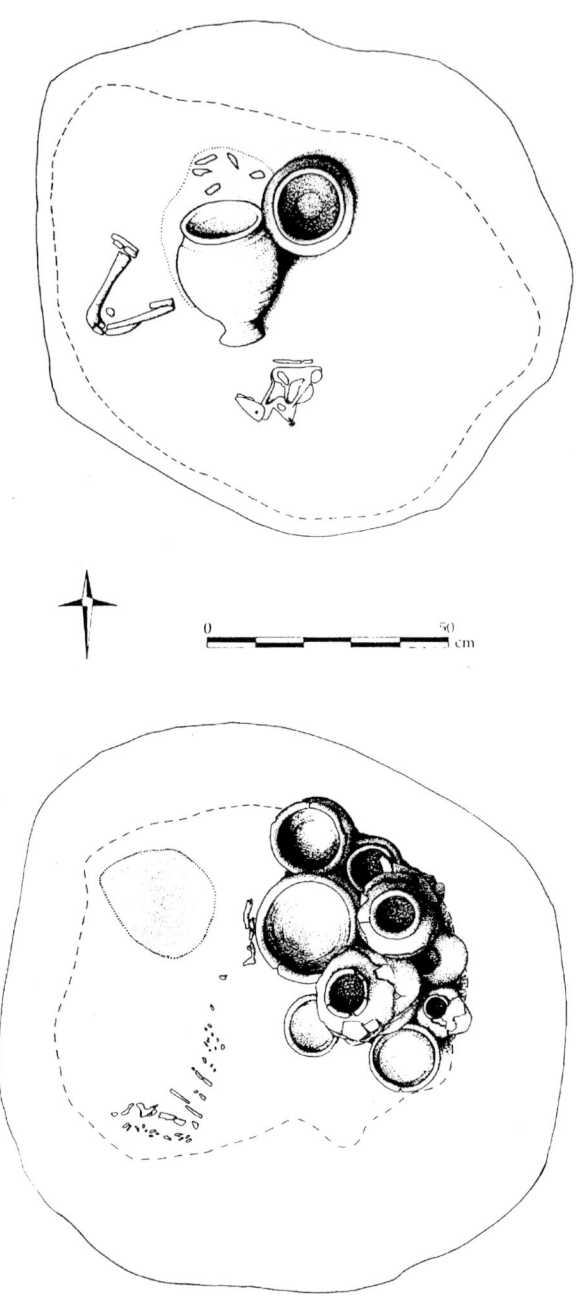

*31 Hinxton, Cambs. Two Aylesford/Swarling burials where cremations within small ring-ditches were accompanied by pots and metalwork (brooches, tweezers, nail cleaner, disks and chain), deposited in a bag of animal fur.* © Prehistoric Society

## Grave layout and coffins

At Hinxton all the graves had a protective cover, with the charred plank of one surviving, and at King Harry Lane several graves were covered by wooden planks. Of some 250 inhumations excavated at Burton Fleming and Rudston in Yorkshire the great majority were crouched or contracted, lying north-south and facing east, and were sometimes in coffins. This disposition was generally maintained in the Arras and Durotrigian cultures and was also common in cist graves, for example at Harlyn Bay, Cornwall, where crouched burials of the fourth to first century BC were arranged in rows. At Rudston, however, Arras-style burials mostly lay east-west or west-east, and their bodies were more extended, but as one family seems to be related to both rites, this change is seen as a religious or similar cultural development rather than a tribal difference.

At Flagstones, Dorchester, three of the burials were in old storage pits, and there were four slightly later ones in normal graves. In the pits were laid layers of rubbish and articulated human and animal skeletons (horse and cattle). All the graves found in these recent excavations were unfurnished but the site had continued under Max Gate, home of Thomas Hardy. The author became involved in the discovery of a cemetery there in 1884 when crouched bodies were found, one with three brooches on its forehead and three pots, and others with four and three pots respectively. One of these had what Hardy described as 'a filmy substance like black cobweb adhering to the inner surface'. Hardy's description of the bodies tightly packed in oval graves 'strongly suggestive of chickens in the egg' is a nice summary of this pervasive style.

## Grave goods

Many of the human remains found in settlements are discovered with parts of animals and other items that might have been deliberately placed, though they are difficult to distinguish from ordinary rubbish. Complete crouched burials in disused pits generally have no obvious grave goods.

Within the Arras culture grave goods indicate much variation in wealth and status. The majority have few if any artefacts, usually just iron brooches or similar personal items, but a few notable examples are exceptionally wealthy. In addition to carts these graves include metal shield fittings (with wood and leather occasionally visible), swords (mainly plain but some with ornate handles and scabbards), iron tools such as hammers, files, tongs and knives, and jewellery that included brooches, bronze, jet and shale bracelets, pins, and beads of shale, jet and glass. Where sexable, those with beads and small rings (ear and toe rings) were female, as were those with spindle whorls. Well-known early excavations of this

32 The Durotrigian 'Whitcombe Warrior', one of 12 crouched burials, nearly all with joints of meat, pots or jewellery. The 'Warrior' had a sword with bronze scabbard mount, metal rings, spear, iron hammer and file, brooch and spindle whorl.
© Dorset Natural History and Archaeological Society

culture include the King's Barrow, a small mound with an inhumation, two pig skulls by the head and a horse on either side, with cart and horse fittings, and the Lady's Barrow, another inhumation with an iron mirror, cart and horse fittings, and pig bones by the skull. Six more cart burials with a wider range of artefacts including complete but dismantled carts were excavated at Garton Station and Kirkburn. The Kirkburn cart burial, lying within a wide square ditch, had a mail coat, bronze toggles, pig bones, decorated bronze and iron linch pins over each wheel and horse fittings such as decorative terrets, strap-unions, yoke and bits. Slightly later, a group at Rudston had similar burials, with swords, spears, knives, spindle whorls, tools and pig bones as grave goods. Use of carts and square barrows have parallels in northern France, and continental examples extend as far east as Hungary in their general form, although with significant local differences. Crouched burials, for example, are British characteristics, and some grave goods are local variants of continental artefacts. Thus brooches, superficially similar to foreign examples, have different fastening mechanisms, the provision of numerous pots is in the regional tradition, pottery and metal work is of local manufacture though with continental connections, and unlike the continent, where men often had the full weapon set of sword, spear and shield, there was usually only one item (mail coat, shield, dagger, spear or sword) to indicate status.

Throughout much of England there are occasional discoveries of single rich graves, both men and women having elements in common with the Arras burials. A few scattered examples include Owslebury, Hants, where a male inhumation, the foundation burial for a cremation cemetery, had a sword, spear and shield; Fordington (Dorchester) where a burial was accompanied by a horse and bit; Whitcombe, Dorset, where a Durotrigian cemetery included a young man with sword, brooch, weapons and tools (**32**); Newnham Croft, Cambridge, with brooches, rings and an ornate bracelet though no cart; and Deal, Kent where a warrior in a cemetery had a crown, brooch, shield and spear. A man from Ventnor, Isle of Wight, with a sword in a sheath, a shield, and iron rings, also fits this geographically diverse group. Rich inhumation burials of women, characteristically with mirrors, are thought to be the female equivalent of these male grave. The best known of these was found in a cist grave at Birdlip, Glos, with beads, brooches, rings, bangles and bronze bowls. Others include Lytchett Minster, Dorset, where a woman was accompanied by a bronze bowl and glass beads, and was near a man with a sword, tankard and horse equipment; there are also fragments in various contexts in Dorset. The most recent Dorset find was from Portesham, where a large grave held a woman with her toilet set, a bronze pan, three pots, a knife in its sheath and pig and lamb bones (**33**). Like Birdlip, examples from St Kevern, Cornwall, and Plymouth were found in cists and with jewellery. Though most cist graves have less evidence of social stratification and obvious wealth, burials within them

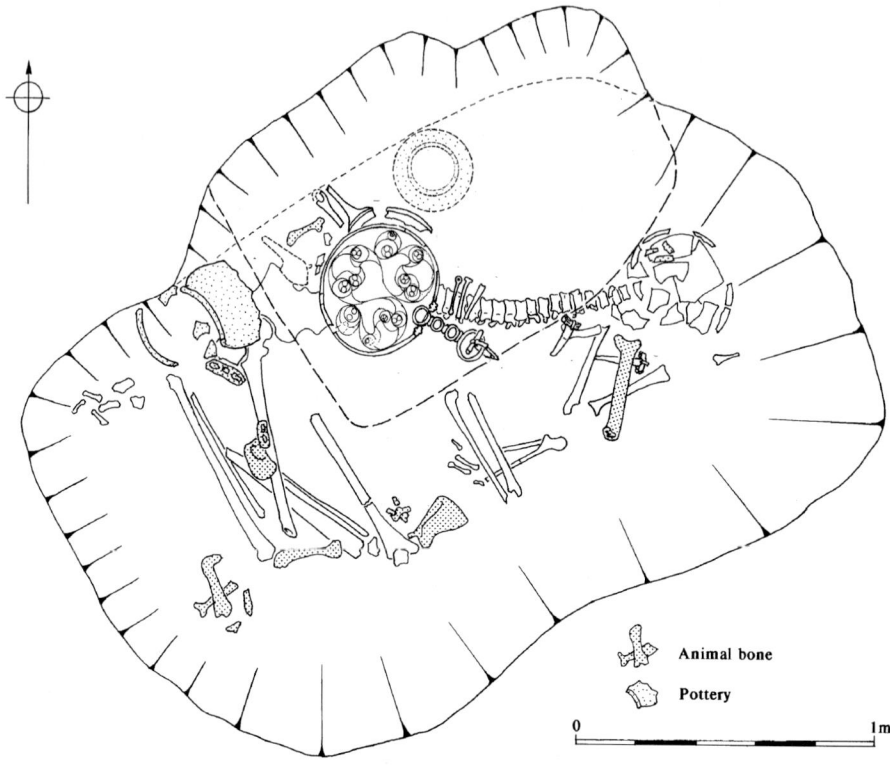

*33 The most recent Dorset find was from Portesham, where a large grave held a woman with her toilet set that included an ornate bronze mirror, a bronze pan, three pots, a knife in its sheath and pig and lamb bones.* © Dorset Natural History and Archaeological Society

were clothed and so often had worn brooches etc. With 130 inhumations in cists at Harlyn Bay, Cornwall, the largest such cemetery, personal ornaments consisted of imported brooches, bracelets, pins, and beads, as well as spindle whorls and some unusual locally produced slate tools. Artefacts indicate sporadic trade with south-west Europe and with similar cultures in south central England. Similar but different mirrors occur with Aylesford-type cremations of women in eastern England. These include Dorton, Bucks, in a wooden box with three amphorae, Rivenhall, Billericay and Colchester in Essex, this last with two jugs and a bronze cup and the standard Aylesford cremation urn, Aston, Herts, Chilham Castle in Kent, Thetford, Norfolk, and six examples from King Harry Lane (below). These lack the fine jewellery that generally accompanied the western examples, the mirrors here being just one luxury in otherwise normal wealthy graves, not a distinguishing feature for an exceptional group of women, an example of one element of the burial rite having variable significance within contemporary groups.

Graves of this Aylesford/Swarling tradition, with both rich and modest types using cremation accompanied by feasting but not fighting equipment, were part of a distinct cultural change visible in south-east England from the mid-first century BC. This change included the introduction of wheel-made pottery, coinage and large permanent settlements away from the old hill forts. Mortuary practices reflect the rise of chieftains, even kings, with attributes including ornate clothing and jewellery, personal grooming and access to imported luxury goods such as wine and fine tablewares, rather reminiscent of stages of Bronze Age culture. The introduction of cremation as well as the use and choice of grave goods at this time is not fortuitous for, as the availability of Roman goods reminds us, this part of Britain was in touch with Rome through politics and trade, and tastes were being formed by a desire to emulate this sophisticated foreign culture. Burial customs would be affected as much as, for example, drinking habits when wine was available, although in both cases practices were adapted to suit native habits. This tradition was first identified with Belgic migrations described by Caesar and, although its origins would appear to pre-date such events, it is hard to totally disassociate disastrous events in Gaul from this incursion of new wealth, commercial adventurousness and advanced diplomatic activity. This is most clear in the élite Welwyn and Lexden sub-groups of this culture, but the ordinary cemeteries demonstrate careful and consistent rites, which became more popular in the region as a whole in the years around the Roman conquest. Characteristic grave goods are multiple pots, brooches (mostly with women and often burnt, a sign they were worn during cremation) and occasional other personal ornaments. Of the type-sites from which the culture is named, Aylesford had three cremations in wooden buckets or tankards accompanied by 4-6 pots each, one of them also with three brooches and bronze wine-serving equipment, and six other cremations with extra pots each. Swarling had 19 cremations, one in a bucket and the rest in urns, several of them provided with extra urns and brooches.

At Westhampnett, one of the earliest cemeteries of this type, almost all graves had a pot, often more, though these were not used for the cremated bones. Grave goods included at least 45 brooches worn to fasten cloaks, some in pairs and joined by small chains, predominantly but not entirely with females. Pottery and metalwork were both influenced by continental styles. There was also gold foil, an iron bracelet, belt hook, knives, latch lifter and iron fittings of several wooden vessels. It was noticed that although there were no clear demarcations for grave goods, men had more than women, and older people more than younger. Acid soil had destroyed all the uncremated bone on this site but quite a lot of animal joints had been burnt on funeral pyres. Where identifiable these were usually pig or sheep/goat, or occasionally cattle, all apparently immature. It is evident that here leg of lamb or piglet was preferred and was generally reserved for adults.

At Hinxton cremations also include men, women and children. All were accompanied by pots, some just single but one having nine fine vessels that compare with the table settings found in early Roman graves and another having a bag of objects (including four brooches, tweezers, nail cleaners, a chain, two discs and a decorative terminal) that had been on the pyre. These two richer graves also had meat (sheep and pig) which, like the pots, had not been burnt. Brooches in two other graves had also been through the cremation process. Rather similar cemeteries have come to light in Bedfordshire, with meat, iron discs and toilet implements turning up quite often. At Milton Keynes too a small late Iron Age cemetery that carried on after the Roman conquest had eight cremations, mostly with grave goods that included tableware, brooches, meat (mostly lamb, with some ox and pig). The richest one was a female with five brooches, glass beads, a latch lifter, a nail cleaner, sheep bones and six pots.

The Welwyn graves, more aristocratic but in the same tradition, have a lot of grave goods in large pits. These artefacts include amphorae, containers for the wine and oil that were part of the reward for good relations with Rome. Other hallmarks of these graves are bronze, glass and silver tableware (especially items associated with serving and drinking wine), tripods, spits and fire dogs for roasting. Other small items might be included, but weapons are virtually absent and personal ornaments rare. Outstanding sites of this type include Snailwell, Cambs, with amphorae, wine jugs and other imported vessels, a shield, an armlet, burnt fragments of decorated bone cheek pieces, joints of beef, ham, a chicken and a piglet, the cremation being placed on a couch with bronze and iron fittings (**34**). A grave at Baldock had a bronze cauldron, an amphora, fire dogs, buckets, bronze dishes, bear claws (from a bearskin cloak?) and a pig. At Welwyn Garden City there was a grave with amphorae, gaming counters and board, wood, bronze and silver vessels, more bear claws and pots, in a deep vault with graves around it. Most artefacts were deposited as whole objects with the collected bone, but fragments of fire-distorted metal and decorative bone showed that other things, including elaborate biers, were burned with the body.

Even more extravagant were the slightly later (just pre-Conquest) Lexden group. Lexden Tumulus, Colchester, lay within the late Iron Age dykes that defended the town of Camulodunum. Below the mound was a vault more than 2m deep and 8m square. Finds with the cremated remains of an adult male are the most Romanised collection in Iron Age Britain. They included the bronze figurines of Cupid, a wild boar, a bull and a griffin, various ornaments, fittings, scraps of decorative sheeting (much of it probably from a large oak chest), a pedestal, a (lamp?) stand, a wooden box and casket, a Bronze Age palstave wrapped in cloth, chainmail with its buckles, hinges and silver studs, decorative silver mounts in the form of corn stems, trefoils and bars, a silver medallion with the bust of Augustus, gold tissue, stitched pieces of leather, many iron fittings and

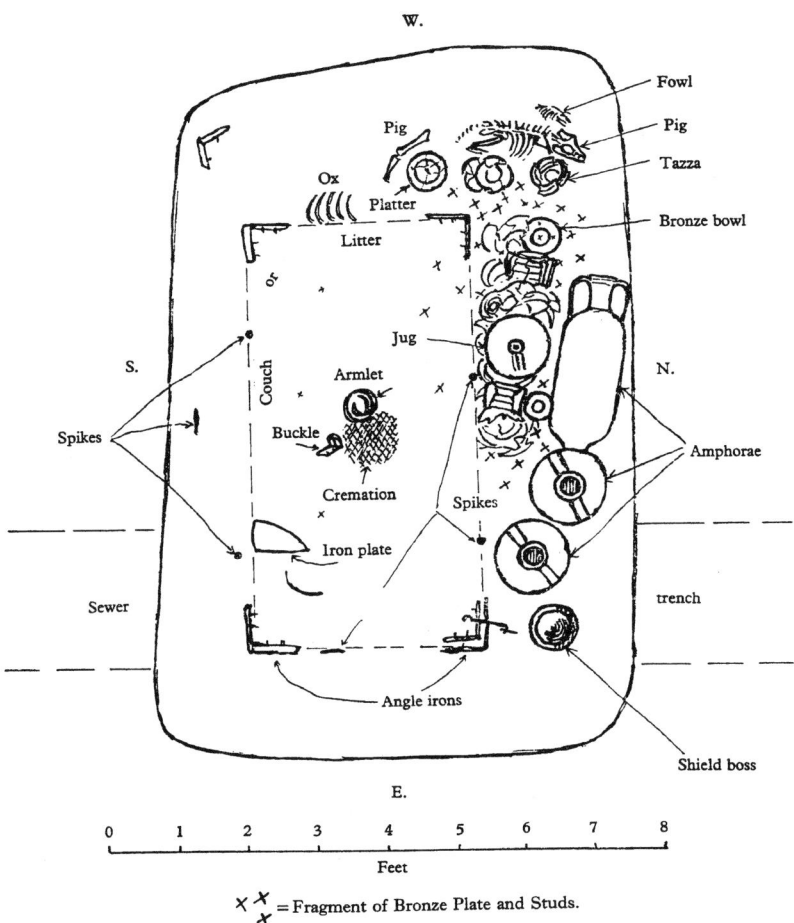

W.

Fowl

Pig

Pig

Tazza

Ox

Platter

Bronze bowl

Litter

Jug

S.

N.

Armlet

Spikes

Buckle

Amphorae

Cremation

Spikes

Iron plate

Sewer

trench

Angle irons

Shield boss

E.

0   1   2   3   4   5   6   7   8

Feet

×ˣ× = Fragment of Bronze Plate and Studs.

*34 Snailwell, Cambs, where late Iron Age cremated remains in a deep pit were laid on a couch and accompanied by feasting regalia and armour.*
© Cambridge Antiquarian Society

nails, parts of a folding chair, and broken pot and amphora sherds. Many of the pieces would have come from furniture such as a couch for the cremated bone, but, apart from the usual effects of decay, the whole grave had been ransacked in the past. Lots of the items were broken, fragmentary and scattered and some of the richest artefacts no doubt had been removed. Such a burial, packed with gifts, status symbols and insignia that must have come straight from Rome can be assumed to be of a king of the Catuvellaunian tribe, perhaps Addedomarus if the dating is right. The medallion of Augustus may have been an imperial gift, and the folding chair was reserved for those with authority directly bestowed by Rome. A disturbed neighbouring site known as Lexden Mount may have been similar, and so too are burials known from the Ivel valley in Bedfordshire. At Stanfordbury, dating to about the time of the Roman conquest, there were two huge pits. One contained six amphorae, Samian cups, bronze bowls and jug, a flute, gaming pieces, a spit, tripod and fire dogs to cook the meal. The other had amphorae, glass and Samian vessels, a casket and jewellery. One grave nearby at Old Warden had Kimmeridge shale pots and a bucket, and another had a mirror and an amphora.

Politically, this whole rich group of Welwyn-type burials belongs to tribes that were particularly important to Caesar and later Romans, amphorae in particular being goodwill gifts. It is even now suggested that the individuals buried thus may be the result of diplomatic ties involving taking noble children to Rome, giving them a Roman education and training, and then returning them to rule their homelands. Somewhat similar graves are thinly scattered through the free German world in the first three centuries AD and can perhaps be seen as results of the same Roman policy, though there it was less successful. In any case these are graves where we see the old Iron Age aspirations and expressions of dominance through the feast and hospitality enhanced by the Roman world, happily ignoring the threat that world would soon be to their whole lifestyle.

## Relationship to earlier and later sites

In a few places Bronze Age sites might attract Iron Age burials, and a few Iron Age cemeteries continued without interruption into the early Roman period. In some cases sites were reused in Roman or Anglo-Saxon times after they had been neglected for some time. Examples of different periods of use include King Harry Lane, where pottery finds suggest Bronze Age burials, then an Iron Age cemetery continuing after the Roman conquest with no change apparent in the rituals. From the mid-seventh to eighth century there was a small Anglo-Saxon cemetery here. Westhampnett cemetery was situated on a low hill with a Bronze Age barrow, and this site too was used again for Roman and Anglo-Saxon cemeteries. At Flagstones, Dorchester, a site which had been deserted from the middle Bronze Age was used for Durotrigian burials, and at Barrington, Cambs, a single Iron Age burial was close to a Bronze Age barrow on a site that became an Anglo-Saxon cemetery (**35**). At Deal too Iron Age burials were overlain by an Anglo-Saxon cemetery, and a horse burial at Fordington, Dorchester, was followed by Roman burials and then a medieval church.

## Examples

### King Harry Lane, Verulamium (St Albans)

The cemetery contained 472 Iron Age and pre-AD 60 burials, all but 17 of them cremations. Many were arranged within rectangular ditched enclosures each with a rich central burial. The cemetery had suffered much from ploughing, so only the deep grave pits were intact, many burials being reduced to piles of cremated bone on the ground surface and the bases of pots that had accompanied them, suggesting the original protection of mounds. Of the cremations, 192 were in pots though quite a few, including some of the richest, had no container. Apart from joints of meat and a few odd items such as gaming pieces, dice and bits of bronze distorted by heat, most of the grave goods, even personal items such as brooches, were placed in the grave, not on the pyre. Two amphorae had been smashed just outside the grave, but otherwise most vessels were placed carefully. A regular nick had been taken out of about ten per cent of the rims in antiquity and four were deliberately pierced. Several of the pots were well used, repaired or imperfect in some way, a feature of grave goods throughout the ages.

The burials seemed to be fully representative of the families entitled to use this ground. In many cases poor survival made it difficult to distinguish male, female and child, but analysis was good enough to be sure of a fair number of each, and to

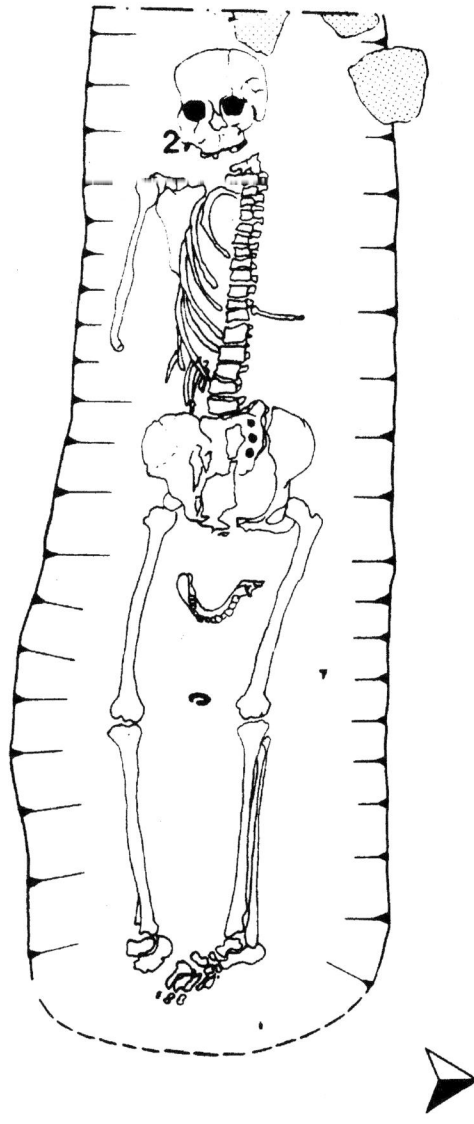

35 *A possible late Iron Age burial within the Anglo-Saxon cemetery at Barrington. Her jaw has been put between her legs after the body had decomposed.*
© Cambridgeshire County Council Archaeological Field Unit

81

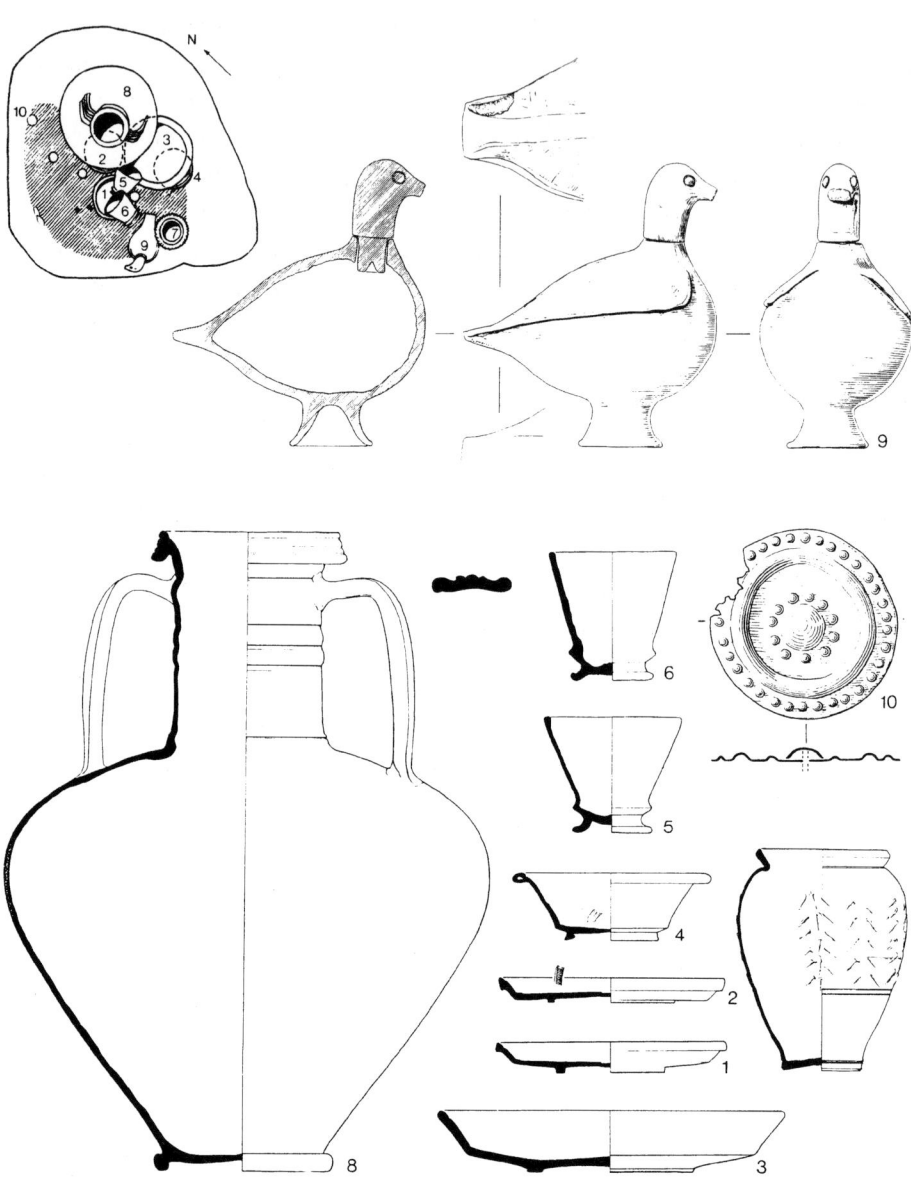

36 *Cremated remains from King Harry Lane, grave goods including three platters, three cups or beakers, a flagon, bronze fittings of a wooden board and a flask in the form of a duck.* © English Heritage

see that grave goods were quite evenly distributed between the sexes and age groups. There was a surprising lack of sex-oriented preferences — brooches, for example, were found in male graves, as were toilet implements and even a cosmetic grinding set. None were exceptionally wealthy compared to Welwyn-style burials, but the central graves could be impressive. Pottery was the most common grave good. There were 700 examples of this, about 30 per cent of them imported tableware, the rest being good quality, mainly wheel-thrown, local pots. The oddest of these pots was in the form of a duck (**36**). Analysis of soil samples from the six amphorae gives their contents as olive oil and fish sauce (two examples each), wine, and a sweet liquid made from reducing wine must. An exceptional feature of this cemetery was the number of brooches, 237, of iron and copper alloy. Other personal items included 15 knives, six mirrors, three bracelets, a finger ring, a belt of bone with an iron buckle, five sets of toilet instruments, three spoons, two pairs of shears, two hammer heads, two keys, an iron needle, two spindle whorls and an unguent bottle. Several of the groups of nails are thought to belong to gaming boards, one grave had 21 bone pegs from a board game, and there were cremated remains of similar pieces, glass counters and dice in others.

# 5 Roman burial: the first two centuries

Let my pale corpse the rite of burial know
And give me entrance to the realms below.
*Homer. A plea by the dead Patroclus to his sleeping friend Achilles*

# Roman burial: the first two centuries

The Romans found both ancient and new burial traditions in Britain and quickly added their own rites derived from the customs of the Mediterranean world. All of these customs were to influence each other in the years that followed but they remained identifiably separate for at least two centuries. In broad terms, the old rites of burial in pits and ditches survived in rural areas especially in northern and western Britain, and intrusive Iron Age rites such as clothed inhumation with food in the Wessex area were also persistent. The newer Iron Age cremation rites for the élite became more extreme and widespread in the south and east, whilst the classical rites of Rome were adopted in military areas, villa estates and trading centres.

The basic features of Roman burial in Britain up to the mid-second century were cremation, use of a receptacle, table place settings, food offerings (or symbolic tokens), with only a few personal items apart from those needed for the journey to the afterlife (boots, lamps and coins) (**37**). Where found, personal items are most commonly brooches, reflecting continuation of Iron Age dressed burials. Cemeteries had to be outside the settlements they served but were not separate or forgotten. They lined the main routes into the towns, with the best positions being next to the road and as close as possible to occupied areas. Thanks

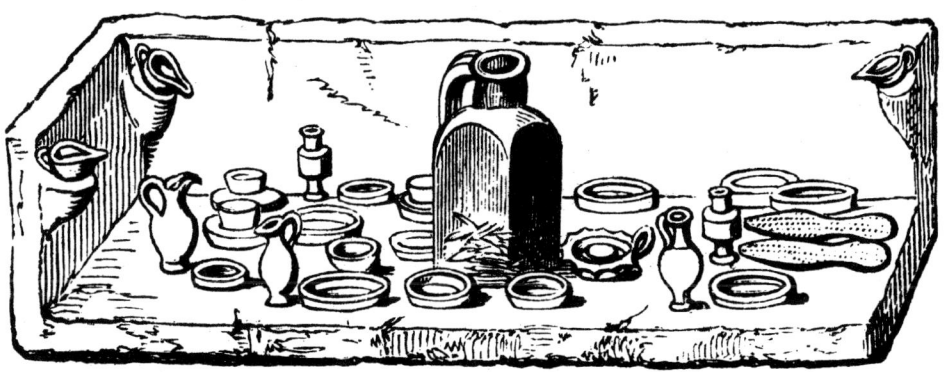

*37 This nineteenth-century drawing of a burial at Avisford, Sussex, is a somewhat idealised version of the excavated remains (note the shoe soles, hobnailed in brass, shown in their entirety) but gives a good idea of the grave goods accompanying elaborate Romanised burials. The cremated remains are in a typical glass urn within a stone coffin, with serving equipment for an elegant banquet, shoes and the lamps still where they were placed*

to the Romanised classes the number of surviving burials is higher than in earlier years but the pattern is localised, much of the countryside being barely represented, suggesting that native rites still predominated.

## Classical rites

The new classical rite left a considerable literature as well as obvious physical evidence which is relatively easy to recognise, date, and even to some extent interpret. It is thus possible to look beyond bald excavated evidence, both at the beliefs and hopes that drove the mourners' ceremonies, and at aspects of those ceremonies that meant so much at the time but which leave little trace 2000 years later. Problems in fact come with too much information. The Romans themselves were as confused, contradictory and even cynical in their professed beliefs as any other sophisticated and disparate population. Attitudes within Rome itself spanned the extremes, from fastidious segregation (strictly forbidding cremation or burial within the city), to a macabre incorporation of elderly dead males into State and family events.

As in many aspects of culture Roman customs in death mixed Greek and Etruscan philosophies and traditions. Cremation and inhumation were both used, though Cicero and Pliny described inhumation as a primitive rite that was being superseded despite some notable families who chose to retain it. Grave goods included vessels of pottery and bronze, weapons and lamps. There were various speculations on the actual life after death. These included Elysium for a select few, where sport, music and feasting were enjoyed, the rest becoming shadowy but beneficial spirits if properly respected, but capable of causing damage if neglected. The existence of the *Manes*, spirits of the dead, was not disputed, but *where* they lived caused confusion. Close to the burial, where they could be visited and where they needed food and drink explains the home-like touches such as plates of food and lamps left burning in the graves. But there was also a long-lived tradition of a journey to the murky afterlife, graphically if sarcastically recorded by Lucian of Samosata (below), and apparent in well-known features of burial such as the coin for the ferryman and hobnails from boots provided for the journey. As the years progressed there was less encouragement from the educated élite, who were expressing doubt about any sort of afterlife and thought ideas of resurrection were ridiculous, whilst the Stoics and Epicureans were openly scornful. Still, it was this élite that expected the most elaborate provisions in the old style for themselves, for this showed proper respect, a matter of family honour as well as affection. This class too could be quite open about recommending belief in a punitive afterlife as a way of controlling the lower orders.

Actual procedures recorded in Rome began with washing, anointing and dressing the body, for death was believed to bring pollution and without purification and correct burial the soul would not properly depart. Professional undertakers carried the body, burnt and buried it and took part in the mourning. According to the old laws, fuel should be planed wood and the pyre should be quenched with wine. There would be a funeral procession to the graveside, in early days taking place at night, a custom which continued for children and the poor. Cremation of the corpse and bier with gifts and personal possessions was usually in a special cremation area. Bones and ashes were collected by relatives and placed in pots or other containers according to wealth. Various purificatory procedures followed. A funeral feast was eaten at the graveside and again at the end of mourning, when libations were poured over the grave. Later anniversaries might be celebrated in similar ways. Continued care for the dead was important, partly due to fear of spirits walking, and offerings of food, drink and flowers were regularly made. Provision was sometimes made for lamps to be lit at the grave on certain dates, especially the *Parentalia* in February and *Lemuria* in May, when Ovid says small gifts such as violets or corn might be placed on pot sherds in the road.

Many literary accounts fill out our pictures of burial for the upper classes. Polybius in the second century BC describes a typical aristocratic funeral in which the body is carried to the forum, the son celebrates the dead man's achievements and virtues, and a lifelike mask is kept with other ancestors in the house and brought out at later ceremonies to help impersonate the dead. Diodorus Siculus records the use of actors involved in similar impersonations. Suetonius describes an actor who imitates Vespasian and he also mentions the cost of the emperor's funeral, 10,000,000 *sesterces*, probably enough to pay about 10,000 legionaries for a year. Just a modest respectable funeral would cost more than many people could afford and so burial clubs with monthly payments were used. Even slaves could join these, and provision was made for their effigies to be buried if their bodies were not handed over, thus avoiding the ignominy of anonymity. Such clubs could also ensure a good turnout for the funeral: one at least is recorded as providing a jar of wine, but only for those who attended the ceremony.

One particularly useful written source is the second-century AD provincial Roman, Lucian of Samosata. He wrote as a cynical outsider, mocking what he saw on extensive travels that included Gaul though not Britain, and presumably he was fairly accurate or his humour would not have hit home. His irreverent attitude was not untypical of educated opinions and is perhaps a clue to some of the changes in belief and practice apparent in the second century. He is scathing about general beliefs in life after death derived, he says, from 'Homer, Hesiod and other mythmakers', and he mocks at the grief which parents of a young man (rather naturally, one might think) show at his death, though 'they have not one whit of definite knowledge as to whether this experience is unpleasant and worth grieving about or, on the contrary delightful and better for those who undergo it'. He describes popular current beliefs in Hades, a place under the earth which is 'large and roomy and murky and sunless', ruled over by Pluto and Persephone, with Furies, Tormentors etc to help them. Their land is surrounded by huge rivers, and the dead have to cross Lake Acheron, which is guarded by Pluto's nephew and his three-headed dog, with help from the ferryman. They reach a meadow filled with asphodel and the well of Oblivion and are judged by two sons of Zeus. The very good go off to the Elysian Fields, the bad to the Furies for terrible punishment while most 'wander about in the meadow without their bodies, in the form of shadows that vanish like smoke in your fingers. They get their nourishment, naturally, from the libations that are poured in our world and the burnt offerings at the tomb; so that if anyone has not left a friend or a kinsman behind him on earth he goes about his business there as an unfed corpse, in a state of famine.'

His sarcastic descriptions of the treatment of the body agree with much of the archaeological evidence we have for Romanised burials and fill out details this cannot supply. Corpses, he says, are washed, anointed with perfume and 'crowning it with pretty flowers, they lay them in state, clothed in splendid raiment, which very likely is intended to keep them from being cold on the way and from being seen undressed by Cerberus'. There are loud cries of mourning, tearing of hair, cheeks and clothing and rolling around in the dust. The dead youth in this scenario laughs at all this carrying-on, asking 'what is use of your pouring out the pure wine? You don't think, do you, that it will drip all the way to Hades? As to the burnt offerings you yourselves see that the most nourishing part of your provender is carried off up to Heaven by the smoke without doing us in the lower world the least bit of good.' He would even have laughed out loud, according to Lucian, except that he was constrained by a winding sheet and fillets binding up his jaws. After three days of this mourning relatives tempt the bereaved to join the funeral feast, portions being provided for the departed.

The classic Roman funeral, therefore, adhered to rituals that expressed respect, grief, affection, remembrance and lasting care, alongside provisions for purification and other measures to ensure the dead caused no trouble to the living, even if beliefs in the afterlife were vague, contradictory and sometimes non-existent.

## Burial types

The direct impact of these classical traditions can be seen on some burials in Britain. The bulk of the population who practised crouched inhumation without grave goods and those who already used intrusive rites distinctive to particular regions continued with their customs. By the end of the first century, however, many towns had Romanised cemeteries (**colour plate 8**), and similar

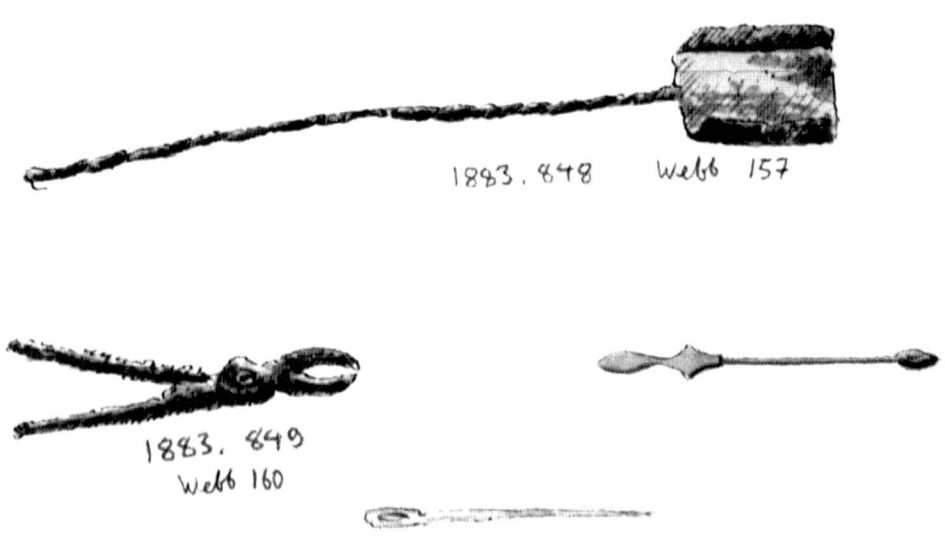

1883.848   Webb 157

1883.849
Webb 160

*38 Shovel and tongs used in the cremation ceremonies at Litlington, Cambs.*
© Cambridge Antiquarian Society

rapid change was associated with villas in southern Britain, the changes probably initiated by families of foreigners and emulated by the native upper and middle classes. In the north, the only known burials are associated with Roman towns and military sites. Britons in the south-east, where the ruling classes already used cremation, reacted in an interesting way to the Roman Conquest, a process which stripped them of real leadership in society but provided greater access to material goods, territorial rights and new status within Roman systems of government. These groups fused regional styles of burial, which became more extreme if anything, with key elements of classical Roman burial, demonstrating enjoyment of both worlds. By the end of the first century, the upper classes were followed in these changes by the wealthier and more cosmopolitan elements of the middle class, so that rites such as box burials become far more common, standardised and less richly furnished later on.

Cemeteries where the classical rites derided by Lucian were followed include those serving villa estates. These were often walled, and would have been filled with trees, flowers, pools and wells of the kinds described lyrically in Roman accounts, for example Trimalchio's wish to have 'every kind of fruit growing round my ashes and plenty of vines'. Several examples of such walled cemeteries are known in Kent, and they are found by roadsides in Cambridgeshire, Essex and Hertfordshire. Pyre remains, and the ritual shovel and tongs (**38**) used to gather bones from them, were features of the cemetery at Litlington in Cambridgeshire, associated with a large and magnificent villa. This was a long-lived cemetery, used from the first through to the late fourth century, with a mixture of rites. Within walls of flint and brick more than 80 cremations were in neat rows, about 1m apart and parallel to the Roman road. Several of these were in nailed and locked boxes accompanied by place settings, typically a flagon, storage jar and Samian cup (**colour plate 9**). Others were covered by tiles, or were in tile- or flint-lined holes (**39**). Heaps of woodash, enough, according to the nineteenth-century excavators, to fill five carts, were evidence for cremations being carried out within the cemetery but away from actual graves. Uniformity and strict following of this rite of place-setting and cremation, with scarcely any other grave goods, points to very Romanised origins, possibly an immigrant official whose family maintained a long-lived residence.

Litlington cemetery contrasts with another found only about three miles away and on the same Roman road, at Guilden Morden. This too was associated with a villa, not yet investigated but obviously a more modest affair than Litlington. The interest of this site lies in the mixture of rites represented, again over a very long time span, as locals adapted to new fashions. It is one of the few rural

*39 An urned cremation and accessory vessel covered by a tile, from Litlington.*
© Cambridge Antiquarian Society

*40 An inhumation slumping into a boxed cremation burial at Guilden Morden, Cambs.*
© Cambridge Antiquarian Society

cemeteries where continuity from the Iron Age can be seen, for cremations, two
with brooches, date from the first half of the first century AD. In the mid-first
century, whether just before or just after the conquest could not be recognised, an
inhumation had imported Roman pots and sheep bones, and an urned cremation
was accompanied by hobnails, bronze bangles and an iron chain. Shortly
afterwards another cremation in a hinged box had a place setting of a jar, flagon
and Samian bowl, and an iron lamp, and another had five Samian dishes, a flagon,
iron lamp and hobnails with an urned cremation. Cremation was used alongside
inhumation well into the third century, with a total of 139 cremations to 147
inhumations (these being mostly but not entirely third-fourth-century), the
confusion of burial rites including a cremation that was cut through an
inhumation and many graves intercutting or overlying others (**40**). Several
cremations had no container or grave goods, and the graves were a great contrast
to the fastidiously orderly Litlington cemetery just up the road.

Other rural cemeteries rapidly adopted Romanised burials for a broader
spectrum of their population. One ordinary cemetery which demonstrates how
the basic Roman provisions for the dead were used in a prosperous agricultural
area of south-eastern Britain is Skeleton Green near Puckeridge, Herts. This site
was occupied in the late first century BC/early AD, then deserted for a few years
before a small cremation cemetery was enclosed by a bank and ditch in about AD
90. Unlike Guilden Morden, there was uniformity in the burial rite. The whole
cemetery was investigated and 52 cremations excavated. Ten of these had all the
grave goods and remains buried in large wooden boxes, often with iron fittings,
and six were casket-burials, in which cremated bone was placed inside much

smaller boxes with locks and delicate bronze fittings such as lions' head mounts. These were the richest burials on the site, and one of them had a coin, glass beaker and intaglio within the casket. Textile impressions suggest cloth lining or wraps in the caskets, and incense burning was noted. The only other personal items were a finger ring and a fragment of mirror. Animal bones were included in nearly half the cremations and all five inhumations, mostly fowl (especially with women) but there were also many sheep and some ox (but only with the men). Of the 44 fairly complete cremations, 27 had the standard feasting set of an urn, a Samian bowl and a flagon, and many of these also had additional dining ware such as a beaker, cup or bowl. There was a rather similar group of boxed cremation burials at nearby Baldock, where animal bones included fowl, calf, pig, sheep and red deer, some of the food being included on the pyre and some placed separately in the grave. Other grave goods here were brooches, sometimes in caskets, a glass jug, a wooden board holding joints of meat, bronze pins, and hobnails.

In other regions of Britain local customs scarcely altered with Roman rule. The Durotriges of Dorset provide a good example of a specialised inhumation rite which developed from continental prototypes in the late Iron Age and then persisted. Their burials had standard types of grave goods (pots, meat or jewellery) in almost all graves, much as they had done in the years preceding the Conquest. Later ones became a bit more varied, but generally the impact of Romanisation was slight before the late second century. A group of sites near the Roman town of Dorchester includes Fordington Bottom, Poundbury, Maiden Castle and Alington Avenue, mostly dating to around AD 50-100, the period when the town of Dorchester was replacing settlement at the great fortress of Maiden Castle. Fordington Bottom was a small and humble family cemetery, consisting almost entirely of burials in a crouched position with usually just newborn lambs as grave goods. Some had pots and one woman had an iron finger ring. The graves were arranged around a small rectangular building, probably the sort of shrine paralleled on Iron Age sites, but rarely with a cemetery. Second-century burials were also crouched but in coffins, and two had hobnails. This site had begun with pre-conquest Iron Age graves, some of them the ones noted by Thomas Hardy at Max Gate (above). Jordan Hill at Weymouth was another Durotrigian cemetery near a Romano-Celtic temple. The cemetery was late first- to early second-century, with over 80 burials in family groups. Some were in cists, and they were accompanied by assorted objects covering the spectrum of food and personal belongings, using Roman objects in their own native way. Most had at least one pot, there were weapons including iron arrowheads, a sword, spear head and sling stones, worn items such as rings, brooches, beads and an armlet, and Roman treasures such as styli and a shale table leg.

Some communities of high social standing used the basic new Roman rites but also followed the traditions of their Iron Age ancestors in ensuring the best

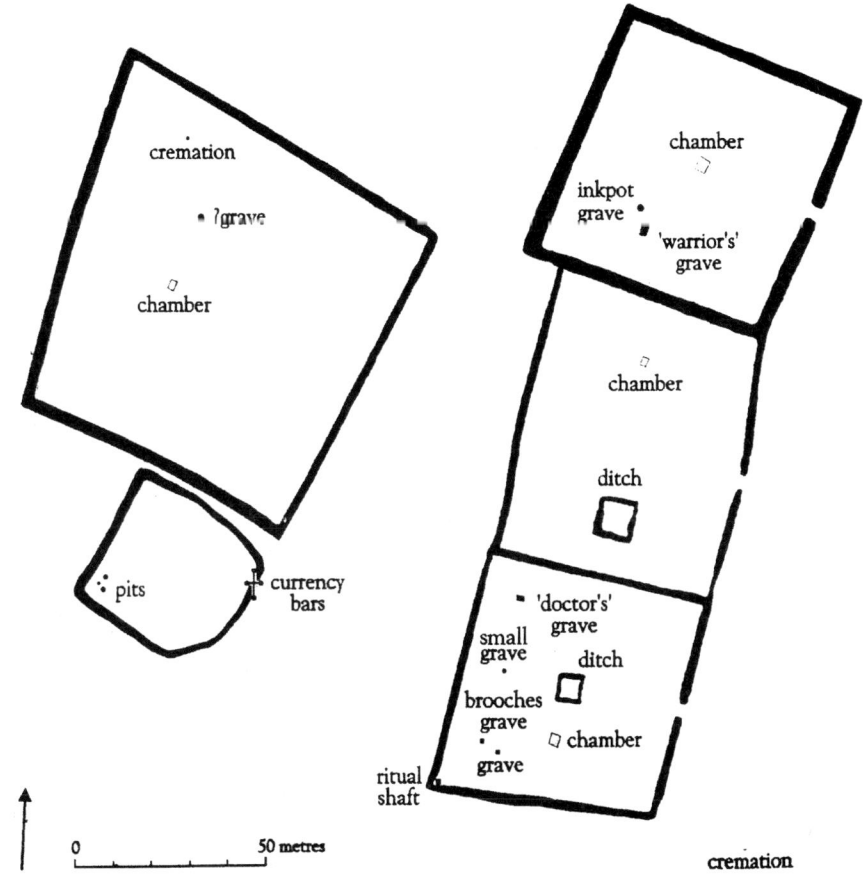

*41 Grave enclosures at Stanway.* © Colchester Archaeological Trust

provisions were made for feasting and other amusements for eternity. The mixture of Roman material goods and Iron Age faith resulted in grave goods of exceptional interest, for they include artefacts found in scarcely any other conditions. The earliest ones, dating to about AD 50-5, are near Iron Age and Roman strongholds, notably at Stanway near Colchester and Folly Lane just outside St Albans.

Stanway (**41**) is perhaps best known for the board games excavated here. One consisted of a folding wooden board and 20 glass gaming pieces in a timber-lined chamber. Other grave goods with the cremation included a dinner service of over 20 pieces, bronze vessels, glass ware, an amphora, brooches, a spear, a shield, and an ink pot — rare and surprising evidence for literacy at this time. In a neighbouring chamber was an equally interesting burial known as the doctor's grave (**colour plate 10**) which contained the only known surgical kit from

Roman Britain, a set of rods with blunt blades, rings with leather loops, scalpels, forceps, hooks, needles and a small saw. This grave also had a folding gaming board made from maple wood with bronze corners and hinges, this time with 13 blue and 13 white counters in position and the opening moves already made. It also had the usual dinner service (11 dishes and cups), an amphora, and a bronze spouted strainer or infuser. The cremation itself was in a box with the medical instruments and game, two brooches, a bead and some textiles. These two unusually well-preserved graves were probably typical of secondary graves that were grouped around very large chambers which seem to have been ceremonial resting places for the great figures of society before they were burnt. These resting places were once covered by turf mounds that collapsed into the chambers when their timbers rotted. Finds in them were smashed fragments only, but enough to show about 20 pots per chamber, plus a glass perfume phial and beads.

A similar rite has been recognised at Folly Lane, St Albans, and there was another probable example at Cambridge. Both of these involved the stately laying out of a body in a huge chamber with subsequent cremation and burial in a separate grave, leaving the original chamber packed with broken tableware, amphorae, religious items, the remains of the feast and furniture. At Folly Lane, at about the same date as Stanway, a shaft nearly 7m square and 3m deep, massively revetted with layers of timber, held the smashed remains of this feasting beneath a demolished superstructure. Beside it was a pit that held the pyre debris, which in this case included a coat of iron mail, horse trappings, ivory furniture decorations and more burnt and broken feasting remains. The Cambridge site was of similar size and construction but with one apsidal end and stairs on one side. Its fill contained more than 250 wine flagons, great numbers of glass and Samian vessels, furniture fittings, gaming pieces, a bone flute, an intaglio of Bacchus, complete animal sacrifices (horse, cow, sheep and dogs) and other unusual animal bones such as cat, duck and hare, again comparable with Folly Lane. The timber shrine over this site was eventually burnt and piled into the chamber along with more feasting regalia. This was not just because some extremely good times were part of any mourning but because the site, whose destruction dated to the mid-second century, was evidently part of a long-lived cult within the Roman town, the association of death and religious worship, like the rites followed here, being in the Iron Age rather than the Roman tradition.

## Barrows

At Stanway and Folly Lane, though the sites were flat when excavated, there was evidence for original mounds above the graves, and it is possible that when the Cambridge chamber was still a cavity there was a similar upstanding monument.

1 *Mulfra Quoit. The megalithic stones of this chamber tomb overlook wide areas of Cornish moorland. Nineteenth-century excavations failed to find any remains in a pit within the chamber. Any covering mound has long gone.* © Cornwall County Council

2 *The timber chamber inside a long barrow at Haddenham, Cambs, preserved by wet Fenland conditions.* Cambridge Archaeological Unit

*3   Barrows covered in contrasting gravel emerging through the peat at Over, Cambs.*
Ben Robinson

*4   Flint kerb under a barrow at Week Down.* Author

5 *A burial in a ring-ditch at Barnack near Peterborough had the classic attributes of a Beaker warrior grave*

6 *A wrist-guard studded with gold, a dagger, bone pendant and a beaker, from the Barnack ring-ditch*

7  *Barrows in East Anglia have mostly been destroyed by ploughing. Those that are left, like this one at Kennett, Cambs, are still so vulnerable they need a physical barrier to protect them from arable agriculture*

8  *A cremation within a tiled cist, equipped with food, drink and lighting, one of the exotic types of burial introduced to first-century Colchester.* © Colchester Archaeology Trust

9  *A typical place setting accompanying an urned cremation at Litlington, Cambs. Drawn by Mrs Webb in the early nineteenth century.* © Cambridge University Museum of Archaeology and Anthropology

10  *Excavating the Doctor's Grave at Stanway, Essex.* © Colchester Archaeological Trust

*11 The Bartlow Hills in 1821, drawn by Richard Relhan.* © Cambridge Antiquarian Society

*12 The Officer's Tomb, High Rochester*

13 *Excavation of a second-century cemetery near Godmanchester included a burial in the typical green glass urn, with a Samian dish and wine flagons*

14 *Excavation of a boxed grave at Milton, Cambs. A storage jar has been used for the cremation, which is accompanied by two small flagons, both deliberately holed to 'kill' them and so not actually containing sustenance in a literal sense*

15 *Religious pipeclay figurines accompanying a baby at Arrington, Cambs. Deep burial, a lead-lined coffin and plenty of religious symbols should have ensured a safe journey to another life for this hydrocephalic child*

16 *The cremated remains of a child at Godmanchester were placed in a Samian pot together with her bronze bracelets, food vessels and figurines of a bull and mare*

17 *London Road, Godmanchester. Typical graves in a late Roman managed cemetery, with parallel rows of west-east coffined burials and scarce grave goods, found in their hundreds or even thousands on roads leading out of towns*

18 *Tombstone of Aurelia Aureliana, wife of Ulpius Apolinaris, who died at Carlisle, aged 41. Now on display in the Museum of Antiquities, Newcastle.* Photograph by Lindsay Allason-Jones; © Courtesy of Museum of Antiquities, Newcastle

19 *A tombstone found near Colchester still had traces of gesso adhering which has made it possible to reconstruct its original colours. The depiction is the standard image of a Roman soldier killing a naked barbarian, commonly used by auxiliary troops. This first-century example commemorates a soldier involved in the earliest phase of occupation but the same motif was popular in the later years. It reads 'Longinus Sdapaze, son of Matygus, a man on double pay from the First Cavalry Regiment of Thracians, from the district of Sardica, aged 40, of 15 years service, lies buried here; his heirs under his will had this set up.'* Reconstruction © Leg II Aug

20 *Excavating an early timber coffin at Atlantic House, London.* © Maggie Cox/Museum of London Archaeological Service

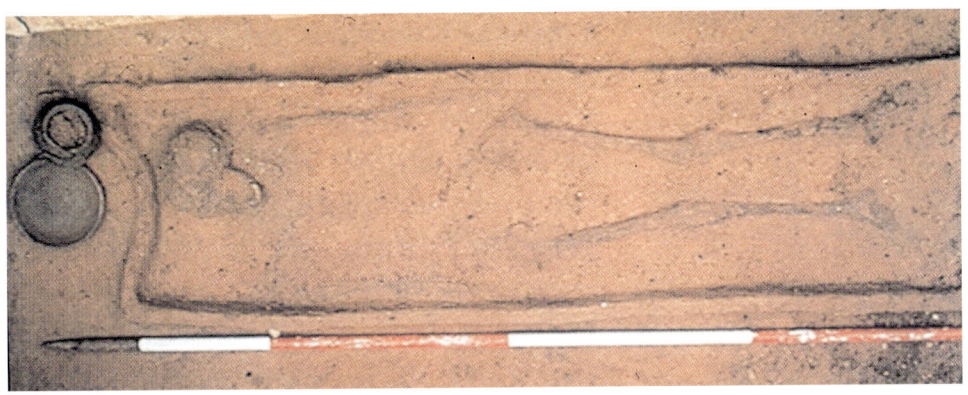

*21 In the sandy soil at Springhead, Kent, wooden coffins were also found with their nails and other fittings. The bones were dissolved but they too could be seen as dark stains. Many graves were equipped with jars, flagons and platters, and a few also had coins, bracelets, finger rings and hobnail boots, and one had a mirror. Note the pots deposited outside the coffin.*
© Union Railways (South) Ltd

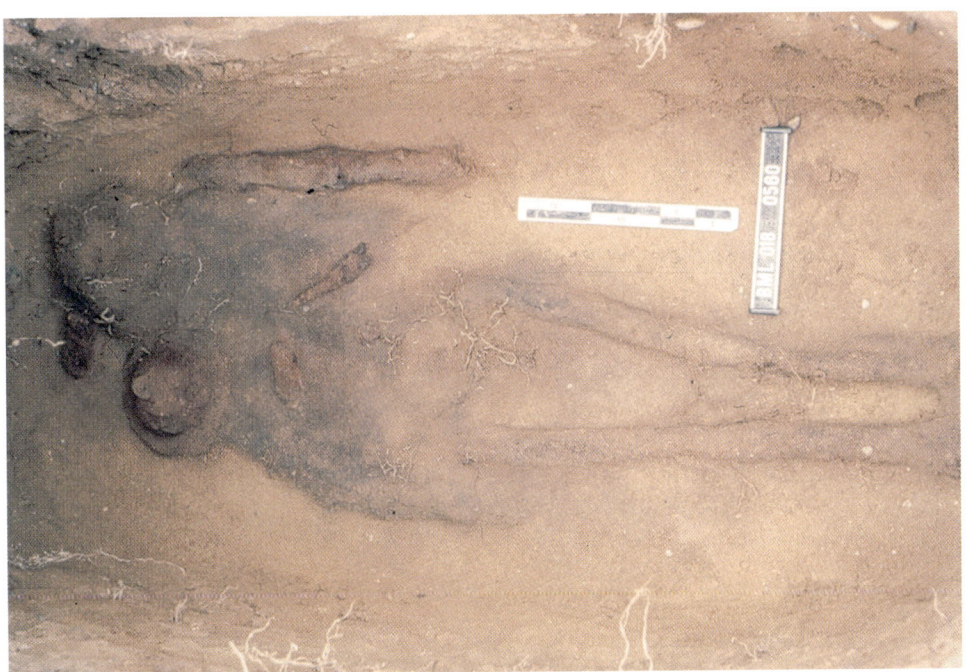

*22 The latest work (2000) at Sutton Hoo uncovered a sixth-century cremation and inhumation cemetery in which bodies and coffins survived as dark stains. A sword and a shield can be seen with the coffined body of this man.* © Suffolk County Council Archaeological Service

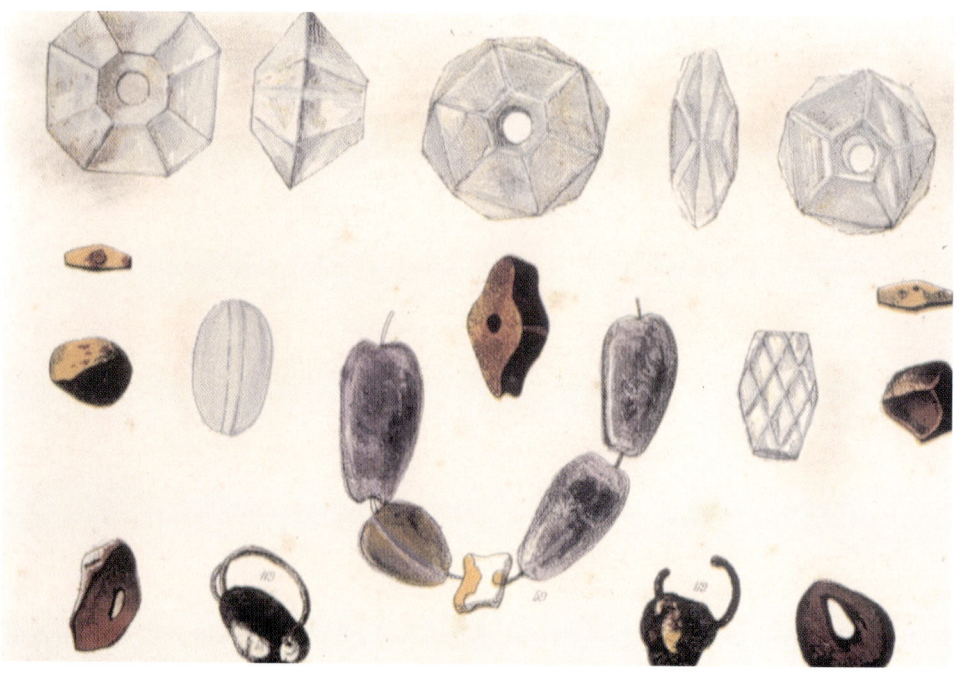

*23  Beads of quartz, amethyst and glass from Little Wilbraham.*
   © Cambridge Antiquarian Society

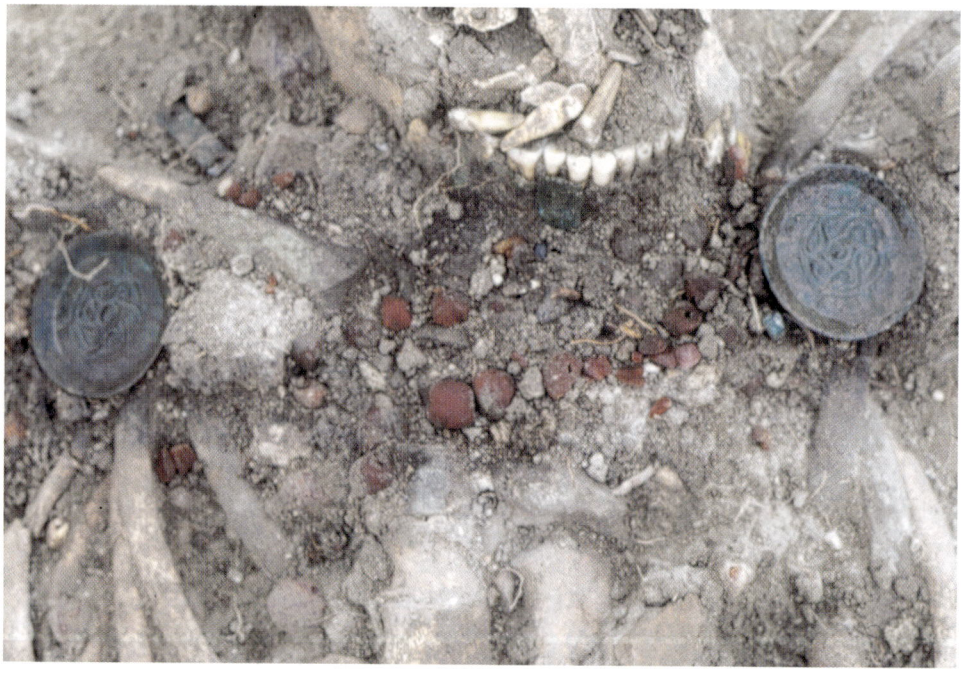

*24  Brooches and amber beads on a woman at Barrington*

25  *These freshly excavated grave goods from Swaffham Prior, Cambs, are a very typical group of items (amber beads, knife, brooch and wrist-clasp) from an Anglian grave*

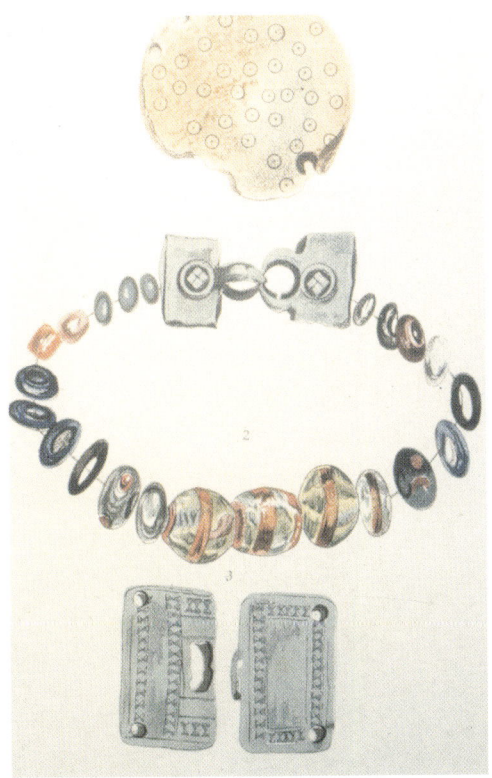

26  *Glass bead necklace and wrist clasps from Barrington.*
© Cambridge Antiquarian Society

27  *Man and horse buried together at Lakenheath.* © Suffolk County Council Archaeological Service

28 Recording an 18-month-old child at Barrington, buried with a complete pot, one large pot sherd and 15 beads

29 (below left) Gilded brooches, silver wrist clasps and crystal beads from Barrington

30 (below right) Seventh-century necklace with silver rings, glass beads, and gold pendants, one containing a crystal, from Barrington

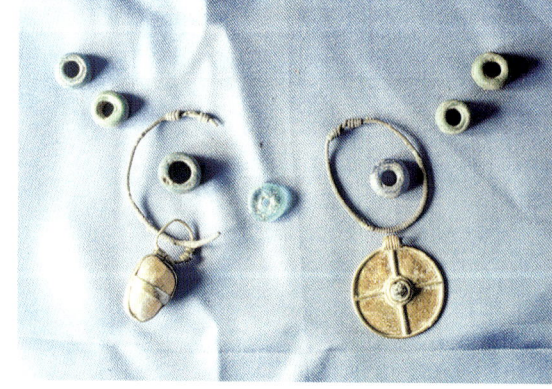

31 Excavation of the Barrington bed burial

32 Late Anglo-Saxon grave stones
   in the churchyard at Elton,
   Peterborough

*33 An eighth-century cemetery at Sedgeford, Norfolk, with graves carefully laid out and all heads to the west. In more crowded parts of the cemetery there was orderly intercutting of earlier graves.* © Sedgeford Historical and Archaeological Research Project

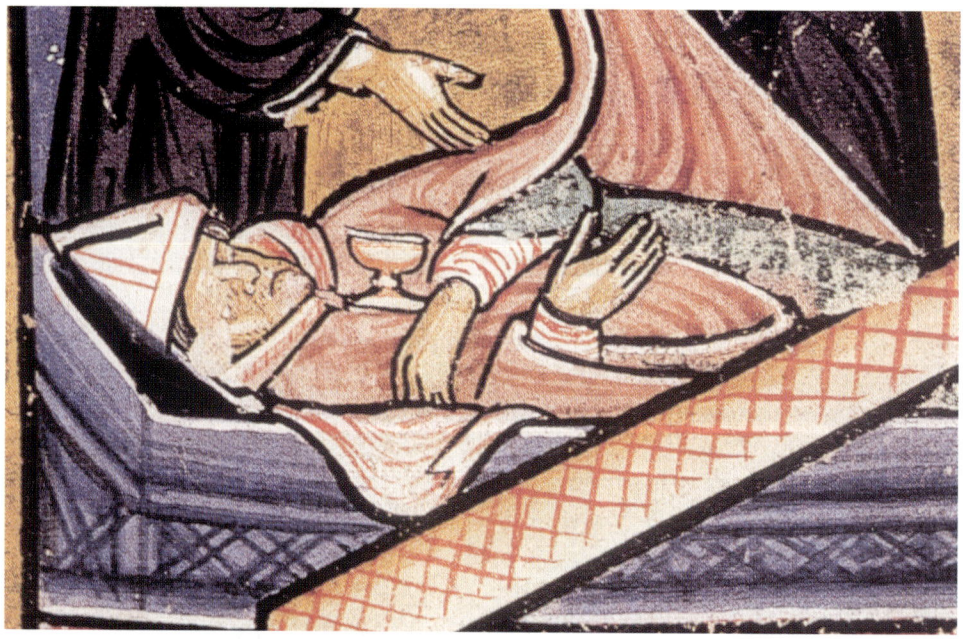

*34 A detail from the late twelfth-century illuminated* Life of St Cuthbert. *Note how he has been given a mitre, communion cup and more elaborate textiles than in the early twelfth-century drawing (81).* © By permission of the British Library, BL Yates Thompson Ms 26, 77

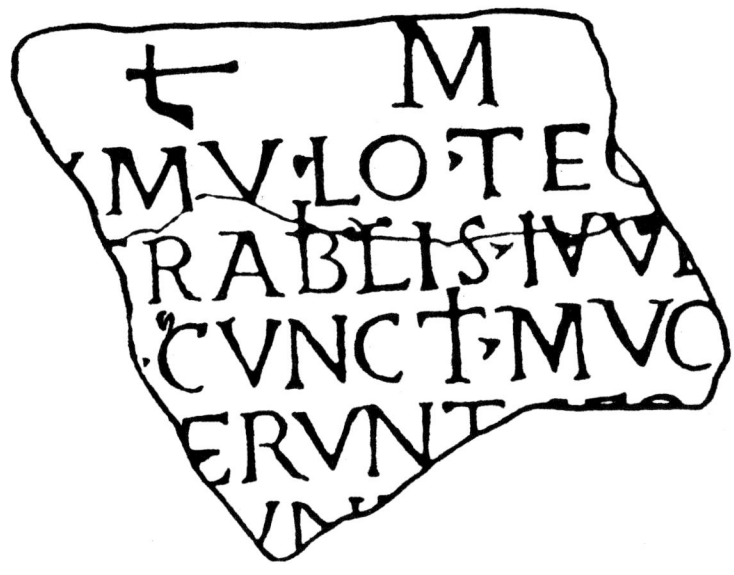

*42 Part of a Purbeck marble tombstone found in Colchester, now in the Fitzwilliam
   Museum, Cambridge, inscribed 'To the spirits of the departed; in this mound (*tumulo)
   *lie buried the bones of a young man, much regretted . . . everyone . . . Mucianus.'*
   © Administrators of the Haverfield Bequest

Mounds are also noted on inscriptions on tombstones (**42**). This makes them part
of the strange revival (perhaps more correctly the reintroduction) of barrow burial
in this part of England that was also seen in the late Iron Age. Roman burial
mounds, unlike those of the Bronze Age, are rare and restricted to specific
localities and a very limited social élite who followed a closely defined rite. In
Britain about a hundred are known, nearly all from the south-eastern area where
richly furnished cremations were already the practice (**43**). Their origins are
problematic. They seem to be inspired by the great mortuary mound Augustus
built for himself in Rome in AD 14, itself inspired perhaps by a romantic mixture
of Etruscan precedents, accounts such as Homer's description of the mound
raised for Patroclus, and the poetry of Virgil. The role of literature was probably
significant in the spread as well as the reinvention of barrow burial. We know that
Homer and Virgil in particular were widely read and they are both studded with
references to burial rites involving barrow building and the importance of
ancestral graves. This does not however explain why the custom should have been
taken up by such a scatter of wealthy provincials, nor why the burials they contain
should follow a particular class of Iron Age rite. Soldiers may have played a part
in spreading the fashion for some barrows have military connections and they

*The 6 Barrows near Stevenage 10. July 1724.*

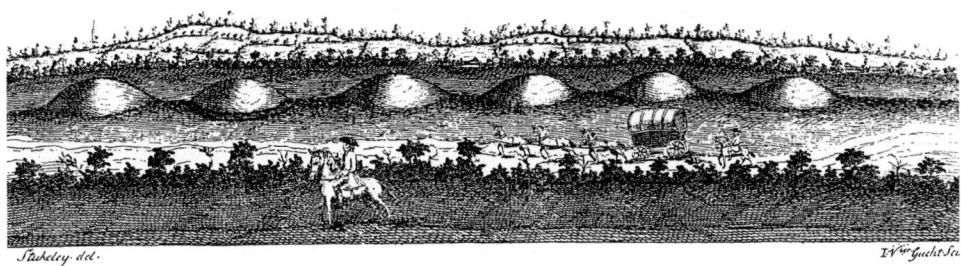

*Stukeley del.*                                                                                 *I.Van Gucht Sc.*

*43 The Six Hills at Stevenage, Herts, drawn by William Stukeley in 1724*

seem to belong to individuals or families with official status within the Roman administration. These barrows are typically taller than in the Bronze Age, with a conical flat-topped profile, and are often near to roads and to villas. They are thought to have been built for single central graves, but as it is usually only the central area that has been excavated this impression could be wrong, and certainly secondaries often occur. The cremation rite is consistently used for primary burials, very often with lamps and tableware of an exotic nature. They ranged from simple graves such as that at Emmanuel Knoll, near Godmanchester, Cambs (**44**) to the amazing wealth and size of Bartlow Hills, in the same county.

At Bartlow there were originally six or seven mounds, of which four remain, the largest being still over 15m high (**colour plate 11**). The reports of early nineteenth-century excavations show that the cremated bones were placed in glass urns and then in large, locked wooden chests or, in one case, a brick cist, each with a lamp left burning. Grave goods mostly related to feasting, with plenty of exotic glass, bronze and pottery flagons, cups, bottles and other items for the table (**45**). There were also perfume phials, a miniature enamelled cauldron, strigils, and an amphora. Thanks to dry conditions within the chalk mounds, a wooden tankard, a wicker bottle, a wreath of box leaves, flower petals (probably a rose), a sponge and even the contents of vessels, identified at the time as frankincense, wine with honey, and blood with milk, had been preserved. Signs of official rank were a folding chair and a gold signet ring. The chair, similar to examples found at Holborough Knob (below), Lexden, Verulamium and in Belgium and Bulgaria, was a ceremonial item used by high-ranking civilian and military officers, a definite sign of official status. Only the centres of the mounds were investigated, and so little is known about their structure or development. Their steepness

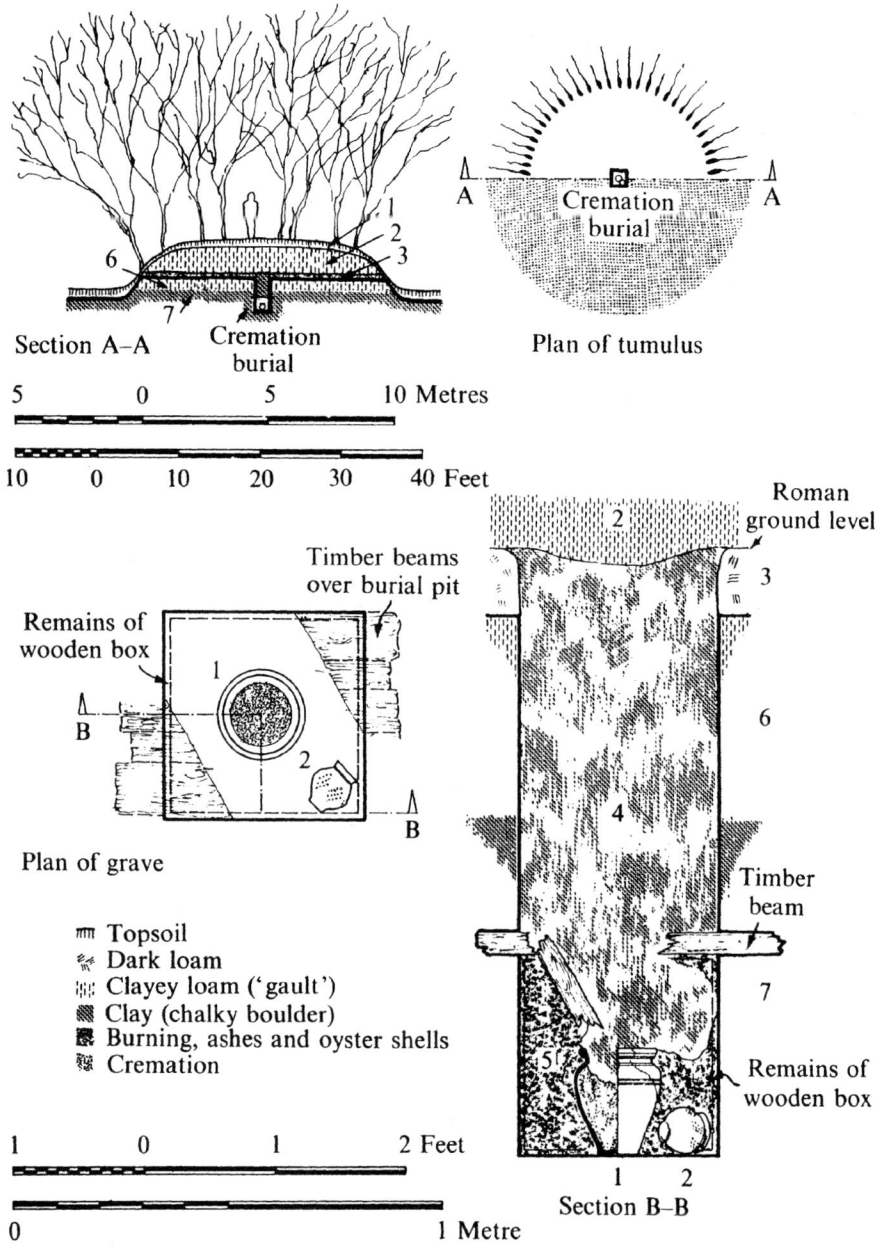

Section A–A  Cremation burial

Plan of tumulus

5   0   5   10 Metres

10   0   10   20   30   40 Feet

Timber beams over burial pit

Remains of wooden box

Plan of grave

Roman ground level

Timber beam

Remains of wooden box

Section B–B

᠁ Topsoil
᠁ Dark loam
᠁ Clayey loam ('gault')
᠁ Clay (chalky boulder)
᠁ Burning, ashes and oyster shells
᠁ Cremation

1   0   1   2 Feet

0   1 Metre

**44** *A simple boxed cremation burial in a shaft beneath a small mound at Emmanuel Knoll near Godmanchester, Cambs. Reconstructed by Michael Green from early twentieth-century records. © Cambridge Antiquarian Society*

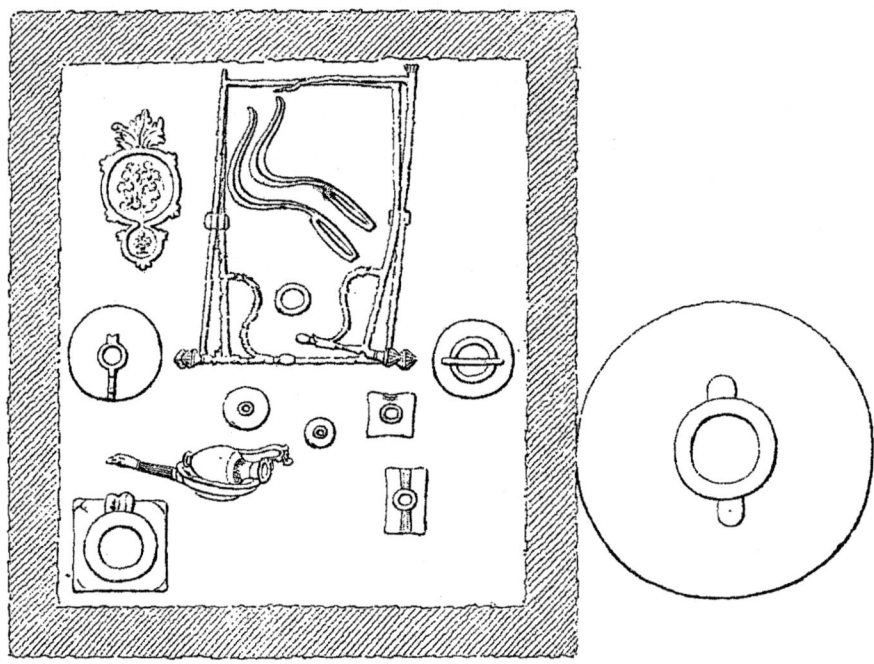

*45 The grave within the largest mound at Bartlow. Note the folding chair and strigils, symbols of Roman life-styles and power used within an Iron Age tradition. An amphora is outside the chest, and feasting equipment and an ornate bronze lamp are inside, along with cremated remains in a glass vessel*

suggests the use of revetting or retaining walls on the Italian model, and fourth-century pottery brought up by burrowing animals from top levels must mean they were heightened in later years, probably by descendants living in the nearby villa.

A rare variant on these barrow burials has a stone retaining wall, like Italian mausolea, and was probably chosen by foreigners to this land. Examples are known from Sussex and from Kent, where Holborough Knob had a primary male cremation of a man. He had with him a folding chair like that of Bartlow but with a cushion, meat (including fowl), glass vessels, all of which had been on the pyre, and five amphorae, 'smashed in a welter of resinated wine'. Another, in a military context at High Rochester, a fort north of Hadrian's Wall, is known as 'the Officer's Tomb' (**colour plate 12**). Also at High Rochester is a group of very small mounds over cremations of a quite different kind. These were humble memorials to soldiers and their families, an auxiliary unit stationed on the Wall for several generations. These were the *bustum* type of burial, better known in the

Rhineland. The body on its bier was burnt over a pit, the bones were collected and perhaps placed in a pot, all the remains were pushed into the pit and sealed with a clay mound, surrounded by a ditch and marked with a post. They measured between 1.2 and 4m in diameter. The only artefacts in the graves were nails from the biers and from boots, pots, either whole or deliberately broken, and the occasional coin. These tiny mounds may well have been the normal soldier's grave on other parts of the Wall, for with any ploughing or other disturbance they would disappear. Reddened earth within the Officer's Tomb suggested that here too the cremation was carried out in situ.

## Grave goods

The most consistent items in Roman graves (pots, food, coins, lamps and boots) were all taken from the Greeks, who in turn had taken on yet earlier traditions. They, for example, had coins placed in the mouths of the dead from the fifth century (apparently because that was where they normally carried wrapped-up small change) and provided shoes for the journey for centuries before this. Intended functions are unclear, for many artefacts might serve different purposes: food and drink could sustain spirits in the grave or on the journey, and lamps, which are known from as far back as the Mycenean tombs, might light the way or illumine the grave for eternity. In either case, it was symbolism that counted, with the degree of literal belief depending on the individual.

Pots were the usual receptacle for cremated remains, and it was normal to use ordinary domestic wares (and not necessarily new or well-made examples). Straight-sided green glass urns, which do seem to have been specially made for the purpose, were popular in more prestigious graves. Sometimes the ashes were placed directly in the ground, but it is likely that originally some organic material such as leather, cloth or wood was normally used (Hector's cremated bones were wrapped in 'soft, purple cloths' in a golden box within a barrow for example). Typically the cremations were in urns that were sealed in some way, accompanied by one other pot (**colour plate 13**).

Box burials were one distinctive tradition in which we see the material goods of the Roman world used in ceremonies that recall aristocratic rites spreading down the social scale to aspirant middle classes amongst the Romanised natives. The containers were sometimes just wooden boxes, often with nails or iron fittings to strengthen the corners or to fasten them, or they might be smaller caskets with bronze fittings and/or decorative lion headed studs, or substantial wooden cists. Many of these graves are exceptionally well furnished, particularly with glass and rich tableware, and the lamps and hobnail boots discussed below. The earliest of these are found at Colchester in the mid-first century. In the late first/early second century they become numerous, serving small rich family groups near towns or on country estates, as in Litlington, Skeleton Green and Baldock (above). At Girton, on a road leading out of Roman Cambridge, there were at least three such burials, the richest of which had cremated bones in a wooden casket with boar's head studs, Samian plates and cup, glass vessels, a lead-glazed bowl and an iron lamp. Probably more typical was a much simpler boxed cremation in a small mixed cemetery at Milton, also near Cambridge. Here, the cremation was in an ordinary storage vessel within a plain wooden box, with two small wine flagons, both deliberately holed to 'kill' them (**colour plate 14**). Variations of these boxed burials are also sometimes found under Roman barrows.

Apart from pots used to hold burnt bone the most common early grave goods are place settings for food for the dead, obviously relating to a funerary meal eaten at the graveside which features in so much classical literature, where the dead received their own token share. The importance of symbolism is shown by the way the setting is often later replaced by a single pot, by the 'killing' of pots by smashing, holing or chipping their rim (suggesting the pot itself was more important than contents, especially as some are stacked the wrong way), and by leaving the dead with inedible portions of animals enjoyed by the relatives. Moderately wealthy graves in the south-east are commonly accompanied by up to four pots, generally a jar, a flagon, a bowl, a dish, or a selection of these.

Lamps in graves, some (as at Bartlow, and probably at Guilden Morden) known to have been left alight when the grave-chamber was closed, are a poignant offering, whether intended to light the journey to the underworld, to cheer the gloom for the spirits in their tomb-home, or, like candles today, as a symbol of hope and eternal life. These are most commonly found in the form of iron hanging lamps, made only rarely of terracotta, and we can imagine that candles or lights of other ephemeral materials were once extremely common. This ancient custom was to be long-lived, for lights can still be found burning on graves around Europe. In England it is originally found in urban and military centres, before spreading through the Trinovantian/Catuvellaunian territories and fusing with other customs of elaborate cremation that were already common among wealthy natives. The more elaborate urban cremations often had lamps. The most outstanding example was a group of eight in a woman's grave recently discovered at Great Dover Street, London. One was decorated with a gladiator and one with the Egyptian god Anubis, guardian of the Underworld and an indicator of a priestess of Isis, who is known to have had a temple in London.

Another homely touch in many graves was the inclusion of hobnail boots. This custom was to persist in varying degrees into the inhumation graves of the fourth century, although it virtually disappeared in the 'managed' cemeteries late in that century, presumably because shrouds replaced normal dress in the grave and shoes were only provided as deliberate grave goods. To some extent it may just reflect the occurrence of shod shoes, which were not worn in Iron Age Britain or in the Mediterranean world but were common in Gaul and the Rhineland. They were popular around small towns and in rural areas where farm-workers would find them comfortable, and are a useful indicator of the Romanisation of natives of all classes. In the second century most examples are with quite rich, often boxed, graves, along with lamps, coins and glass phials, but with later inhumations they usually occur with the middling range rather than the wealthy ones. When they occur with cremations they are sometimes found complete, that is added to the grave as a whole pair after the body was burnt, as at Guilden Morden where they are described as being tucked into the top of the cremation urn to keep everything else in place. At Skeleton Green some boots were cremated while others were placed as whole pairs in the grave pit. During the fourth century there were worn hobnail boots in many graves outside the coffins, as if the bodies were dressed differently and their normal clothes were left beside them. Similarly in Cambridge there were burials of babies in ritual shafts within the town which were supplied with shoes that would only have fitted older children. Obviously we are looking at more than the accidence of normal dress. It is worth remembering a much later reference to the custom which comes in a Norse saga, 'Gisli the Outlaw', in which, just before a body was laid in a barrow, a priest says 'tis the custom to bind the Hell shoe on men, so that they may walk on them to Valhalla'.

Coins, although well known in literature, are quite rare until the mid-second century when they become synthesised with the native custom of providing useful artefacts. The custom declines in the third century and reappears in the fourth. Although a widespread custom it was usually confined to only one or two graves per cemetery.

Imported pipeclay figurines, most commonly of children's busts but sometimes religious, are often found in children's graves in the most Romanised areas, notably London, York and Colchester. These are likely to belong to immigrant families, whether bureaucrats, soldiers or merchants, perhaps bringing the artefacts with them as part of a household shrine. One exceptionally exotic burial was a baby buried 2m deep next to Ermine Street at Arrington, Cambs. Although only a few months old and suffering from hydrocephalus the child, wrapped in a pink and blue woollen shawl, was in an over-sized lead-lined coffin with a box of imported pipeclay religious figurines including a Germanic mother-goddess, an Asiatic nature god and animals suitable for sacrifice. In this case there was no attempt to provide the child with anything practical, instead concentrating on its spiritual wellbeing with what looks like the contents of the family's domestic shrine, within an expensive grave from which no spirits could wander (**colour plate 15**). Further up Ermine Street a rather similar second-century child's grave, this time a cremation, was found within Godmanchester. Here the cremated bones of a small girl, her two bangles and a tiny gold rivet were within a Samian jar. She had a place setting of three more pots, as well as pipeclay figurines of a horse and bull, items thought to symbolise sacrifices for gods the deceased girl might meet (**colour plate 16**).

During the second century the cynicism of sophisticates such as Lucian of Samosata was perhaps becoming more widespread. The mass of the population did continue to deposit grave goods, but these are personal items that were customarily worn rather than artefacts of religious or even symbolic nature. Mixtures of grave goods now included bracelets, pins, beads and rings, mainly with females, especially adolescent girls, though men quite often had brooches as cloak fasteners. The best collections are from Colchester, generally thought to belong to an immigrant population.

## Food and wine, flowers and incense

Sprinkle my ashes with pure wine and fragrant oil of spikenard
Bring balsam, too, stranger, with crimson roses.
Tearless my urn enjoys eternal spring.
I have not died, but changed my state.
*Ausonius*

Even if a dead person is buried with fragrances he will rot, perhaps later, but he will rot all the same.
*St Augustine, late fourth century*

Ausonius' epitaph reminds us that, whilst organic offerings can play only a small part in the usual archaeological record, there is much evidence to show how important they were in the burial ritual. Many classical authors refer to roses and violets, and a flower was found at Bartlow, as well as a wreath of box leaves (above). There were leaves around a head in a lead coffin at Shaftesbury which were thought to be a wreath, and box is recorded at Chesterford (Essex) and Roden Down (Berks).

Anointing of the body with perfumed oils and the use of aromatic resin, fragrant spices and incense are well attested in Roman literature and throughout its provinces (as in the gospel accounts of Christ's treatment after crucifixion). Their considerable expense is seen in a letter of Younger Pliny in which, mourning the death of a young girl, he says that the money her wealthy father had intended for clothes, pearls and jewellery would now be spent on incense, ointments and perfume. The custom persisted throughout the Roman period and its extravagance was one of the complaints of church fathers such as John

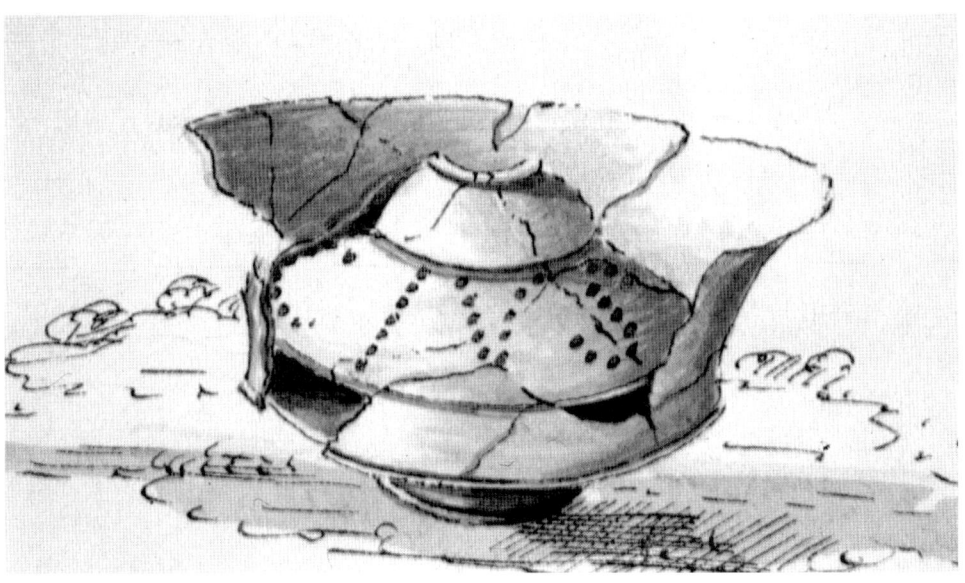

*46 An incense burner from Litlington cemetery.* © Cambridge Antiquarian Society

Chrysostom. In addition to glass phials which would have held perfumes and oils suitable for such anointing, there is a growing body of evidence for the use of such exotic substances in Roman Britain. Funerary incense burning is suggested at Skeleton Green and at Colchester, and a perforated pot from Litlington is interpreted as an incense burner (**46**). Lumps thought to be frankincense were found at Weston Turville (Bucks). At Aston Rowant, Oxfordshire, there was a seventeenth-century discovery of a Samian platter and other vessels, one of which held an aromatic liquor described as still having a strong scent. Another pot, stopped up with lead, held the cremated bones. In one of the Bartlow mounds a wickerwork bottle contained incense that smelled of frankincense or myrrh, and lumps of aromatic resin, probably myrrh, were found with the baby from Arrington, its face ringed with perfumed chunks which the author can vouch were still fragrant when crushed. It is perhaps worth noting here that we missed these in the field and they were only found during investigation of the skull in the laboratory, for they looked just like gravel. Innumerable other cases have probably gone unnoticed. With the Great Dover Street burial in London too there were eight tazzae that were sooted as if incense had burnt in them. The woman here had been cremated in a *bustum* (linked with Eastern auxiliaries and rare in Britain outside military sites and the large towns) with grave goods including many food remains. Amongst these were hundreds of stone pines, a food sometimes found on high-status occupation sites in London and Rome and linked with the Vestal Virgins as well as with temples of Mithras at Carrowburgh and London. Found too were several figs, an almond, a date, charred grains of barley, various types of wheat, a whole chicken, the bones of hens, cockerels and a dove. Foodstuffs in general were doubtless far more common than the archaeological record can normally show, and careful work at St Albans for example demonstrated that wholesome supplies of cabbage, wheat, hazelnuts and lentils were all cremated, counteracting endless references to joints of meat.

## Reuse of earlier sites

Though nowhere near as significant as it was to become in the Anglo-Saxon period, the reuse of earlier sites was often a feature of Roman burial. Prehistoric sites such as hill forts and barrows were used for temples and for minor rituals such as offerings of coins, and they might be the sites of apparently ordinary burials. Examples include Roxton, Beds, where a cremation in an old and broken pot was inserted in the edge of a ring-ditch, and Pakenham, Suffolk, where eight cremations were on the edge of a Bronze Age barrow.

Cemeteries with Iron Age antecedents sometimes went out of use and then were brought back into use after a period of neglect. At Westhampnett the Iron Age site was used more than a century later without disturbing the original cremations. The site was later used by a small Anglo-Saxon cemetery. A somewhat similar process is apparent at King Harry Lane (above) where the rich Iron Age cemetery continued in use for a small group of 20 cremations.

# 6 Roman burial: the third and fourth centuries

Take, O take him, mighty leader,
Take again thy servant's soul,
To the house from which he wandered
Exiled, erring, long ago.

But for us heap earth upon him,
Earth with leaves and violets strewn,
Grave his name, and pour the fragrant
Balm upon his icy stone.
*Prudentius*, 348-405, trans. Helen Waddell, 1929

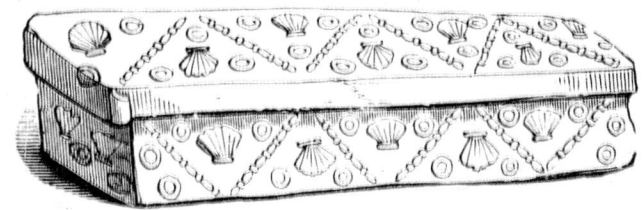

# Roman burial: the third and fourth centuries

Inhumation was introduced from the continent from the mid-second century when it started to take over from cremation in the large towns, was rare until the third century and only became almost universal in the fourth. In the form we see it in urban contexts it represents a new rite derived from the more sophisticated religions of the East. It started in Britain in towns and military areas, but in the countryside the situation is more complex. There, inhumation, usually crouched and without deep graves, was already the normal rite, and the two traditions resulted in more varied patterns than are found with more Romanised parts of the population. Burials close to town limits filled cemeteries with, in some cases, thousands of bodies (**colour plate 17**).

Probably due to the use of professional undertakers and municipal by-laws these burials became remarkably standardised, and for the first time nearly all members of certain communities, even the babies, were buried in the same way. The great majority lie extended on their backs, often in nailed wooden coffins but with a few high-status ones of stone and/or lead. There is evidence for the use of shrouds, but others must have been dressed in normal clothes for functional buckles and brooches are also known. There is a sharp decline in use of grave goods in the fourth century, especially in the orderly urban sites.

## Religious beliefs

The change to coffined inhumation, scarcely any grave goods, tidy rows and regular west-east alignment, in areas set aside for burial of the whole community, is seen throughout the Roman Empire. It is independent of political, economic or cultural upheaval, being rather one of the rare occasions when we can link changes in burial practice with religion. By the second half of the fourth century in Britain the strongest influence was the Christian Church, but the change had begun much earlier in the Mediterranean world, when Christianity was still a minor and private affair. Attempts to understand the origins of this change, whereby ancient eastern traditions including Judaism were mixed with mystic religions and sun worship, plus novel Christian attitudes and practices, need to begin well outside the remote British province.

The reasons behind the changes are not really understood, though there is evidence for the growing influence of eastern mystery religions, which for historical rather than theological reasons favoured inhumation. There were followers of these in the Roman world from the first century, for Isis was introduced by Caligula, and Claudius permitted worship of Cybele. In Britain both of these appear, for example on Hadrian's Wall and in London, but membership was restricted, often to males of particular classes, and some aspects of these cults (such as self-castration in the case of Cybele) were hardly tempting whatever the offers for life after death. The influence of these religions presumably explains some of the exotic inhumation burials (not restricted to noviciates, as women and children are represented). We cannot assume that an individual buried with one form of rite was committed to a particular religion, for fashion, social emulation and the convenience of professional undertakers and municipal authorities must have played a part. Yet it is from these eastern religions that the inspiration and example came. When one of these, Christianity, became the state religion in the fourth century, its practices were widely adopted and, it can be argued, became *the* major influence over cemeteries of this date (**47**).

If we do accept that the bulk of fourth-century inhumation burials were according to the Christian rite we need to examine the influences that created the form so dominant at this time. Inhumation was to return with Christianity in the later Anglo-Saxon period and is still commonly followed in Britain today. These influences include specifically Christian attitudes, Jewish traditions, other Eastern cults, the continuing appeal of older Roman rites, and the resurgence of even older Celtic forms. Arguably the clearest of these influences was Jewish custom. Up to the end of the fourth century Christian burial followed Jewish traditions of underground catacombs outside towns and the use of separate areas; Jewish customs in general were followed until Paul emphasised differences, and early

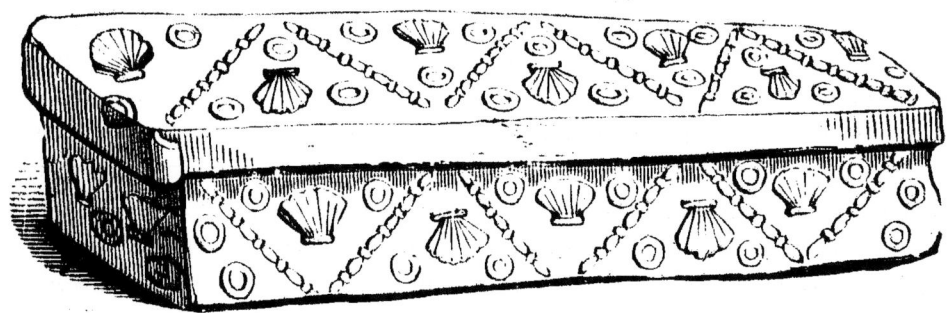

*47 A richly decorated lead coffin from Colchester. Scallop shells, like the emphasis on physical protection of the body, relate to Christian beliefs but are also found in other imported religious beliefs*

Christian communities thrived most in areas where Judaism was already strong. Athanasius states that Christian burial follows Jewish rites, and Tertullian describes Christian burials including anointing with spices, though incense and wreaths were sometimes forbidden. Like later Christians people were consciously following the example of Christ's burial, and Jerome for example described burying the dead in linen, like Christ, as one of the duties of a priest. They followed customs such as the use of a plain shroud and no other clothing or grave goods, elaborate preparation and anointing of the body, careful avoidance of any intercutting or other disturbance of graves, and the optional use of wooden coffins. Although found in other cultures, these were important parts of burial technology in Jewish practice, reflecting fear of the dead as pollutants and the need to protect the living. However, the official Jewish attitude that the dead body is unclean, and that even an 'olive's bulk' of a corpse could pollute, was defiantly not adopted, often to the disgust of contemporaries for this was also the usual Roman view.

Another attitude to the dead, which Jon Davies (1999) interestingly argues entered medieval Christianity via a competing and strictly unofficial Jewish belief, was the prehistoric tradition that the bones of important ancestors are filled with magical and sacred properties. This led to a long-lived secondary burial tradition, as seen in the many parts of Europe, including Britain, in the Neolithic period. The attitude was anathema to official Jewish thought at the time of Christ, but occasional biblical references show it was current as a folk tradition, and at Beth Shearim, for example, the second-century AD necropolis was still a site where disarticulated bones were visited and regularly rearranged. In this culture the dead are intercessors in the afterlife, and they need continuing care by the living. Their presence could legitimise land holding and affect the fertility of this land. Much Jewish law was concerned with restricting what we might see as black magic (consulting and providing offerings for the dead, for example), for these had been part of Canaanite practice, but there was always popular pressure to revert to older customs. In Christianity, the revival of cults of the dead and of sacrifice appear more strongly. Related beliefs and practices (such as saints and martyrs interceding for the living) become respected if disputed theology, others (such as calling up spirits) definitely did not, but were practised (even today) nonetheless.

The cult of saintly relics in caskets can be seen as a continuation of this tradition of reverencing, consulting and rearranging the bones of significant individuals. Extreme reverence for the remains of martyrs became particularly important in the foundation of shrines/churches within cemeteries, a practice which could lead to wholesale shifts in population, as the centres of towns such as St Albans moved away from their Roman sites onto what had been extramural burial grounds. A common scenario in Gaul was for graves to cluster around the tombs of saintly individuals, and for their mausolea to be virtually used as churches. This started a movement for settlement outside city centres in some places, as habitation moved to be around the mortuary chapel/church. The cult of martyrs made early churches in towns (often reusing old sacred areas) virtually into mortuary chapels, attracting first the burials of the rich founding families and later a more general congregation. This blurring of a distinction between mortuary chapels and places of worship was to be a lasting feature of the Christian church.

The Christian concept of death was that it was not polluting but was a matter of joy. In the early centuries, especially during periods of persecution, faith in immediate and blissful new life became so strong that Christian leaders had to start teaching and even legislating against suicide. The very early Church expected a rapid Second Coming that made careful burial irrelevant, but St Paul played down such expectations in favour of more individual resurrection. This literal concept of life after death was a key attraction of early Christianity and preachers were much concerned that all members of the community be given both baptism and proper burial to ensure it was achieved. Infants were specifically targeted for both rites and appear fully for the first time in the buried congregation due both to these concerns and to Christian teachings against the common Roman practice of infanticide. The preoccupation of Christians with physical rebirth in popular though not official thought was well recognised by contemporaries. Eusebius for example writes of how burial of martyrs was prevented.

> For those who had been strangled in jail they threw to the dogs, and watched carefully day and night that none should be cared for by us. They threw out the remains left by the beasts and by the fire, torn and charred, and for many days watched with untiring guard the heads of the rest, together with the trunks, all unburied.

The custom clearly started early on in the life of Christianity for in the 150s the Jews of Smyrna would not release one martyr for fear his bones would start a cult. Where bones of the martyred dead were recovered, they were often not treated like the other Christians but more like the old prehistoric ancestral bones. They might be moved over great distances, or could be adopted as a local cult like the old genii loci.

Elements of Roman rites also continued. An important one, the funerary meal, perhaps in the mortuary chapel rather than at the graveside is certainly recorded. Even the custom of leaving food and drink by graves must have persisted for it was necessary for St Augustine to condemn it, though connected items such as pots and animal bones become rare in well-managed cemeteries. Some aspects of even older Iron Age rites reappear at this time together with new forms such as decapitated burials. Some rural customs, such as the mutilation of bodies, crouched burials, cist graves and the habit of wearing or taking hobnail boots, occur far more frequently away from the large urban cemeteries though scattered examples do creep into these, perhaps with migrant labour. This may be because all those buried in them had fully bought into the strictures of one faith, but it is more likely that it was the professional undertakers who ran the cemeteries on behalf of town councils who ensured uniformity in line with the state religion. The countryside always lagged well behind and had much more variety. There were always a few cremations in some old-fashioned areas, and there are even sites in some very Romanised areas that continued to prefer the old rites. Examples include King Harry Lane, Braughing, and military sites near Hadrian's Wall.

By and large however the new rite was so widely accepted that areas that never adopted cremation shift directly from Iron Age style crouched inhumations, a process seen just outside Dorchester in cemeteries such as Alington Drive and Poundbury. These can perhaps best be described as middle-class cemeteries serving a country town that had long been Romanised but was distant from the exotic influences that appear in trading and military centres. This is the context for Poundbury, the principal British cemetery for which an essentially Christian population is argued.

## Monuments and memorials

Mausolea, often big enough to live in, would be used by many generations of a family and its dependants, and had practical uses during the ceremonies and meals held to remember the ancestral dead. Their remains are often found in managed urban cemeteries, including small towns such as Cambridge (**48**) and Dorchester. At Poundbury there were ten mausolea, square or rectangular enclosures with stone and mortar foundations (**49**). Painted plaster on the walls included lifesize human figures with tunics and draped garments, and views of townscapes. In one group three generations of men were depicted. Similar evidence to Poundbury was found at West Tenter Street, London, where mausolea had burials grouped around them and at York where the larger ones had plastered stone walls and cement floors. There were even mausolea near Cambridge (where building stone has to be transported for about 40 miles), including some with monumental carvings like the lion and other figures from Girton (**50**). These mausolea are also found associated with villas, such as Litlington and Lullingstone. Stone and lead coffins are often found in them (**51**). Quite a few of these were eventually turned into churches on both urban and rural sites, for example at Lullingstone and Colchester. Another cemetery at Colchester was a site with a specifically Christian character containing a small Roman church in one corner. This was built over an important grave within a timber vault, which can be seen as a founder burial for the church. The church itself is described by the excavators as a 'funeral banqueting hall', used for memorial services and funeral meals, with a timber

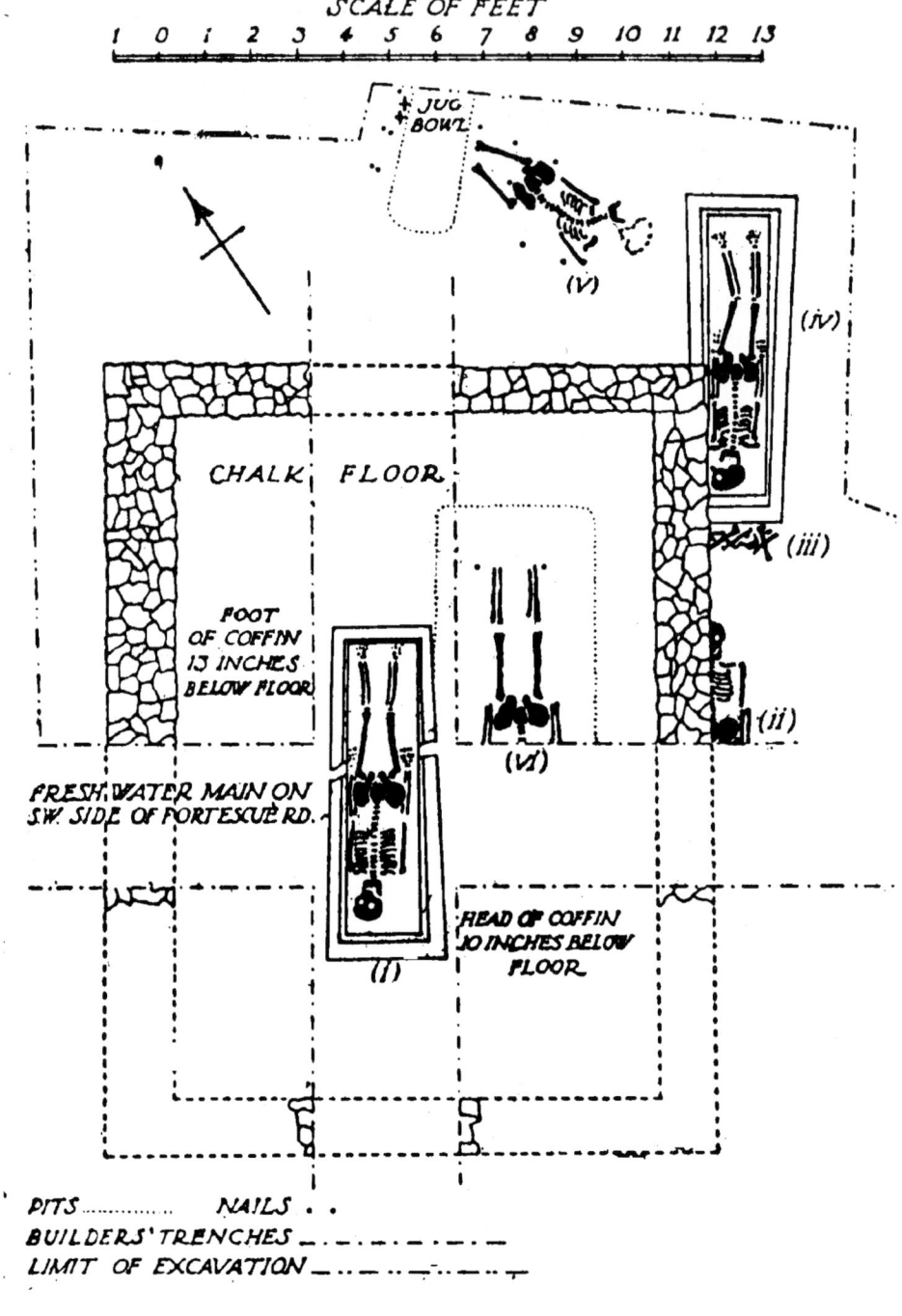

SCALE OF FEET

CHALK FLOOR.

JUG
BOWL

(V)

(iv)

(iii)

FOOT
OF COFFIN
13 INCHES
BELOW FLOOR

FRESH WATER MAIN ON
S.W. SIDE OF FORTESCUE RD.

(vi)

(ii)

HEAD OF COFFIN
10 INCHES BELOW
FLOOR

(i)

PITS ............... NAILS . .
BUILDERS' TRENCHES _ . _ .. _ . _ .. _
LIMIT OF EXCAVATION _ .. _ .. _ . _ .. _ . _ _

48 *Successive burials on a road out of Cambridge culminate in a single lead-lined stone*
*coffin within a mausoleum. Earlier graves were ignored, even one in a stone coffin.*
© Cambridge Antiquarian Society

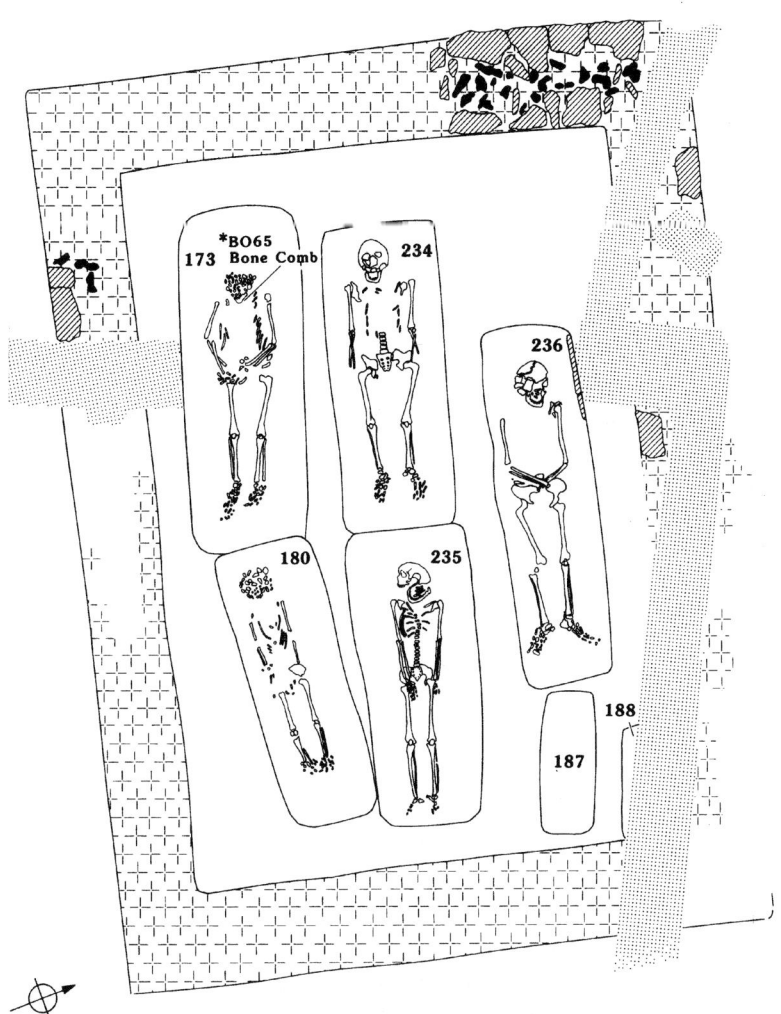

*49 A family mausoleum at Poundbury, Dorchester, originally containing two men, two women, a child and two babies, all in nailed wooden coffins. The only grave good is a comb in one woman's hair. The building was decorated with painted plaster and stood until the late fourth century. © Dorset Natural History and Archaeological Society*

structure later built on as a kitchen. An apse and two aisles were then added, and afterwards the nave extended. The overlaps in form and function between this early church and the old pagan style of family mausoleum are striking.

Graves in cemeteries were marked in many ways, their positions apparent for long periods to judge by the lack of intercutting graves. In a few areas, nearly always linked with the military, tombstones were used, often engraved with the

*50 A stone lion's head that decorated a mausoleum at Girton. © Cambridge Antiquarian Society*

*51 A stone coffin that came from a mausoleum at Litlington but was moved to the church, a common location for antiquarian finds*

name, age and place of origin of the person commemorated (**colour plate 18**). These are a valuable source of personal data, most interestingly seen on Hadrian's Wall where the scale and long period of occupation by the army together with abundant stone suitable for carving meant that quite ordinary people including children (**52**) were recorded, sometimes in touching detail. At South Shields was found a stone in memory of Regina, a Catuvellaunian ex-slave woman who ended her days married to a man from Palmyra stationed on the Wall, a reminder of the

52 *A young child, Pervica, is commemorated on a tombstone that combines native style with Roman custom. Originally from Great Chesters on Hadrian's Wall it is now on display in the Museum of Antiquities, Newcastle.* Photograph by Lindsay Allason-Jones © Courtesy of Museum of Antiquities, Newcastle

mobility of individuals at this time (if often not through their own choosing). Descriptions of social status are an important element of the inscriptions, as well as family relationships and rather uninspiring virtues. This is somewhat surprising as the status celebrated often appears quite humble. Auxiliary troops and freed men and women seem most commonly commemorated in this way (**colour plate 19**). The London tombstone of Claudia Martina even records her marriage to a slave. Only rarely are events or causes of death given (**53**).

Most graves had far less to mark them. Tile-tombs, such as those found at York, and fourth-century cist graves, were designed to be visible above ground, and holes for wood or stone grave markers have been noted in excavations at Poundbury for example, where one was excavated as two post-holes and two iron loops with spiked attachments. Even more ephemeral markers would be pots (or just sherds) or tiles, as mentioned in literary sources, or a white substance such as the lime used in plaster burials, a normal practice in Palestine (the biblical 'whited sepulchres').

## Grave layout and coffins

The promise of rebirth without a need for worldly goods or sustenance as stressed by Christianity concentrated efforts on care for the body itself, seen for example in the elaborate dressing of hair at Poundbury, the use of a standard white linen shroud, the best and most secure coffin that could be afforded and, probably thanks to confusion with sun worship, a west-east alignment.

London had enormous cemeteries along the roads leading out of it. Excavations on the eastern cemetery have shown that more than 50 acres were devoted to burial here, dating from the first to the fifth century and estimated to contain over 100,000 bodies. Long-lived plots here have made it possible to study the way individual families gradually adapted from cremation to inhumation, often with long periods when both rites were practised side by side and a surprising mixture of customs within single plots. One cemetery, West Tenter Street, was thought to be Christian yet, although nearly all the inhumations were in coffins, their orientation was mixed, and the largest number in fact lay roughly north-south. London has produced a very early coffin in the new fashion, found with its timber still preserved. It was made of rough-hewn reused planks fastened with many small nails without any carpentry joints, and contained a mid-second century flagon (**colour plate 20**).

Roman Colchester also has a large collection of Roman burials (about 1400) from at least seven cemetery areas. The last cremation is after about AD 240, and the earliest inhumations started about 250 so the change was rapid and orderly, more typical of the effects of new bylaws and regulations than religious

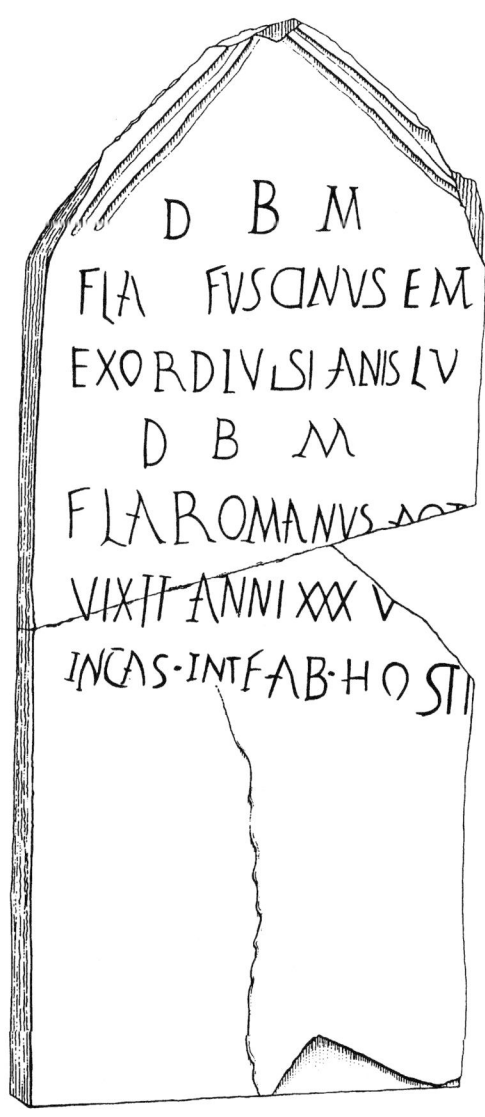

*53 A tombstone found reused in a later building near the fort at Ambleside must have had a dramatic story behind it. The first inscription is straightforward and reads 'D(is) B(onis) M(anibus) Fla(vius) Fuscinus eme(ritus) ex ordi(nato) visi(t) an(n)is LV.' 'To the good spirits of the departed, Flavius Fascinus a retired centurion who lived 55 years.' The second reads 'D(is) B(onis) M(anibus) Fla(vius) Romanus (act(arius) vixit anni)s) XXXV. In cas(tris) inte(fectus) ab hosti(bus).' 'Flavius Romanus, a record clerk, lived 35 years and was killed by the enemy within the camp.' This unfortunate accountant was killed by someone who got into the fort.* © English Heritage motivation or the vague following of fashion. Inhumations on these sites had mixed alignments governed by boundaries around the plots until greater organisation came with west-east burials at a later stage. Overall, about 90 per cent of inhumations at Colchester were in wood coffins, 21 in lead (one with a pipe over the head to pour drink down), and a few stone ones are known. Few lack coffins, and these tend to be careless burials in unusual positions, usually outside the cemetery areas. At Butt Road cemetery the shift to inhumation was early, in the mid-second century, and after this a more formal cemetery layout was adopted, with north-south alignments and plots marked by ditches. The burials at this stage were very consistent, all of them in wooden coffins.

By about 320/40 a Christian church was built at Butt Road cemetery, and alignments then changed, apparently immediately, to west-east. This meant taking great care to avoid intercutting north-south graves, but without other changes to burial ritual as families continued to own and use plots. There were few grave goods among the 669 burials here, and these are very varied. Family groups were identifiable, some showing continuity with earlier plots, and they included the burials of very young children. A few graves were marked with timber posts or stones and tile fragments. In some cases graves were dug deliberately large so they could be opened for another family member, and a few were stacked as much as four deep. Graves without coffins were extremely rare. Apart from an infant and graves excluded from the main cemetery all at this time had their heads to the west, lay flat on their backs (though the legs were sometimes moved a little to accommodate the coffin) and the arms were to the side or resting on lap or hips. Seven were in lime plaster or gypsum, only one, a child, being completely covered and with impressions of a shroud surviving. This child was in a lead coffin decorated with scallop shells and St Andrew's crosses. In total there were nine fragments of textile recognisable, one silk and the rest linen, all thought to be shrouds not clothing, though occasional bodies were wearing jewellery.

Poundbury, although only outside a small town, includes a cemetery that exhibits some of the clearest Christian characteristics. Its huge number of burials (some 4000) were almost all west-east, in regular rows, mostly in wooden coffins, with some of them stone- or lead-lined and packed with gypsum. One had a St Andrew's cross and another had letters scratched inside the coffin which can be read as the Christian dedication *i(n) n(omime tuo) D(omi)ne*. Poundbury is also one of the best cemeteries for seeing how carefully bodies were laid out before burial. This shows most clearly in some gypsum-packed lead coffins where, for example, hairstyles were oiled and dressed especially for the burial. One elderly man seemed to have had his receding hair treated with henna and combed forward to cover the bald area. A woman's naturally fair hair had an elaborate style composed of five and six strand plaits, one wound around her head and the other coiled in a bun, with a fringe in front. Some skulls still showed how the hair had lain, and on these it appears that men had hair combed forward while on women it was drawn back, with a centre parting. Careful combing and dressing with oil seems universal. Men, women and children were buried throughout the cemetery in family groups in which genetic characteristics were shared. Outside the Christian area at Poundbury there continued a quite disorderly layout of graves, with alignments governed by existing enclosure boundaries. These fringe cemeteries included several examples of facedown, crouched and decapitated burials comparable with those in rural cemeteries, as well as including their boots and other grave goods (**54**).

A few coffins in the main cemetery were lined with lead, and some of these as well as some plain wooden ones were packed with plaster or gypsum. This plaster was either poured in to create a whole or partial cast, or was bound to the body with a shroud. It may have been seen as a preservative and/or antiseptic, absorbing noxious liquids and inhibiting bacterial action and it is certainly helpful to the archaeologist in preserving both the casts of linen, showing that a shroud was now normal, and organic remains such as hair. It is mostly found in the fourth century,

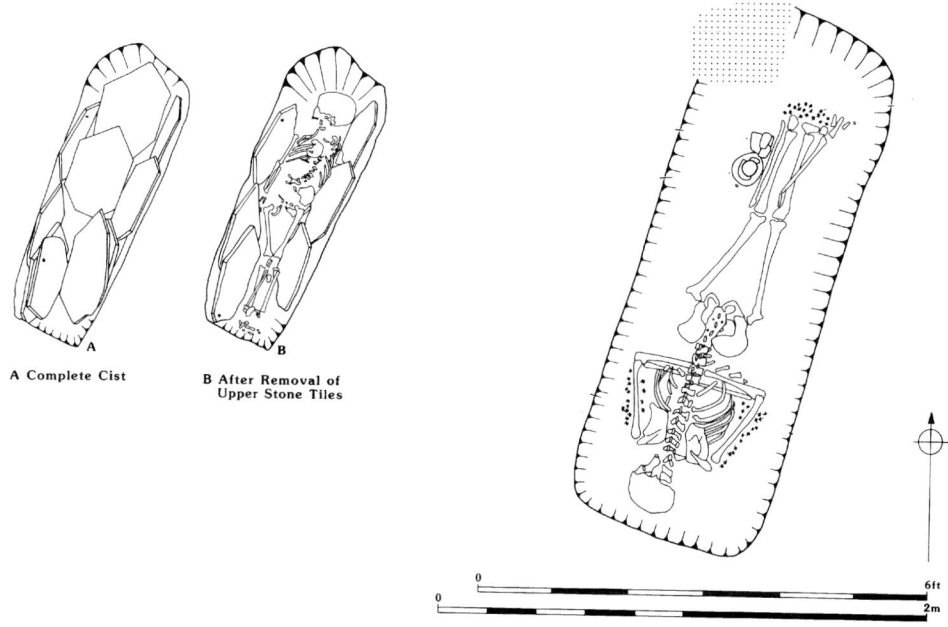

A Complete Cist     B After Removal of Upper Stone Tiles

*54 Late Roman burials in the peripheral cemeteries at Poundbury continued older traditions. The child on the left, in a cist made with roof tiles, had been born deaf and was buried face down, as if its spirit might be fearful. The man on the right had hobnail boots on his feet and an extra pair under his arms as well as two pots. There was no sign of a coffin. Neither follow the west-east pattern of the Christian cemetery.*
© Dorset Natural History and Archaeological Society

121

*55 Stone coffin from York, in which a man was wrapped in 'a coarse linen cloth, fragments of which still remained', within a cedar lining*

generally in urban areas and in rich and specifically Christian contexts such as Lullingstone and Icklingham. At York itself, where a considerable Christian population is known, one part of cemetery had 20 plaster-packed stone or lead coffins without grave goods, all in rows and with their heads roughly to the west. In one, stone slabs covered a wooden coffin, thought, when found in the nineteenth century, to be cedar, within which the plaster had preserved a coarse linen shroud (**55**). Similar burials occur at London, for example, where eight fourth-century plaster graves in one area were only partially covered, so the symbolism of the white cleansing powder was perhaps more important than any notion of corporeal preservation in preparation for resurrection. Despite many Christian connections the custom began in pre-Christian North Africa and Egypt (though it only becomes common in the third and fourth century AD), also being used in graves in the Rhineland, where it gained a strong Christian link through use in martyrs' burials. Quite a few such plaster graves, however, do not lie west-east or have grave goods, so probably there were other rich immigrants who were not Christian.

Even urban cemeteries had areas where older customs persisted, for paganism was not banned until 395 and there would still have been places where such state rules could be ignored. There were parts of Poundbury where mixed rites of older customs were found and nearby, at Maiden Castle Road, there were even late fourth-century skeletons flexed or crouched in the Durotrigian tradition. Seven of these had hobnails in the grave, two had pots, two had the bones of young sheep and one a chicken, remarkable evidence for the continuation of the old rites in a very Romanised area so late in the Empire. One burial even had a bracelet and a ring with intaglio. Typically, this was a young woman, for it is generally they who carried on the custom of being buried with jewellery for longest.

In rural areas there were more variations within the cemeteries and more old-fashioned reliance on sustenance being provided for the life beyond the grave (**colour plate 21**). Mixed rites persist throughout this period, though the survival of greater numbers of ordinary inhumations suggests that there was more widespread use of deep graves than in earlier years. It may be that this is one factor in the quite sudden appearance of mutilated bodies, usually decapitated or lying face down with arms and legs often sprawling or bound, with few signs of respect. These suggest older customs and punishments that could be undetected in centuries when the ordinary rural population is invisible in death. Decapitation for example has been reported from every late Roman rural cemetery in Oxfordshire, including more than 10 per cent of burials at Cassington. These decapitated bodies, like those buried prone (face down), are an interesting phenomenon with no obvious explanation. Occasionally the beheading was from behind, with an axe, and probably represents execution, but usually the head was removed from the front and with great care in severing the vertebrae. These heads were almost certainly cut off after death, after blood had stopped pumping out. In many cases the body was then buried with normal careful burial, with the head in various positions but no other sign of disrespect. In these cases the cause of this treatment may be linked to a wish to release the spirit of the dead, possibly due to fear of witchcraft or the walking dead. Others, especially those face down, often have unusual positions within the grave or marginal situations in the cemetery, and few grave goods, though there are exceptions to this which may be due to mistakes by undertakers, explicable when dealing with shrouded bodies, heavy coffins or night-time ceremonies. It is noticeable however that these deviant forms of burial rarely occur in managed urban cemeteries, and they indicate different religious practices and attitudes to certain corpses which continue well into the Anglo-Saxon period (**56**). Other features particularly observed in Oxfordshire and apparent in many areas are variable grave alignment, often relating to boundaries, and the occasional continued use of cremation. Many informal arrangements were also made for burial in the countryside. In Bedfordshire there were inhumations in old pits at Odell, in a well at Sandy and on a yard surface at Newnham. Quite a few made use of Bronze Age round barrows, as at Dunstable Downs, Galley Hill (Streatley), and, following the single cremation found on the edge of a ring-ditch at Roxton, the unaccompanied inhumation of a woman in a similar position on the same site. Elsewhere such inhumations are not rare: they have been noted for example in barrows on White Horse Hill (Bronze Age), and Waylands Smithy and Hetty Pegler's Tump (Neolithic).

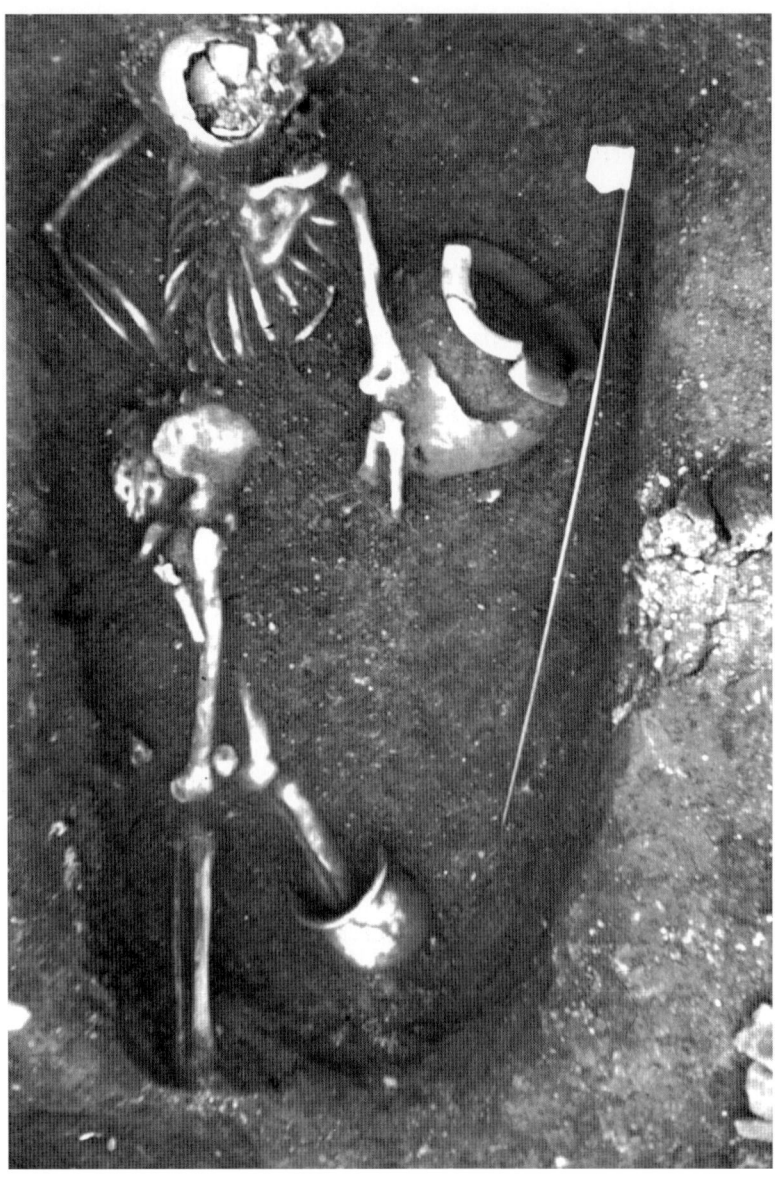

*56 A prone and awkward burial of a man with his feet removed within the walled town of Cambridge. Though apparently a careless burial, its location and deliberate disrespect to the corpse indicate unusual practices.* © Cambridge Antiquarian Society

It was normal for large rural cemeteries to continue in use without any of the reorganisation seen in towns. In Cambridgeshire the cemetery at Guilden Morden continued in use without any sharp changes, some cremations belonging in the later period just as there had been inhumations earlier on. Inhumations here are described as lying in all directions except for west-east, and they intercut each other at random. At least three were decapitated, one with her head in her lap, another (her body partially burned in the grave) with it at the feet (**57**), and one replaced in the right position. Others lay oddly, though quite a few were in coffins with an eclectic mixture of grave goods. These included glass phials, bronze, shale and bone bracelets, brooches, a finger ring, a coin in a child's mouth, some amulets including a bell on a child's wrist, a possible priest with a sceptre that had a phallic amulet hanging from it, ferrule and a pile of charred grain. There was also a woman with charcoal scattered by her leg, a custom which, like the burned grain, will reoccur in Saxon times. Several of the inhumations were in nailed coffins, two also had angle irons and one had loops for careful lowering into the ground, but there were many impoverished burials, and at least six skeletons had been dumped in a ditch 'without any attempt at seemly internment' according to the excavator. The whole cemetery therefore includes a huge range of rites and variations in status during its long history, which was completed with a few early Anglo-Saxon graves. As in earlier centuries this is a contrast to Litlington where the cremation cemetery was succeeded by about 250 more orderly inhumations, often in nailed coffins. Many had coins, and there were brooches, beads, bracelets and pins, though these are difficult to disentangle from finds with cremations.

In northern England cremation continued to be a normal burial rite for the military. Forts on Hadrian's Wall feature pyre debris, often in small quantities, as if actual burial was the least important part of the funerary ritual, a factor noted elsewhere on the Roman frontier. Often just a token amount of bone was placed, while still hot, in a small square hole, sometimes with fragments of pot. These sites were constantly reused and holes intercut.

## Grave goods

Rarity of grave goods, even clothing, was also a feature of eastern cults before Christianity was common, and in this period inclusion of jewellery is an exception not the rule. It generally became limited to the most vulnerable not the most prestigious in society: children and young girls. Other occasional grave goods include a single pot, some food (animal and bird bones are quite often found and there are occasionally shellfish or eggs), a coin, or an unworn personal item. For the first time grave goods, though increasingly scarce, are more common in rural than urban contexts.

Grave goods were not forbidden by Christianity nor, as far as we know, by other religions of the time. Yet concepts of a more spiritual type of afterlife seem to have made them generally redundant, and the use of shrouds in particular stopped the use of ordinary items associated with dress, such as fastenings.

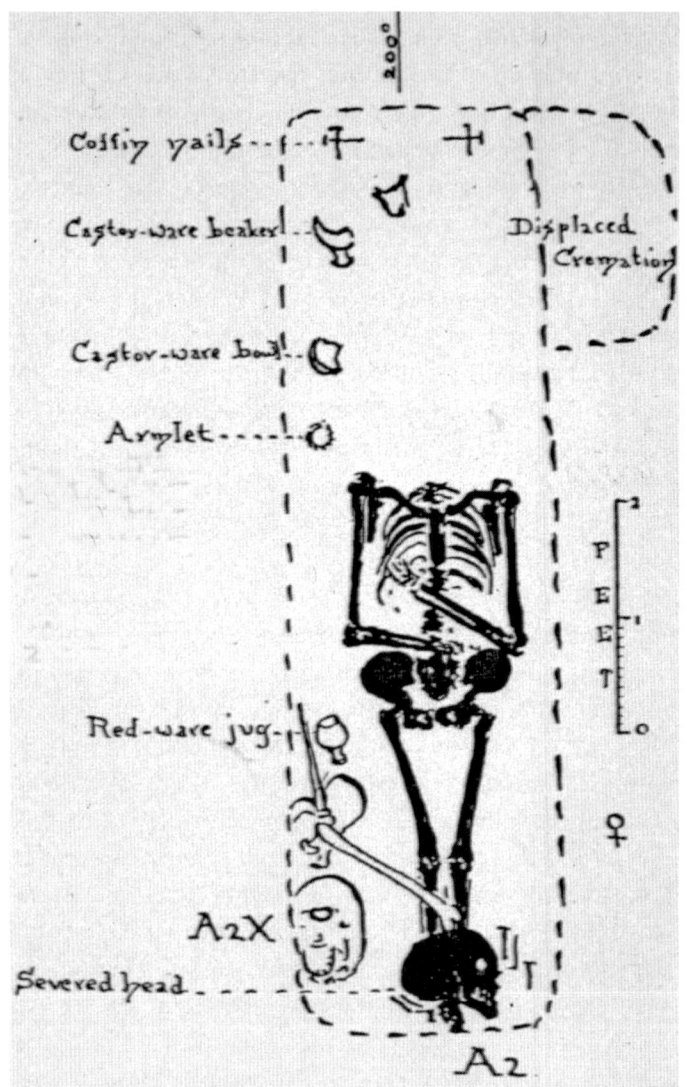

57 *The coffined burial of an elderly woman at Guilden Morden, Cambs, disturbed after death and her head placed at her feet.* © Cambridge Antiquarian Society

Brooches disappeared when bodies were no longer buried wrapped in cloaks but, as bracelets were probably worn constantly in life by some adolescent girls, these were not removed after death. There could be exceptions; a woman in York can be presumed to be Christian from a strip of bone on which a motto reads 'Sister, hail! May you live in God', but her grave was very fully furnished with earrings, bracelets, armlets, mirror and glass jug. Elsewhere some grave goods are specifically Christian, such as a bronze-sheeted wooden vessel decorated with biblical scenes and found with a child at Long Wittenham.

The change was fairly gradual, for inhumations of the late second and third century are often still quite richly provisioned. Butt Road, Colchester, is a good site to see where the dramatic shift away from grave goods came in a well-organised cemetery. With the earlier north-south burials more than half had some sort of grave goods, most commonly a pot (sometimes inverted, some on top of or outside coffin), or hobnails. Interestingly (and providing further evidence for professional undertakers making choices on behalf of the family), pots deposited as grave goods were anything up to 200 years old when they were buried. This was highly confusing for the excavators, and eventually it was decided that the answer was that undertakers were reusing cremation urns from the same cemetery. Other grave goods were a mixed bag. A few women had jewellery, there were two styli and a wooden writing tablet at the feet of one man, and a child had a purse containing a chain with good luck charms (coins, a bell, a horned phallus, an African head in amber and a pierced dog's tooth). Foreign influences in this highly Romanised area therefore seem to have changed the rite from cremation without noticeable impact on grave goods, the impression being that the cemetery was principally run for the convenience of professional grave diggers, with just a few extra items added for personal reasons.

In the fourth century this cemetery moved around a church. The proportion of burials with grave goods dropped to seven per cent, and these were mostly personal adornment with young girls, men only wearing finger rings, and all graves were oriented west-east. Most of the jewellery was in boxes or wrapped and placed near the head (perhaps deliberately hidden), but elaborate hair pins (not typical of ones used in life) and combs on the heads of women and children (and one man) were probably to keep neatly dressed hair in place, an important part of the preparation of the body. Only 13 (1.5 per cent) had pottery or glass vessels, even less than found at Poundbury, so the teachings of St Augustine and others like him against the provision of food and drink for the dead must have been having some effect. Other rare grave goods included an unpierced coin, boots on one body, hobnails in the graves of six others and a few amulets such as a bead, old coin or bell. Thus pagan customs were not quite dead, especially for the most vulnerable, but were no longer considered normal behaviour. Though not common, the use of amulets, especially bells, obviously had great significance to individuals and gave much offence to the religious authorities. There were many strictures against their use, and eventually this became a capital offence, women being particularly liable to this condemnation. The church father John Chrysostom specifically condemned anyone who entrusted children to the protection of bells, but they were still placed in children's graves in the catacombs of Rome, and in Britain at rural sites such as Guilden Morden as well as sophisticated Colchester.

Elsewhere in Colchester yet another third-/fourth-century cemetery, with 34 mainly west-east burials in coffins, had very few grave goods except with children. This also became the site of a church, later St John's abbey. Food remains are especially rare, though some flagons and similar vessels are stoppered, so perhaps the very ancient custom of providing a drink for the departed was dying hard after all.

Poundbury is an instructive site for the changing pattern of grave good deposition. After a period of neglect, following use from the Iron Age into the second century, its stable burial rituals ignoring cultural changes in these years, separate enclosures were laid out in the fourth century. Two of these came to be used for a cemetery for over 1000 people who all seem to be buried in the Christian tradition, while in other areas there continued a more local rite. In the Christian area grave goods were very rare, those that occurred being mostly bracelets or bone combs, with occasional glass beads, spindle whorls, knives, pins etc, found with young women and children. The only object associated with men were single coins, mostly in the mouth in the old tradition. In other areas (where more mixed rites were also noted) there were grave goods such as pots, worn jewellery and animal bones. Hobnails representing three sorts of footwear were found on men, women and children. These burials are comparable with those in rural cemeteries.

At the other extreme of Romano-British practice there are a few clearly exotic burials. Centres such as London, York, St Albans and Colchester, where the families of expatriate civil servants, military officers or merchants are to be expected, see most of the finds of this class. Examples include a child at St Albans who lay in a lead coffin covered with roofing tiles wearing a linen tunic embroidered with gold thread and wrapped in a woollen cloak. He/she held an iron staff decorated with beads, had a coin in the mouth and a wooden toy box with coloured beads, rings, Mediterranean seashells and a phallic amulet. More spectacularly, the lead coffin of a girl recently found at Spitalfields, London, dating to AD 350 or later, was decorated with scallop shells. Her grave goods included several glass vessels of various types and she also had a stoppered glass phial and dipper outside her coffin, presumably containing perfumes or unguents associated with preparation of her body for the grave. She was remarkable for the traces of cloth in the lead coffin, for one garment was of silk damask from Syria decorated with gold thread, and another of wool may have been her shroud. She had a tiny box made of pieces of jet and jet-like substances, and the silt beneath her body contained fig seeds. Leaves of bay were used as a pillow. Otherwise the large cemetery of Spitalfields was highly orthodox, with all the bodies in neat west-east rows and no intercutting. This is the pattern being found around innumerable Roman towns, even small ones such as Godmanchester, all with coffined graves, regular orientation, a paucity of grave goods, great size, and whole communities buried together.

Further records of plant remains and other organic materials are disappointingly rare despite the abundant literature on the importance of flowers and anointment of the body. Apart from the burials described above, examples include Scole, Norfolk, where a child was buried in a coffin preserved in wet peat which had leaves of box and seeds of deadly nightshade (not a local plant in that area). At Dartford too, plaster round a girl's body preserved hair that was fixed with pearls, and the remains of an aromatic substance. The best evidence for the use of precious oils, perfumes and other aromatic substances are the glass phials found in rich graves, mostly with young women and in stone or lead coffins or cists, quite often with other foreign aspects to the burial.

At the other extreme it is worth remembering how many small towns have single or groups of quite casual burials in ditches and other features on the fringes of settlement. Farms too, as in earlier and later years, have burials in ditches, especially in the corners of fields, with little to show what ceremonies attended them.

# Examples

## *Cirencester*

In contrast to the well-managed urban cemeteries was one just outside the highly Romanised town of Cirencester. Here, in the mid- to late fourth century, there were 421 inhumations and three cremations which, with a few exceptions, belonged to a more disadvantaged section of society. Pathological evidence suggests many of those buried here belonged to the nearby amphitheatre as gladiators, acrobats and so on, though labouring in the nearby stone quarries could explain some of their problems, and a cemetery for retired legionaries has also been suggested. The demography of this cemetery was certainly very strange: 241 males, 96 females and 62 children. Although there were five stone coffins, used for men, women and children, most have no evidence for a coffin at all. Most lie approximately north-south, aligned on neighbouring features such as the Fosse Way. One child had jewellery but otherwise the only grave goods were occasional coins on the eyes or in the mouth. There were several examples of prone burial and decapitation, and one looked as if her arms were tied behind her back.

The numerous cases of injury and unusual stresses indicate a tough life style, and the graves reflect a lack of sophistication as well as wealth. In one area in particular several men had healed fractures, supporting the suggestion that they were gladiators. Unusually, osteoarthritis in Cirencester women was as widespread though not as severe as it was in men. Also unusual were the indications on many women's bones of heavy labour when they were young. Arthritic hips, wrist and shoulders and osteoarthrosis of the knee were also common, due to falls, heavy lifting and other physical stress. Further evidence for a hard lifestyle were the fractures still visible on at least 53 men and six women.

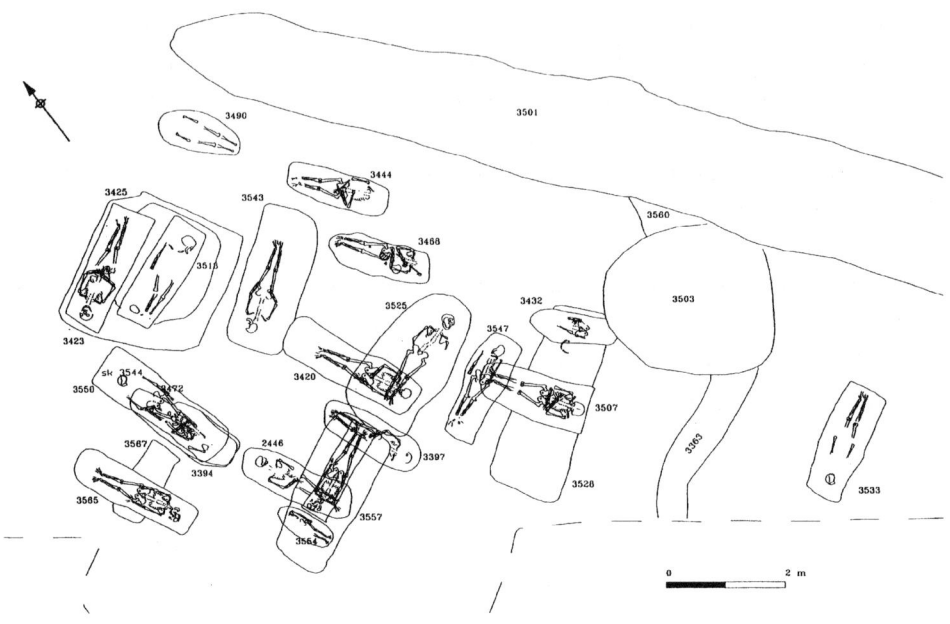

*58 The rural cemetery at Foxton.* © British Gas Transco

Most of these were broken ribs but there were also many fractures on forearms, six fractured metacarpals (perhaps from punching an opponent's head or raising a hand in self-defence) and two broken noses. The many head injuries caused by blunt and sharp weapons and the broken shoulders indicated violent attacks. Some of the sharp cuts to the head and limbs had healed, though others must have proved fatal. Evidence for fighting, including hand to hand sword combat, seems incontrovertible. Women had far fewer such injuries, but even they had bones damaged by instruments in a way that looked to the bone specialist, Calvin Wells, more like assault than accident. Several of both sexes had osteochondritis in joints, probably caused by over-vigorous use of feet and knees in adolescence before their musculature was strong enough to protect them, which would be consistent with, for example, acrobats or gymnasts. In addition to all their other problems, this population was heavily exposed to lead, which in some of the children was high enough to have caused death.

*Foxton*
Away from urban areas old traditions persisted to a greater degree, although even there they were adapted. One example of a small family cemetery, that illustrates subtly shifting patterns of burial rites in the third and fourth century (roughly AD 250-400) within a conservative rural settlement, was excavated next to a modest

villa at Foxton, Cambs (**58**). Here there were 23 skeletons within a ditched enclosure, next to a square temple that was associated with a large hoard of fourth-century ironwork. There were eight earlier third-century burials, the men lying west-east and the women east-west, all in nailed coffins within deep graves. One of the men had a lead-lined coffin and as grave goods had a Nene Valley pot and two geese and a chicken in black burnished bowls. He was buried clothed and still had a buckle at his waist. Later in the same century there were two groups of graves, one with ten burials lying south-north, again probably all in coffins. These included two decapitated older women. Slightly later were five bodies in shallow graves, this time with their heads to the north. Grave goods apart from chickens were sparse throughout the life of the cemetery. One of the decapitated women had a bracelet and comb, but there were no grave goods at all in the last phase apart from chicken bones with one child. Also on this site were human remains in ditches and pits in the older rural fashion. Some were contemporary with the cemetery (perhaps those unrelated to the villa owner) and some were later, reflecting the more chaotic years of the fifth century in eastern Britain.

# 7  The early Anglo-Saxons

They suffered the earth to hold the treasure of warriors, gold on
the earth, where it yet remains, as useless to men as it was of old.
*Beowulf*

# The early Anglo-Saxons

New burial customs are a highly visible element in the early history of Anglo-Saxon England, the change from late Roman graves being as distinctive as any of the upheavals brought about by the ending of the Roman Empire. In the west of England late Roman-style graves persisted but elsewhere Anglo-Saxon rites took hold, starting in the fifth century in some parts. Christian cemeteries disappear in these areas, surviving Britons either adopting Anglo-Saxon dress and burial customs or reverting to the Iron Age-style crouched inhumations which may well have been continuing in remote areas through the later Roman years. Many of these burials too are probably 'hidden' in cemeteries, where bodies without grave goods are not rare.

The normal custom once again was for clothed burial with a wealth of grave goods. But the emphasis was now on the disposal of each person's own possessions in a way that made their identity clear both to those who attended the final rites and to the gods they might meet in the afterlife. Aspects of status, wealth, sex, age and tribal affiliations should therefore be readable from the grave goods. In its simplest terms the new custom meant that women were buried with abundant jewellery and men with weapons. Inhumation and cremation were both practised. Cremations were usually buried in urns with items either burnt with the body or deposited separately afterwards. Sometimes the cremated bone was just placed in a shallow hole in the ground and probably only a small fraction of these have been recovered. In East Anglia cremations in aristocratic graves were sometimes wrapped in linen and buried in bronze bowls, but the great majority were in earthenware pots, many of them highly decorated with motifs and symbols, probably all holding meanings we are only just beginning to unlock (**59**). Some urns had lids (**60**) made to match.

Within these common customs there is more variety in the detail of Anglo-Saxon burials than was the case in earlier periods. Grave cuts, the way the body lies, the choice of objects and the way they are arranged can all vary within what should be a straightforward deposition with weapons or jewellery. Now that the results of many cemetery excavations are available the importance of local customs is becoming more evident, and certain regional variations have always been obvious. At the time that Bede was writing, in the early eighth century, he was able to distinguish three distinct tribal areas which he famously ascribed to original settlements by Angles (in eastern England), Saxons (southern and central

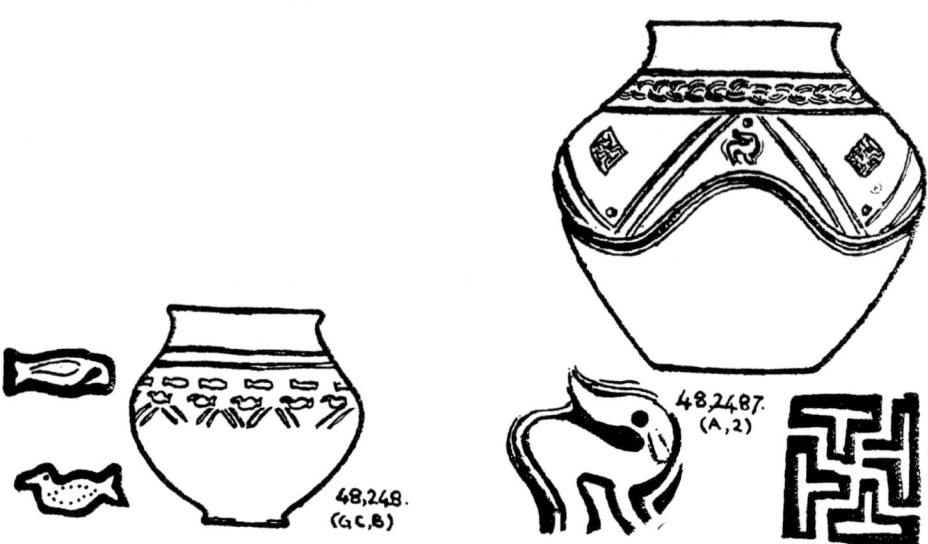

*59 Birds and dogs decorating cremation urns from Lackford.*
© Cambridge Antiquarian Society

England) and Jutes (mostly in Kent), to which we might add Frisians and Franks. The differences are reflected in dress and fashion details such as brooches, and elements in the burial rite, as well as in dialects and place names, and they were evidently real in the late ninth century, when Alfred became king of the 'Angles and the Saxons'. Quite how much these differences originated with ethnic origins is much disputed but in the forms they appear in the burial record they are mainly due to ongoing sixth-century cultural connections, themselves no doubt affected to more or less an extent by historic homelands. For example, East Anglia and other Anglian regions have Danish connections, seen in items of dress, decorative motifs and weaponry, and dynastic connections which appear in mythical form in Beowulf. Late in this period there is much Frankish influence at the aristocratic level, some of it mediated through the kingdom of Kent but some of it straight from Gaul, for we know of missionaries and members of the royal family who were welcomed in both these lands. Kent itself, as well as other areas further along the south coast, notably the Isle of Wight, had more connections with continental Europe, especially the Franks of northern France. These connections can be seen in the wealth and variety of grave goods imported from this Frankish area, which was itself a product of Roman technology, religion and customs, continuing under a Germanic regime. They are clear too in styles of art, in dynastic marriages such as that of Ethelbert, King of Kent, to Bertha, a Frankish princess, and in the claims of Frankish kings to have some sort of sovereignty in southern England.

Wealth and continental connections in Kent at this time are obvious at cemeteries such as Buckland near Dover, where over half its great quantity of brooches was imported from Europe. It held at least 24 swords, various exotic weapons and considerable gold and glass, evidence of several élite families benefiting from the superiority of Kent at this time. Artefacts show that contacts were two-way, with numerous Anglo-Saxon items found in Europe and many examples of styles changing under the influence of continued travel across the sea.

Meanwhile, outside the areas of Anglo-Saxon influence the old pattern of west-east extended burials with no grave goods continued the same normal tradition. Most western parts of England (Wiltshire is a notable exception) have few cemeteries of the Anglo-Saxon type, several counties having virtually none before the seventh century. These were regions where, together with a few areas in the east (such as around St Albans), Romano-British power was still organised enough for military resistance and where British enclaves survived. In between there are counties where Anglo-Saxon

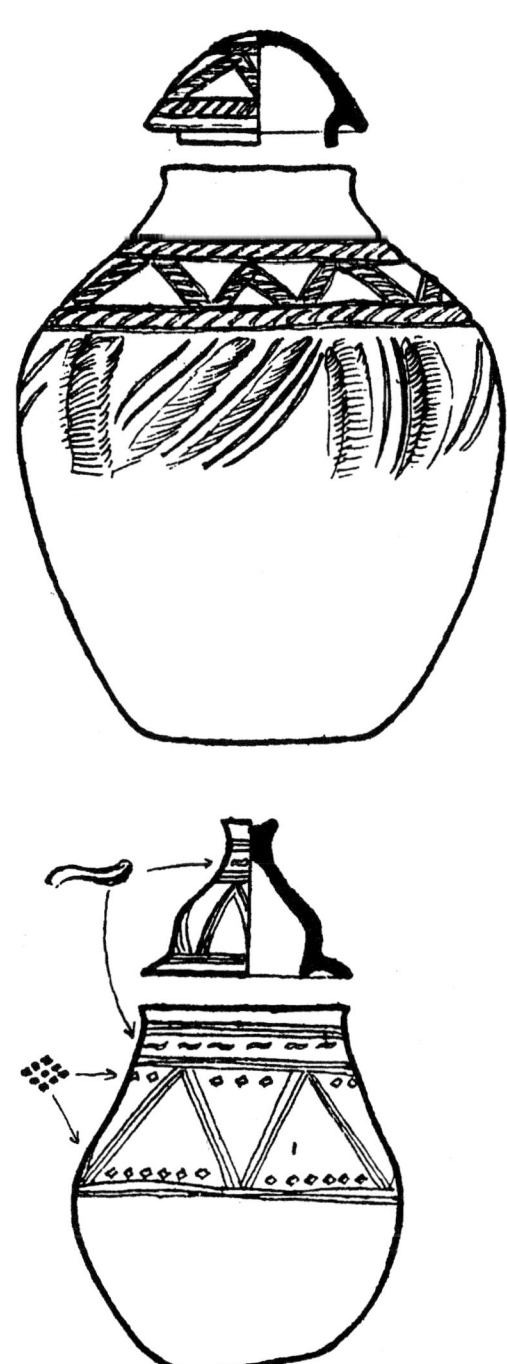

*60 Cremation urns from Lackford, their lids made to match.* © Cambridge Antiquarian Society

elements are sparse and there is evidence for mixing with the native population. At Wasperton and Stretton-on-the-Fosse in Warwickshire, for example, Anglo-Saxon graves were mixed with others that either had no grave goods, nothing diagnostic, or were positively Romano-British in character, with their hobnail boots and decapitated skeletons.

Although there is no clear distinction in the preference for cremation or inhumation in time or region, most cemeteries having an element of each, there are some regional variations. Very large cremation cemeteries with a small minority of inhumations are early in origin and concentrated in eastern England, where they are sometimes linked to Roman towns (Girton and St Johns near Cambridge, Caistor by Norwich). They include sites as large as Spong Hill, Norfolk (nearly 2500 cremations), and Loveden, Lincs (1500 plus). Later on cremations in mixed cemeteries can be contemporary or later than inhumations. At Little Wilbraham, Cambs, for example, they are cut into earlier inhumation graves, at Andover they cover a similar time span to the inhumations, and at Apple Down in Sussex they continue into the later seventh century. Mixed cemeteries occur in particular in central England, and inhumations are more normal in the south, the choice of rite in the early stages at least reflecting the continental Germanic customs of their homelands. Later on the easy mix of burial rites is even seen at Sutton Hoo, supposedly the burial place of one royal family over a short time span and therefore a site where conformity might be expected. Here, burials beneath round barrows were split roughly equally between cremation (one on an oak tray or boat, the rest tied in linen on bronze bowls), and inhumation, two in ships, others in coffins or a wooden chamber. On the same site there were two inhumations in coffins with modest grave goods, and one urned and one unurned cremation without mounds, apart from the later execution victims in various postures. Close by, sixth-century inhumations and cremations (some of these in small ring-ditches and with an abnormally high proportion having swords and other weapons) have just come to light. This medley of customs on the most prominent site in England illustrates the breakdown of old patterns as pagan burial came to an end.

At about this time, the early seventh century, a change to a new and again distinctive style of burial is seen. This is the time of the conversion of England to Christianity and we can assume that many of the people buried in the new fashion were Christian even though, at first, there seems to be little in the rite that reflects these beliefs and practices. Tom Lethbridge was the first to recognise seventh-century burials in his excavations at Burwell and Shudy Camps (Cambs), cogently arguing against previous ideas that Christians were buried without grave goods. All the burials of what is known as the Final Phase are inhumations, the majority lying west-east. Many graves have no grave goods and those that do mostly relate to clothing and small personal items (though amulets are surprisingly common), and there are a few objects with Christian symbolism. Grave goods, especially those of the élite, become more uniform across England at this time. Styles and artefacts were now imported from the Mediterranean not the Germanic world, with access at last to elements of Roman civilisation preserved by the Byzantine Empire. Some of the fashions introduced at this time could have come as presents associated with new loyalties that were being forged, spreading through family events such as baptisms and marriages. These, at an aristocratic level, would be attended by rulers of foreign kingdoms, and at a lowlier level would have been focal events for the interchange of gifts and trinkets.

The Christian church did not particularly object to grave goods, though these were to die out as their connotations became irrelevant and other forms of display were available, but, as the new authorities became more confident, there were rulings against burial in the old pagan cemeteries. Such rulings were commonly ignored, and on many sites (like Barrington, below) rich late burials are found; there are probably many without grave goods that belong to this time. In the area of earliest conversion and strongest Frankish influence, Kent, cemeteries such as Faversham, Broadstairs, Sarre and Finglesham go straight through into Christian-style burial with rich grave goods, and occasionally these last into the eighth century, dated by purses of coins. Sites elsewhere that show a change within the cemetery include Lechlade (Glos), where the regular orientation moves fairly consistently from north-south to west-east (**61**). The grave goods here also changed to the new style, though the only actual Christian artefact was a silver crucifix. Recent work at Melbourn, Cambs, also shows a change within the cemetery, from north-south bodies with grave goods to east-west without, and with more narrow sharply cut graves. Elsewhere, pairs of earlier and later cemeteries are recognised within a few hundred yards of each other. This is the case at Winnall near Winchester, Eastry in Kent, Long Wittenham, Desborough, Chamberlains Barn at Leighton Buzzard and Apple Down, Sussex, apparently due to religion and not any other sort of social change.

## Religious beliefs

The religion of the early Anglo-Saxons relates to the Nordic beliefs recorded in the Prose Edda, first written down by the Icelandic scholar Snorri Storluson in about 1220. This account must have varied considerably from the traditions of England in the sixth century but, as it is the only coherent account we have of the gods whose worship is familiar to us as days of the week and various place names, it is worth recalling the story it tells. The basic mythology included an otherworld known as Asgard which was ruled by Woden and his wife Frigg. Thor and Baldr were among their children. Other gods were Njord, father of Freyr

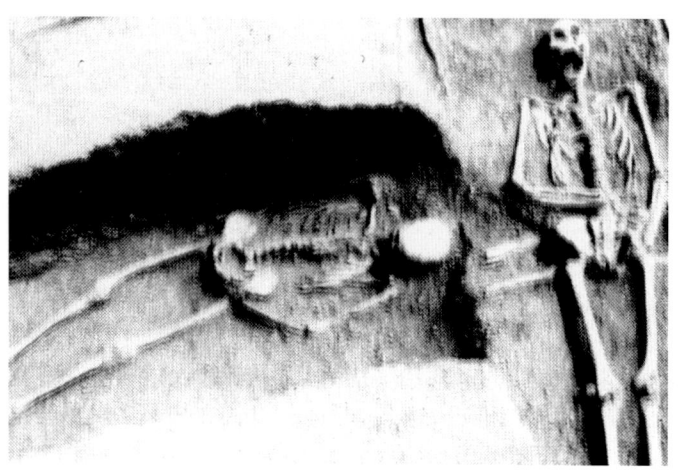

*61 At Lechlade there was a clear change in orientation of burials, seen here where a seventh-century west-east grave lies immediately over a north-south one of the sixth century.*
© Oxford Archaeological Unit

(peace and plenty) and Freya (love and death), Tiw (victory in battle), Loki (cunning and mischief) and Hel, Loki's daughter and ruler of the otherworld for those unfit for Asgard. In Asgard were many halls, one of them Valhalla, home for warriors who would fight by day and feast every evening on pork and mead, and another for the righteous dead. This picture of a happy and energetic afterlife is confirmed by other occasional references such as Ibn Fadlan's tenth-century description of the rituals attending the cremation of a Rus Viking leader. In this, a slave girl who is about to be sacrificed claimed that she was looking into the otherworld, where she could see the activities of her dead relatives and the master she was about to die for.

Baldr's funeral pyre on a ship along with his wife and horse is echoed in graves of this period, and as the god who went down to Hel's kingdom but was reborn every spring he was probably thought relevant at times of death. Thor appears occasionally in graves in the form of his symbol of a hammer, and if some of the sheep/goat bones reported from cremation burials were actually goat (another of his symbols) then many sacrifices were being made in his honour. If it is correct to interpret the sacrifice of horses with Woden then there are many male burials linked to his worship too. Woden's horse Sleipnir was renowned for flying and for travelling between the human world and Asgard. His association with the death of the most powerful in society and especially their transformation through cremation may well be part of a leader's shamanistic responsibilities for maintaining links with the spirit world and influencing it to bring strength and good luck. Other animals found in cremations may also have had direct links with particular gods and their desired properties.

The picture of life after death was fairly consistent with what we can glean about Iron Age beliefs. It was also (apart from specifications for fighting and mead) surprisingly similar to some Roman expectations, except that the Anglo-Saxons seem more optimistic that they personally would make it to the better sort of afterlife. For when we look at Anglo-Saxon visions of death through grave goods it seems that in the inhumations in particular we are seeing folk traditions that take the old ideas to their logical and democratic conclusions. Every free man and every woman of any social standing (and their children) now expected a place in Asgard and so should be dressed and equipped in a way suitable for the endless festivities and so that their identity and status would be unmistakable.

Hints of other beliefs and customs relating to burial are subsequently found in some of the Christian prohibitions, for it was still necessary to forbid pagan customs 400 years after England became notionally Christian. The use of amulets was one particularly important issue with both parties. A long battle was fought which in the end the Church could only win by giving a Christian gloss to some old practices and replacing others with something similar — crucifixes, relics and Christian texts for example. Only against amber does the battle seem to have been won, for it disappears from the later burial record, though this is usually ascribed to fashion or a change in trade routes. According to fourth-century continental complaints, the virulence of early objections to amulets led to the executions of people wearing them against everyday diseases, a severity that was replaced by various ecclesiastical penances. These measures were never wholly successful, which is not surprising as the argument was not that they were ineffective but that it was somehow sinful to use them — even if it saved the life of a child. The late seventh-century *Penitentials* of Theodore, archbishop of Canterbury, also forbade sacrificing to devils, eating food offered as sacrifice and burning grain for the well being of the dead ('whoever causes grain to be burnt, where there is a dead man, for the well being of the living and the house, should do penance for five years'). Bede complained too about Christians who fell back on spells, amulets and secret arts when faced with plague. An eighth-century Synod ordered bishops to ban divination, soothsaying, amulets, spells and so on, but in the 990s Aelfric again had to instruct priests not to 'eat and drink in the place were the corpse lies', and to forbid burning grain near a corpse, singing, and getting the corpse to speak. Even in the eleventh century there were penalties for clerics practising divination through necromancy. In the archaeological record amulets are particularly common in women's graves of the seventh century, and in this early Christian period food offerings are more common than in preceding pagan graves. Burnt grain has been noted in early cemeteries at Marston St Lawrence (Northants), Sandy (Beds), Markshall and Spong Hill in Norfolk, Burgh Castle and at Andover, where carbonised grains of bread wheat were found on the floor of the only two graves sampled. Other burnt material could relate to similar practices, and scatters of charcoal over parts of the body are not at all uncommon (**62**). At Berinsfield one grave was lined with charred oak logs and there were three with charcoal or smouldering wood spreads. Charred wood was found with the aristocratic burials at Asthall and Taplow, and there were several graves containing

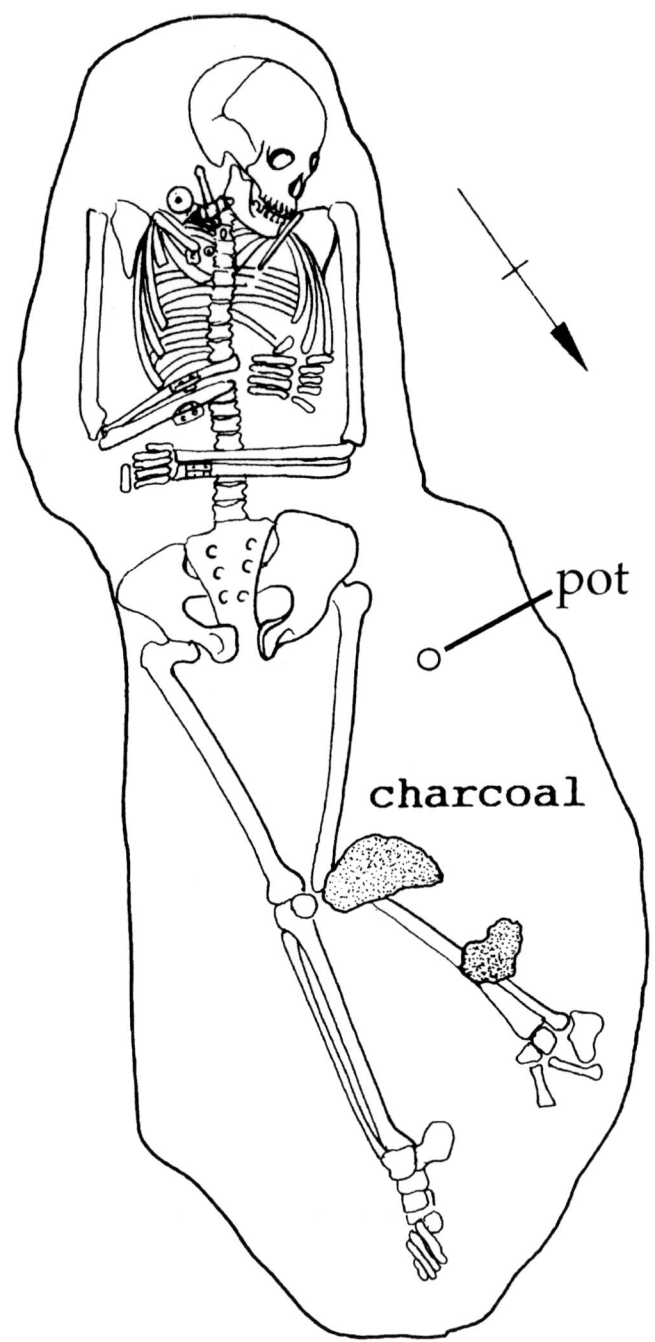

pot

charcoal

*62 A woman at Oakington, Cambs, well dressed with brooches, wrist-clasps and beads, was buried with charcoal over her left leg and a pot sherd near the pelvis.*
© Cambridge Antiquarian Society

pieces of burnt wood at Snape. Charcoal and stone slabs were used to keep an old woman in her place at Soham in Cambridgeshire.

## Monuments/memorials

*Mounds*

> Command men famous as fighters to build a burial mound,
> a conspicuous one, on the ocean bluff, following the cremation.
> *Beowulf*

When Beowulf was dying he asked his friends to bury him in a mound with treasure, the way a real hero should be remembered, and other burials in the poem relate to mounds for royal graves. This powerful and evocative poetry sets a scene which helps us to understand the development of a separate rite of wealthy, even royal, graves for men and women, with distinctive artefacts and an even more distinctive rite, that of barrow burial, in the early seventh century.

Though old Bronze Age barrows had often been reused for quite ordinary burials the immediate inspiration for new royal mounds was probably Scandinavian. In Sweden, Norway and Denmark barrows, often with the burials in boats, were hugely significant, especially for the royal families, and were used to mark territories and centres of government before conversion to Christianity. The change at that point was so decisive that King Gorm, first buried in a mound at Jelling, Denmark, was dug up by his newly Christian son and reburied in a church there. Barrows are found singly, as part of a mixed group of mounds and flat graves, or as one of the options for marking significant graves in normal flat cemeteries. The largest mounds are usually those found singly, apart from the exceptional examples of Sutton Hoo and Snape in Suffolk. Barrow mounds in flat cemeteries are much smaller and are often only recognised as ring-ditches or conjectured from other evidence.

The mounds themselves were not just memorials to individuals and symbols of continuity but would have practical uses as landmarks suitable for festivals, ceremonies and meetings of many kinds. As such they would be sited where communications were good and where there was suitable space for those attending to camp and for their animals to graze. Tara in Ireland, Uppsala in Sweden, Jelling in Denmark, the Tynwald on the Isle of Man and Thingvellir in Iceland were pre-eminent sacred meeting places, but in England mounds probably including Sutton Hoo as well as innumerable lesser sites were used for local moots for centuries to come. How easy it was for a barrow to become a landmark is seen in Hrafnkel's Saga, where a cairn over the dead Einar was 'called Einarsvarda, and the Shieling people use it to mark the middle of the evening'. Here too we see burial mounds keeping their relationship with known local heroes and villains, with stories such as the tale of Gunnar in Njal's Saga, who sat up and recited poems in his barrow.

Large single mounds were nearly always on high points, sited for their visibility over a wide area and also their position on major thoroughfares, in England generally on boundaries rather than at the centre of territories, reminding us of Beowulf's burial on a high headland by the sea. The mounds over princely seventh-century graves on or near prehistoric or Roman sites on the periphery of kingdoms in particular seem to be territorial markers. This group includes female burials though men are more common and their grave goods are the most prestigious for their time: they were equipped with full weapon sets including swords, as well as hanging bowls, grooming equipment and feasting regalia. Women did not have weapons, though swords cut down to make iron weaving battens are sometimes found, but their power through magic is evident from the amulets and other equipment for making charms and spells. Important sites that share locations on sky-lines, routeways and territorial boundaries and have rich artefacts include Asthall, Lowbury Hill and Cuddesdon in Oxfordshire, Taplow (Bucks), Swallowcliffe Down (Wilts), Maiden Bradley and Coombe Bissett (Dorset), Caenby (Lincs) and Benty Grange (Derbyshire Peak District). In Suffolk, Sutton Hoo is on a plateau edge above the Deben, controlling water traffic going upstream to the royal palace at Rendlesham, and Snape was widely visible from sea and river. The largest as well as the richest barrows of course are the Sutton Hoo group, with about 19 mounds, most of them robbed of their grave goods but still with evidence of aristocratic burials, the greatest of all Anglo-Saxon burials being within a ship in Mound 1. The highest of 10 mounds at Snape, originally a Bronze Age barrow, is exceptionally interesting for it dates to the mid-sixth century, well before the tradition was established, and covered a ship burial. It had been robbed before its nineteenth-century excavation but still contained a gold signet ring matched in the Frankish Rhineland, made in Germany but with a Roman setting. Another sixth-century example may be a newly-discovered female burial in a barrow at Newark, Notts, with a bucket with three Roman coins, a pot, silver wrist clasps, a gilded disc from a bag and glass and amber beads.

Smaller barrows of sixth- and seventh-century date, now usually ploughed flat, are being routinely identified in ordinary cemeteries. These include Lakenheath, Spong Hill, Apple Down and Andover. At Lechlade a crucifix on the necklace of a woman within a ring-ditch contradicts the pagan tenor of these sites.

## Other memorials

Excavators often observe that the Anglo-Saxons had little problem in identifying earlier graves, either to avoid accidental disturbance or to locate graves to place another family member, so markers of some kind must have been normal. Many of these need have left no trace, and others are difficult to distinguish with certainty on sites with many earlier and later features, but there are now quite a few cemeteries where memorials are known. Grave posts and slots were excavated at Sewerby, Alton (around the only deep grave, containing a sword and gold-decorated buckle), Barrington (below) and various sites in Kent. Square post structures with central holes covered cremations at Apple Down, Spong Hill, Lackford and Morning-thorpe and inhumations at Melbourn, and there were similar ones from Alton, Carisbrooke (Isle of Wight), Lechlade and Berinsfield. Such features seem to have been used right through from the fifth to the seventh century. It is the seventh-century cemeteries of Kent that had the greatest degree of organisation with elaborate grave design. At St Peter's, Broadstairs, for example, there were nearly 400 graves with heads roughly north-west. Their structural features included posts on both sides or at the head or foot of the grave, floor slots, ledges, upright stone slabs, flints used in the fill, and small circular or penannular ditches.

Pagan Anglo-Saxons did not reach as far west as Cornwall in any numbers, and so forms of literacy and Christianity survived. Gravestones of the fifth to seventh century therefore are occasionally found inscribed with the name and ancestry of the dead in either Latin or the ogham alphabet (**63**).

63 *Inscribed grave stone from Men Scryfa, Cornwall, reading 'Rialobranus, son of Cunovalus'.*
© Cornwall Archaeological Unit

## Coffins

Evidence for some sort of timber coffin is another feature of Anglo-Saxon burial now widely recognised. At Buckland, the collapsed condition of many grave goods, the positioning of flints in graves and the traces of preserved wood below bodies suggest there were coffins or biers for a large number of burials. Andover produced particularly clear evidence for coffins, or at least wooden boxes, in seven of its graves (**64**) where wood remains were visible as dark lines and with sufficient carbonised wood for identification as oak. All but one of these burials was an adult woman with above average grave goods in a deep grave pit. None

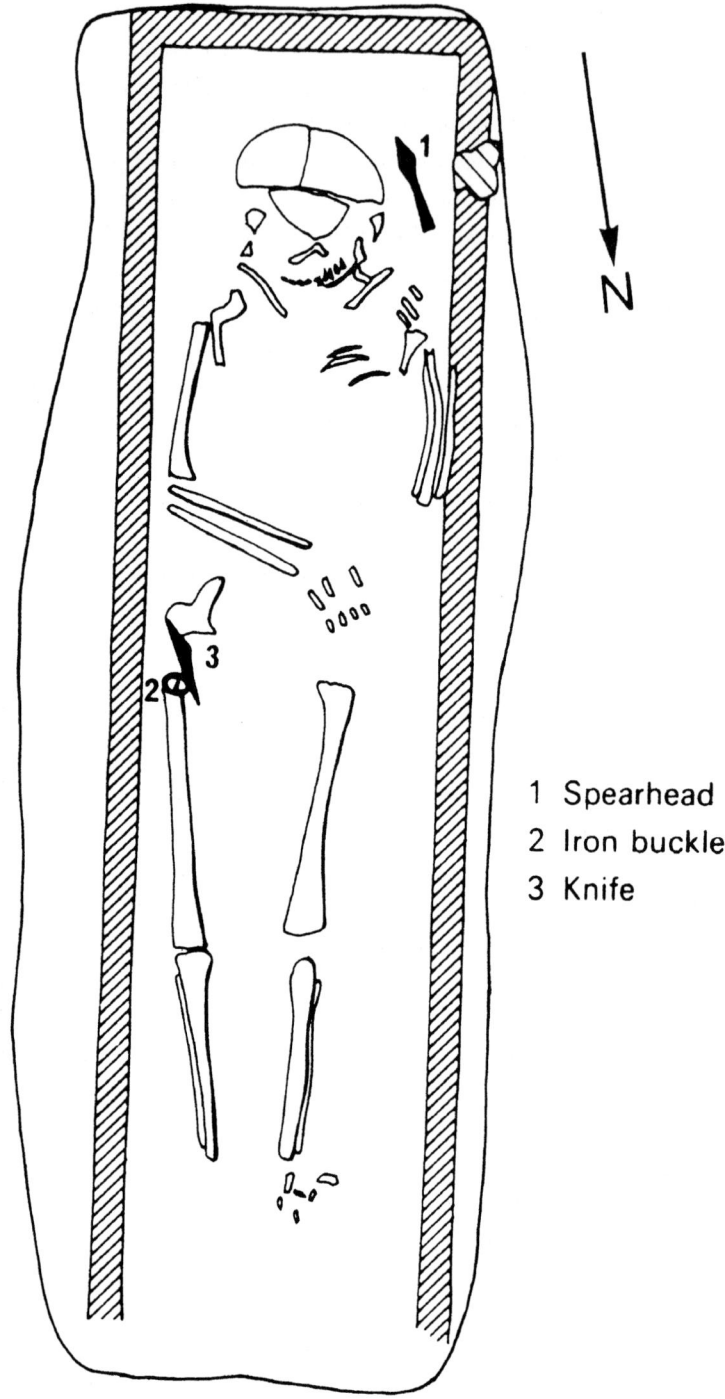

1 Spearhead
2 Iron buckle
3 Knife

*64 Timber coffins were still visible in the ground at Portway, Andover.*
© Oxford University Committee for Archaeology

had nails, and, with one or two possible exceptions, this was also the case at Barrington, where 28 burials out of 149 were thought to be coffined. At Mucking, Essex, this figure rose to 40 per cent in one cemetery, and wooden structures were noted at Standlake, Abingdon, Harwell and Droxford. The richest burial on the site at Lechlade, a girl of 18 with much jewellery, a bag and a bowl containing personal and amuletic items, was in a wooden coffin protected with limestone blocks robbed from a Roman building within a ring-ditch. In the quite poor seventh-century cemetery at King Harry Lane, St Albans, at least four, and probably several more burials had wooden boards over them, as also recognised at Mucking and Empingham (Rutland). Several coffins and biers as well as a dugout boat surviving as stains in the acid sands of Snape and Sutton Hoo (**colour plate 22**) are evidence of what must often be missed in different soils. Only on the richest sites do these coffins involve metal fittings, with occasional nails, clench bolts and other ironwork known from coffins at Sutton Hoo, Sarre, Barton on Humber, Broomfield and Taplow.

Many of the cemeteries with coffins also had graves lined or marked with stones, notably Buckland, where several graves contained large flints covering all or part of the body. Occasionally there is evidence for organic materials used to soften the grave. At Berinsfield one body was covered with a rush mat, at Mucking a coffin was lined with bracken and moss and a shield boss had bracken impressions, and plant stem impressions on a brooch at Sewerby compare with instances in Gaul where grass was used as a shroud. During excavations at Sporle, Norfolk, in 1820 'a kind of woollen cloak was distinctly observed enveloping each body, but which quickly turned to dust on the admission of air'.

Increased elaboration in the design of Conversion-period graves includes charcoal, stone linings and pillow-stones and the use of shrouds, even where the surrender of all grave goods was not yet complete. At Chamberlains Barn one child was wrapped in coarse cloth that was open at the head and tied at the feet, a woman with a silver and bead necklace was covered with layers of textile, perhaps including a shroud, and a crouched burial had traces of sacking under the body.

## Beds

Strange and rare constructions found in the seventh century are wooden beds with iron fittings. These were first identified at Shudy Camps, and then more recently at Swallowcliffe Down, Coddenham in Suffolk and Barrington. The Swallowcliffe Down bed was in a reused Bronze Age barrow. On it lay a young woman with two buckets, a locked box containing silver brooches and spoons, knives, two beads, comb, a bronze sprinkler and other bits and pieces. She also had a satchel decorated with bronze, gold and silver, glass cups, and there were probably other items that had been looted. Older discoveries include Lapwing Hill, Derbys, where a drawing of the nineteenth-century excavations shows the iron cleats of a bed recognisable as decayed wood covered with hair, probably from a hide. On it lay a man with two spears, a knife and a sword in a wooden sheath covered with ornamental leather. There are currently 11 of these beds known, principally in Cambridgeshire and Wiltshire. Most belong to young women and the grave goods indicate not only wealth but also involvement in magical arts, even though they were buried when Christianity was widespread and their graves were among the most prominent and well-displayed burials of their time. Further evidence that such graves were not perceived as un-Christian was a gold and garnet crucifix worn by a woman in a bed-burial at Ixworth. It is quite possible that other all-wood beds were used on occasion, as was found in the grave of a rich mid-sixth-century woman in a mortuary chapel beneath Cologne cathedral, and in Scandinavia, but these have not yet been recognised in England.

## Grave goods

Female graves equipped with worn jewellery (principally brooches and necklaces) and housewifely symbols such as keys, girdle hangers, amulets and spindle whorls, and men with weapons (principally spears and shields, occasionally swords) are extremely common in many areas in the sixth century. The 'head count' for early Anglo-Saxon bodies in East Anglia for example far exceeds that of the Roman or any earlier periods although the time-scale is so short. Both sexes often had knives and belt buckles, and sometimes vessels such as pots, buckets and drinking horns. Grave goods were affected by age as well as wealth, the young and old having more restricted goods than those between about 12 and 40. There is some evidence for food and drink, but nothing like the provisions for feasts and sustenance that preoccupied the Romans. Cremation burials, an older Germanic rite, used similar groups of artefacts but with some use of miniature objects instead of the person's ordinary possessions, and artefacts made specially for burial — that is, badly. Other differences from inhumations that relate to older traditions are the absence of normal weapons except in the most aristocratic graves, the frequent inclusion of grooming equipment especially with men and the considerable number of horse bones. Food in the form of meat joints, if indeed this is how animal bones with cremations should be interpreted, also becomes more common. This more symbolic use of objects as well as the lack of weapons is closer to older continental attitudes to grave goods than the literal interpretation of the need for proper dress in the next world seen in inhumations.

The analysis of some cemeteries has thrown up consistent variables for age/sex/grave good correlation within the individual cemetery, but so far such variables have not held true elsewhere. At Heslerton for example only women over 25 had tweezers or square-headed brooches and burials aged under 12 rarely had knives, but these are not patterns found generally. The same applies to other purely local customs, such as a preference for large graves for male weapon burials at Heslerton, while at nearby Sewerby large graves were used for the display of women with jewellery. Other variations such as the ways the body lay in the grave and precise mix of grave goods changed over time and region and with personal preference and means.

Seventh-century graves, though generally less well equipped, have a wider range of artefacts and included useful items such as shears, spindle whorls, whetstones, iron spoons and tools, and more playing pieces and horse equipment. Ordinary objects, knives and buckles for example, carry on though in smaller numbers, but jewellery and weapons changed with fashion. Brooches are less common, and are worn singly as well as changing from Germanic to classically influenced styles. Necklaces also change style and become less common: amber beads especially become rare. Spectacular large amethyst drops used as beads are introduced (**colour plate 23**), and there are dainty arrangements of glass beads strung with rings of twisted silver wire. Amethyst, though regarded as amuletic by Pliny and other writers, does not seem to have won disapproval in the way amber did. Bede in fact seems to have rather approved of it for reminding the humble of the heavenly kingdom, perhaps the sort of rationale that made it acceptable in seventh-century cemeteries. Pendants of glass, garnets or rock crystal set in gold or silver mounts and amulets of many kinds are found. Crystal was another magical substance that managed to take on Christian virtues and is still found. Weapons in graves become rarer at this time, and the seax replaces the sword. There are iron instead of bronze bound buckets, and exotic containers such as bronze hanging bowls occur in rich graves. One example that demonstrates the changes is Chamberlains Barn where a seventh-century cemetery can be compared with a sixth-century one less than a 100 yards away. Whereas the earlier site had graves of varied orientations and without an obvious layout, the later graves were mostly in rows, with virtually all heads to the south-west. The burials in I were accompanied by amber and glass beads, spears, buckles and knives. In II the proportion of burials with grave goods was much lower but they did still include one weapon grave in a small mound. There were also knives, a lock, six necklaces of silver rings and glass beads, silver-linked pins, a brooch with gold filigree and garnet, a horse's bit, a silver pendant, wooden chests and reused Iron Age pots that were deliberately holed. The body's position in the ground was now standardised in burials instead of the grave goods, but the rich could still take some finery if they wished, and local idiosyncrasy (the Iron Age pots) was tolerated.

Ornaments found on sixth-century women in the Anglian regions of eastern England show that their dress included a gown with long sleeves that often

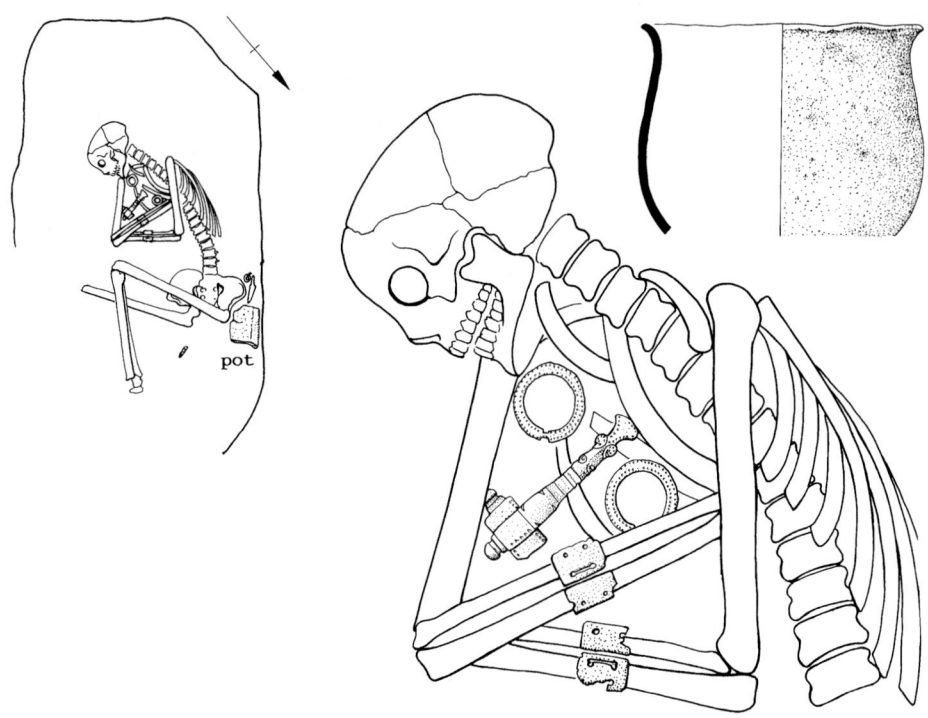

*65 Another woman from Oakington, with wrist-clasps and three brooches. Like **62** she had a pot sherd by her pelvis. © Cambridge Antiquarian Society*

fastened with bronze or occasionally silver wrist-clasps (**65**), covered by another gown fastened on the shoulders with a pair of brooches. In the best graves there might be a third brooch well below the throat to fasten the neck of the undergarment, a cloak, or the folds of the top dress. There would be a belt, either knotted or with a buckle, and to this may be attached a knife and, on higher status women, iron keys, metal objects described as 'girdle hangers' that seem to be some sort of symbolic key, and bags containing odd objects. Brooches were perhaps the most distinctive feature of a woman's dress. Made of bronze, occasionally gilded and/or set with garnets or coloured glass, they could be decorated with elaborate motifs. Their design was affected by the regions where they were worn (for example, round saucer brooches in the Saxon south and Midlands and long cruciform ones in the Anglian east) as well as changing rapidly with time. Fewer brooches are found with very young and old women and they are extremely rare with girls under 12, so their ownership may reflect marital status. When buried, the brooches are sometimes worn-out, broken, in ill-matching pairs or worn singly. It is highly likely therefore that women were buried with the best they could afford to wear in life rather than something devised for ceremonial or the grave, and this personal aspect seems to relate to the other items in inhumation graves, though it does not apply to cremations. It must however have been possible for brooches to be passed on to the next generation, for some young girls have brooches showing more wear than they can have given them.

Beads of amber, mostly imported from the Baltic coast, are extremely common in women's graves in central and eastern England (**colour plates 24 & 25**). Possession of this pretty and magical resin was obviously desirable for women of varying wealth, age and importance. Looking at the arrangements of beads graded in size and mingled with other attractive materials it is impossible to believe they were not valued as decoration, but they also had less tangible benefits. Apart from being involved in the general condemnations of amulets, it was singled out for particular and usually critical comment. Pliny says that peasant women in Roman Gaul wore amber 'chiefly as an adornment and also for its medicinal properties', and attached the beads to babies as amulets. In sixth-century Gaul, women who wore amber were harshly criticised by churchmen; a later Penitential forbids people to 'hang devilish amulets or devilish characters or herbs or amber on themselves' during eclipses of the moon, and the use of amber and herbs attracted frequent objections for several centuries in England and on the Continent. Other beads were of rock crystal (another magical substance already used at this time for 'crystal balls'), and cemeteries with these tend to also be rich in amber beads and ivory rings. Glass beads were also always popular all over England (**colour plate 26**). Occasionally bead threads are found, as at Great Chesterford. These were plied or plaited as whipcord, knotted or whipped at the end, then passed through the springs of brooches. One of the threads was wool and the rest were made of flax.

Bags suspended near the waist of women who generally had many other grave goods often had a ring of ivory (elephant or walrus) to hold open the neck. Within them might be sets of rings, small strips or plates of bronze, fragments of glass and old and broken treasures: odd things suitable for fortune telling and spells. These recall penances imposed on women who have 'performed incantations and diabolical devinations', there being no such shame in the sixth century when the evidence was honourably displayed by some of the richest women in the community. At Oakington a richly dressed girl of 18 lay with her head on a bag of this type in which were a set of keys and bronze fittings (**66**).

Balls of rock crystal, often suspended in metal cradles, also display upper-class women's responsibility for telling the future. Aristocratic graves are particularly rich in these. Giant cowry shells, found with cremations and in boxes with inhumations, are another exotic import in the magical tool kit of powerful women. Bits and pieces collected as amulets included Roman objects,

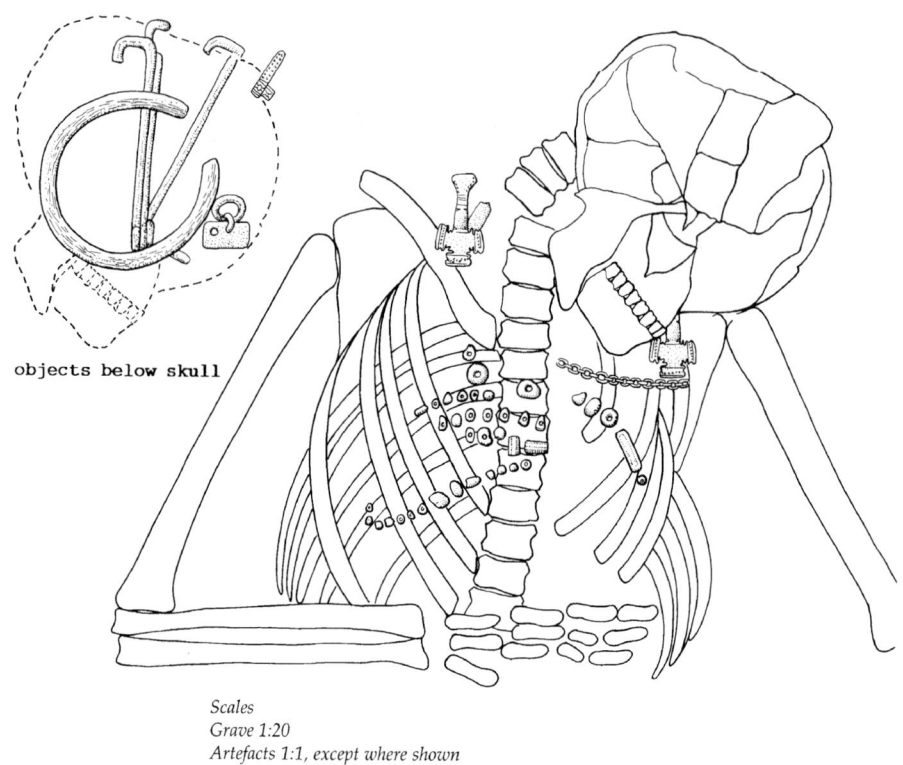

objects below skull

*Scales*
*Grave 1:20*
*Artefacts 1:1, except where shown*

*66 A richly dressed teenage girl at Oakington was buried with her head over a bag with an ivory ring, containing keys and trinkets.* © Cambridge Antiquarian Society

natural fossils, prehistoric flints, pebbles, iron pyrites, horse's teeth and sheep ankle bones (these last two also being used for gaming). Other teeth with amuletic properties are wolf and beaver, and also boar's tusks. Wood shavings around a metal core, like a walnut in a bronze cradle and runes on the back of a brooch, would also be linked to spell-making (**67**). Beads too had protective/magical properties best seen when single beads are fastened around a child's neck or they are found in a box or purse.

Amulets became even more common as Christianity took hold, and they were joined by specifically Christian ones such as crucifixes and thread boxes decorated with crosses and religious scenes. Nearly all these magical items are found with women, and are often the richest graves. One of the finest examples of this feminine status was the woman at Chessell Down, Isle of Wight. Her grave goods included a crystal ball in its silver sling, a silver-gilt perforated spoon (another item associated with spells), a bronze bucket with runic inscription (a queen's duty was to 'hold close a rune-word' in one gnomic

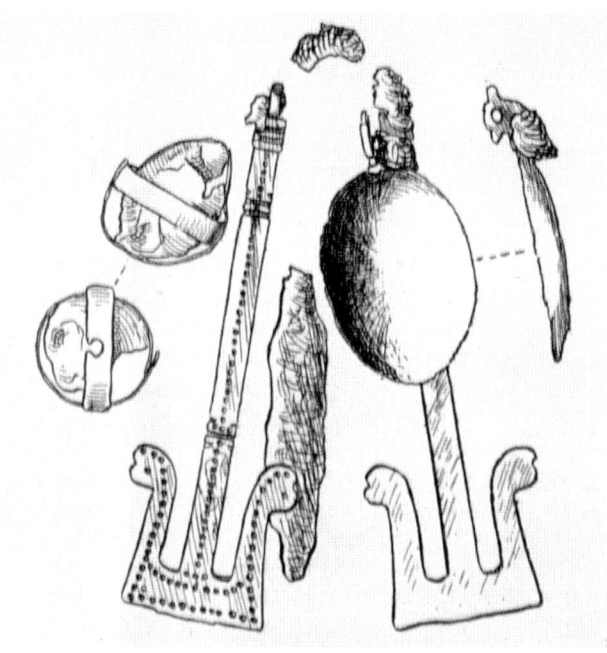

*67 Girdle hangers, spoon, knife and 'wooden' ball in sling, Little Wilbraham.*
  © Cambridge Antiquarian Society

verse), a headdress of gold braid, five silver gilt brooches, gold and silver rings, an iron weaving batten, cups, beads, a buckle and so on. All the items were the most elaborate of their kind. Tacitus, describing Germans in the first century AD, said that women had prophetic powers and advised on political and military decisions. A further clue to such women is found in the (much later) saga of Eirik the Red, just before Christianity became the official religion in Iceland in AD 1000. In this, when people needed to know when a famine would end they invited a famous seeress to the house. Her dress is described in great detail, from her 'hairy calf-skin shoes' to her black lambskin hat lined with white cat fur. It included glass beads around her neck, straps set with stones, and a skin pouch hanging from her belt in which she kept charms for her magic. She carried a knobbed staff decorated with stones and metal, and she ate special food with her own brass spoon and ivory handled knife. Such detail is very rare in the sagas, in which women generally only get mentions for their dangerous beauty or their nagging tongues, and obviously had great significance. Apparatus for her spells is mentioned but unfortunately not described, and gifts were made to her. Her reception was in great state, and no one doubted what she told them. This is surely the sort of picture that lies behind some of the rich female graves.

Games of chance and skill were linked to divination as well as played for fun. The two functions were no doubt often mixed (as today) but there was sexual variation. Women have single playing pieces found with amulets or runes while men have whole sets (teeth/bones or counters of bone or ivory), without any associations other than to leisure interests. In both cases they are linked to richer burials, most commonly cremations. Pebbles were sometimes used in similar ways.

Men had weapons to make their status clear: spears and shields for freeborn men, swords for nobles, and multiple weapons for rulers. These weapons too show wear and appear to be the man's own normal possessions though it seems that the bow and arrow (items very rarely found, one exception being a quiver of five arrows at Lakenheath) were most common, so the symbolism of a spear was significant. This symbolism is reflected in the restriction of full-sized spears to adult males, generally aged 16 or over. In the seventh century weapons become less common, if more varied, with the exception of aristocratic graves, which marked the divine and earthly powers of royalty through a lavish provision for the idealised life to come. Mound 1 at Sutton Hoo is the supreme example of this final flourish of the furnished grave tradition. Here were deposited a sceptre and other symbols of power, weapons and armour (helmet, mail coat and massive shield), adornments such as buckles, baldrics and horse fittings, luxury textiles and furs, coins, sets of silver bowls and other tableware suitable for the Christian *convivia religiosa*. There were also cauldrons, buckets for beer and other essentials of the heathen feast, including drinking horns, wooden cups and a lyre. Burials in the other mounds, though much disturbed, had somewhat similar accoutrements of warfare and festivity, including horses and gaming pieces. Other graves, usually in mounds, have the same type of artefact as Sutton Hoo in a more modest style. One warrior at Wollaston, Northants, provides a very rare example of burial with a helmet with a boar's crest, as described in the poetry. Also in the damaged grave was a sword in a wooden scabbard with sheepskin lining, an enamelled hanging bowl, buckles and a knife.

Children's graves are generally poorly furnished in comparison with their elders, but some provision was often made. In life children were often naked or wore only the simplest tunics or cloaks, and this casual state is reflected in their grave goods. Between 10 and 12 seems about the age that adult equipment is provided, which accords with law codes. A few younger boys had small spears, while some young girls have female equipment such as spindle whorls and keys, though not a full set of these. Items commonly found with children are small pots (looking suitable for porridge bowls), sherds, or a few beads. Cemeteries vary in the detail of grave goods for the very young. At Oakington every child had something, if only a meat bone or sherd of pottery, and children of about 8 and 11 had some of the richest grave goods on the site, but in some cemeteries they have nothing. Even royal children were not well equipped. One of the small Sutton

Hoo mounds contained a child in a wooden coffin, his only grave goods a little spear, buckle and a pin. In many cases children were buried in a grave with adults (both men and women) or with other children.

The age-old tradition of providing food and drink and suitable vessels for these to be enjoyed in proper state was not as important as correct dress in Anglo-Saxon graves. Yet it still had a part to play, especially in cremations in the eastern counties, though our impressions may be skewed by the unequal preservation of organic materials in the ground. At Snape, for example, the unusual standards of preservation in the acidic soil meant that in the grave of a young man in a small boat there were two drinking horns which, lacking any metal ornamentation, would not have been found without survival as stains. Buckets too are found if they are bound with metal, but many others must have been of wood alone and do not come to light. Pottery, generally found with women and children, will survive, but is concentrated in areas where it was plentifully produced. Glass vessels, the majority found in Kent, were a huge luxury given the problems of safe transport. They illustrate the enduring importance of alcohol, perhaps including wine in the small cups, to the social fabric.

Direct evidence for food is inevitably limited. The record is dominated by animal bones, again most common with cremations and in Anglian regions. Except for horse and dog (below) they were the normal food animals of the time and so can be seen as the usual sustaining-in-the-afterlife food supply, but some totemic identification is also likely. Animal bones were found in 46 per cent of about 2000 cremations at Spong Hill, their order of frequency being horse, sheep/goat, pigs, cattle, dogs, birds, deer and bears. Quite a few are thought to have been cremated whole, not butchered for food, recalling Ibn Fadlan's description of the burial of a royal Viking in which two horses, two cows, a dog, cock and slave girl were sacrificed and cremated in a ship, the whole being covered with a mound. Of the 220 cremations examined from Millgate, Newark on Trent, at least 63 contained animal bone (cattle, sheep, pig, horse and red deer), and there were sheep, oxen, pigs, horse and dog at Illington, Norfolk. All age groups might have animal bones, but they were not evenly distributed. There were no joints of beef with children either here or at the neighbouring cremation cemetery at Elsham Wold, though pig and sheep could occur with anyone. Great Chesterford burials included goose, roe deer, cattle and sheep, and two pots with bone fragments. Other food included a pot with three eggs in it, as found also at Holywell Row (**68**). Bird bones, possibly rook, were found in some of the urns at Castle Acre. In a grave at Burwell there were so many hazelnuts that visitors took handfuls away with them; they were also found in bronze bowls at Faversham and Croydon, with cloth tied over the top. Crab apples and onions were found in a hanging bowl in a barrow at Laverstock, beechnuts in a similar one in Hitchin, and unopened oysters at Sarre.

*68 Duck eggs were still in a pot buried with a child at Holywell Row.*
© Cambridge Antiquarian Society

Horses in graves were another long-lived Scandinavian custom that was adopted for rich burials in eastern England, most spectacularly at Sutton Hoo where five burials had horses with them. In cremations they were often whole, were mature animals unlike those used for food, and occasionally had their own urn and grave goods. Several of the horses at both Millgate and Elsham Wold were also cremations of the whole animal and occurred with adults and adolescents. Horses were depicted on cremation urns at Spong and Millgate and their heads feature on cruciform brooches. Horses in inhumations are nowhere near as common but they do occur in quite a number of cemeteries. It was more common for some of the bones or part of the harness to be buried than the whole animal. At Great Chesterford, though, two were found complete, one with its tackle, including a wooden saddle, and at Lakenheath a man with a sword was buried with a sheep and horse that was still wearing elaborate harness (**colour plate 27**). Evidently the horse, whose bones make up a very small proportion of bones on settlement sites and which was used for racing and in games as well as warfare and other practical purposes, was not thought about in the same terms as other domestic animals. This attitude is seen in a gnomic verse in which an essential virtue of a queen is to be 'roomy-hearted at hoard sharing and horse-giving'. It is reflected too in a long-lived taboo in England against eating their flesh. This was not due to Christian teachings, for missionaries from the Mediterranean world were at first surprised by it, though later priests endorsed the prohibition, possibly because it actually had been customary at specific ritual events such as the funeral feasts and therefore was seen as pagan. Occasionally dogs were treated in a similar way, with complete burials in their own grave pits as at Great Chesterford and Barrington.

Fabrics and textiles must have been important in laying out an elegant grave but the problems of preservation are even greater than with foodstuffs. A few sites with exceptional conditions hint at what we have lost. Sutton Hoo as usual is the finest example, for amongst the treasures of Mound 1 were pairs of leather shoes, cloaks, a feather pillow, piles of folded cloth and leather and an otter skin hat. Textile fragments were recognised with nearly all the burials here. Bear claws in two cremations at Elsham Wold are evidence for a bearskin rug, and two graves at Great Chesterford had bases of horn cores, as if a hide lay beneath the body. A hanging bowl containing crab apples at Gally Hills, Banstead Down, was covered with linen tied with string and placed on a pile of leather and cloth, including boots, a cloak and weapons. A bowl found in the latest (2000) excavations at Sutton Hoo held a cremation covered with a wooden lid. At Orsett there were objects wrapped in a checked cloth or bag, and at Fonaby textiles included bead threads, hairs from a cowhide, and some possible goat hair. Examples are found there of decorative tablet weaving using bright wool in red and blue sewn onto sleeves and around the neck, a detail also seen at Mucking and Finglesham. Other feminine ornamentation in the richest graves is gold braid, seen on head-dresses at Sarre, Lyminge and Chessell Down. These are all rich cemeteries but it could appear in an ordinary village cemetery. Thus at Holywell Row a child had an exceptional collection of luxury items including bronze bowls, an iron weaving batten, three brooches with one of gilt set with garnet, beads of amber, jet, crystal and glass, silver bracelets, a finger ring and pendants as well as gold braid.

Old objects, usually Roman but occasionally prehistoric, are another class of artefact commonly found, especially where cemeteries are conveniently close to villas or similar sources. In some fifth-century contexts it is possible that items were acquired as loot or tribute from surviving Romano-Britons, a suggestion made about the numerous glass vessels, bracelets, finger-rings, gemstones and other luxuries at Highdown in Sussex. In other very early cemeteries, eg Girton, Roman brooches are actually worn and it has been suggested these were Roman burials, but it is more likely that, as in sixth- and seventh-century graves, the pieces were just collected for their attractiveness, ancient associations and amuletic properties. Coins were particularly popular, usually perforated and used on necklaces, sometimes in women's bags, and occasionally, as at Great Chesterford, placed as if they were for Charon's fee, in the hand or mouth. A bag of Roman trinkets accompanied a woman in the late seventh-century cemetery at King Harry Lane, easily collected from neighbouring Verulamium, and there are odd and often broken objects such as beads, Samian sherds, rings, gems and spindle whorls. One cremation at Lackford for example contained a Roman finger ring, a spoon, a brooch, a fragment of a bone comb and an ivory gaming piece (**69**). Occasionally older curiosities might also be included, for example a Neolithic axe at Barrington and an Iron Age bead, approximately 1000 years old, at Empingham.

## Relationship to earlier sites

The reuse of earlier sites is a constant theme of Anglo-Saxon burial. Bronze Age round barrows, which play an important part in poetry and storytelling as the homes of dragons and other mysterious forces, were the most popular. The Anglo-Saxons certainly knew of round barrows as places where treasure might be found. In Felix' *Life of Guthlac* he describes how Guthlac came to a mound 'built of clods of earth which greedy comers to the waste had dug open, in the hope of finding treasure there', and in poetry and folklore mounds occur as the homes of elves and sprites throughout the Celtic, Nordic and Germanic worlds. Respect for mounds as 'homes of the Little People' is recognised as a reason for the survival of round barrows in the Irish countryside in living memory. In Beowulf and Guthlac we also read of such barrows being visited to contact supernatural powers and to gain secret knowledge. Extensive cemeteries were centred on them from the fifth to the seventh centuries and single spectacular aristocratic graves of the seventh century often cut into their centres.

The reuse of prehistoric earthworks for burial already occurred occasionally in England and was known in the Anglo-Saxon homelands from at least the third century. As archaeologists become more alert to this phenomenon, mounds or ring-ditches are being recognised on more sites (over half of those with large-scale excavation), and antiquarian references to 'rusty iron objects' and 'coloured glass beads' in Bronze Age mounds can now be interpreted in the same light. The consistency of this 'cultural appropriation' has also become clear, barrows being noted from large cemeteries that begin in the fifth century (eg Little Wilbraham), both ordinary sixth-century cemeteries (Barrington, Melbourn etc) and those with many élite burials (such as Berinsfield and Buckland), humble seventh-century groups and single graves of the highest status (Swallowcliffe Down and

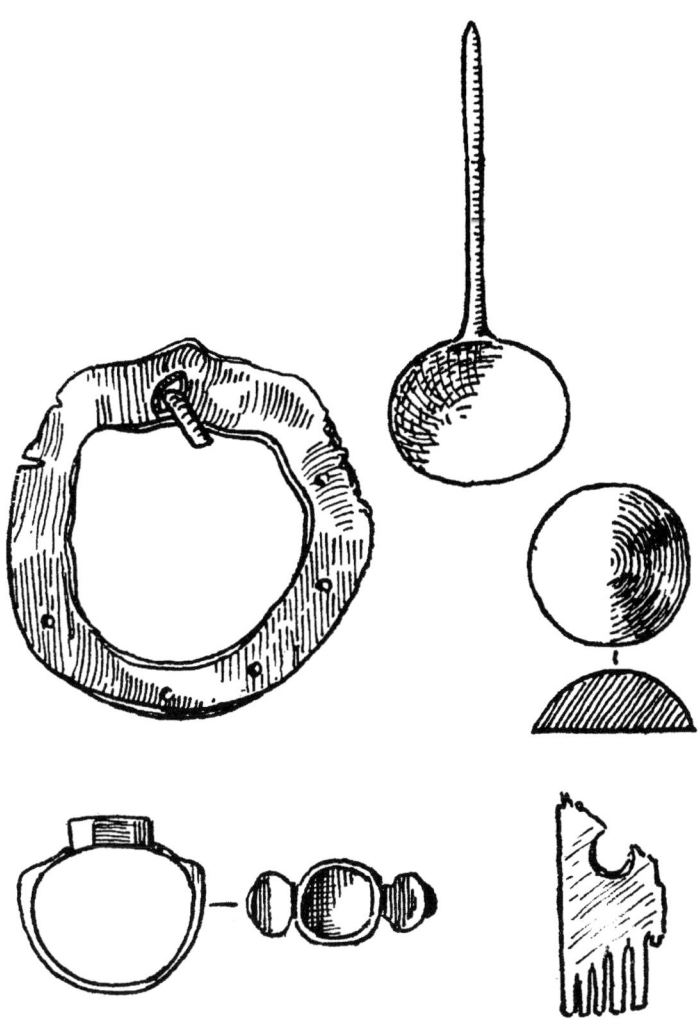

*69 Roman objects amongst grave goods at Lackford.* © Cambridge Antiquarian Society

Snape). Until very recently Sutton Hoo itself was more ambiguous. Customarily thought of as a prehistoric settlement site with Iron Age and Roman fields, the evidence for Neolithic land use principally consisted of numerous small pits containing whole pots, clustered around large trees. In the Bronze Age there were various lines and circles of posts, which could be interpreted, like the Neolithic pits, as ceremonial features. Then, in 2000, excavations close by discovered a sixth-century cemetery which was founded around a Bronze Age barrow. Similarly at Lakenheath, site of the horse burial, a Bronze Age ring-ditch came to light during further work in 2001.

Other monuments (long barrows, hill forts, henges and stone circles) were used, with a preference for sites high up on routeways and boundaries. In some cases areas rich in archaeology of every period would be chosen, as at Lechlade where the cemetery was near a cursus, henge and a group of round barrows, with a major Iron Age boundary ditch and a Roman villa close by. Similarly, at West Heslerton the cemetery lies on a henge, Bronze Age barrows and a Roman/Iron Age triple ditch system. Cemeteries in Iron Age hill forts may have been attracted by visible antiquities but in some areas they could be indicators that the forts themselves were being used again. Highdown, overlooking the sea as well as the Sussex Downs, seems to have been refortified in the fourth century and Roman objects in its cemetery (like the glassware noted above) indicate close but not necessarily friendly relations with Romano-British neighbours. The possible reuse of Iron Age cemeteries is another difficult question, for their burials can be so anonymous. Very close observations and radiocarbon dating are starting to suggest that some graves without grave goods in Anglo-Saxon cemeteries could be disguising earlier burials, for example at Yarnton, where some undated bodies turned out to be Iron Age, and at Mill Hill, Deal, where a rich Iron Age burial with a crown was an indicator that other graves needed careful dating. A single Iron Age grave at Barrington (below and **35**) was hidden amongst Anglo-Saxons. At Croydon one significant Roman grave was in a deep pit within the Anglo-Saxon cemetery, and there are suspicions that some of the unaccompanied bodies could also be of an early date.

When it comes to the use of Roman remains it is more difficult to disentangle mystical motives such as respect for the past and claiming ancestral kin, from the practicalities of making use of good stone buildings and from whatever political situation led to the concentration of early cemeteries next to Roman towns. There may too be cases of genuine continuity as Roman estates were taken over. Another possibility of course is coincidence, particularly where a site has natural advantages such as height or is on a road or river junction. The framework of the Roman landscape certainly had a major impact on the siting of cemeteries. In Cambridgeshire most large cemeteries are on important Roman roads, and they mostly lie close to Roman towns or villas. This pattern is becoming apparent in many other areas, though time-gaps on most sites make it difficult to resolve how the processes of change actually worked.

In some cases the use of Roman cemeteries was similar to that of Bronze Age barrows. This applies to Girton for example, quoted on occasion as an example of continuity but where there were mounds and upstanding mausolea with stone carvings disused for over 300 years. The appropriation of Iron Age and Roman sites in the seventh century, as at Westhampnett and King Harry Lane, must also be due to visible memorials after centuries of neglect. Occasionally the complex patterns of burial hint at some joint use of cemeteries. At Great Chesterford was a cemetery just outside a town, defended by walls in the fourth century and, like Cambridge, evidently important to the late Roman emperors for tax collecting and the protection of food supplies. The Anglo-Saxons were aware of all the Roman burials there and did not disturb them, and distinctive but contemporary west-east burials may even be Roman Christians still present in the fifth century. Cases where we may deduce continuity thanks to a shift in use may be seen in Kent, for example at Eccles, Faversham and Lullingstone, where villas that may or may not have included Christian shrines were used as the sites of the earliest Saxon Christian churches. This model becomes explicable when we see it through a documented case history. The best known of these was St Augustine, who was buried in a church at Canterbury, close to a late Roman cemetery, a choice of site which follows the pattern of early church foundation (with a home-grown saint, typically a martyr, as a foundation burial), in Gaul and Italy. St Mary de Lode, Gloucester, also seems to be a late Roman mausoleum that became a Saxon and then a medieval church, and the same pattern goes for sites such as Wells and most spectacularly St Albans, where there was certainly a 'martyr church' when Germanus visited in 429.

Elsewhere there was more random use of old sites. The upstanding masonry of villas and bathhouses was attractive, whether of humble ones such as Haddon, Cambs, or grander Fishbourne; a cemetery at Catterick was dug into the side of an amphitheatre which overlay a Neolithic cist grave, and temples such as Maiden Castle and Swaffham Prior (Cambs), on high points and associated with many aspects of the past, were natural locations.

## Example

### Barrington, Cambs

During recent excavations on a site that was well known from nineteenth-century records 149 burials were found, their grave goods reflecting Anglian and Saxon types with some Frankish influences. All ages were represented, even the very young often being equipped with grave goods (**colour plate 28**). The site is on a chalk knoll on a ridge, the richest burials being on the skyline. The earliest feature was a Bronze Age ring-ditch and there was intensive Iron Age land use. One burial is thought to belong to this Iron Age phase.

About half the Anglo-Saxon men had spears and (usually) shields, and between them the women had four different costume sets. The cemetery was also used in the late seventh century, most spectacularly by two women in beds. Nine of the graves were marked by posts and about 20 per cent looked as if they had lain in coffins. Diseases encountered included leprosy, TB, osteomyelitis, cancers, sinusitis, leg ulcers, dental problems and the ubiquitous osteoarthritis, as well as healed weapon wounds, breaks and activity related stress. The orientation of graves was varied, though the majority was roughly north-facing. A few graves were deep but most were just shallow scoops with grave goods and bones already lost or broken by modern ploughing. The position of arms and legs often reflected the need to show grave goods to their best advantage, whether displaying jewellery or bags or holding a shield with a crooked left arm. Two were prone and another was contorted, all three being disturbed after partial decomposition. Grave goods included deliberately placed animal bones and pot sherds, though these were difficult to distinguish from those of residual occupation, and a small dog. Sixth-century artefacts included brooches, pins, beads (amber, glass, crystal, jet, stone), chatelaines, keys, girdle hangers, ivory bag-rings, buckles, wrist-clasps, bracelets, finger ring, knives, tweezers, combs, spindle whorls, spears, shields, pots, Roman coins, a bucket and metal-bound boxes (**colour plates 29**). Seventh-century finds were few but rich. One burial on top of the hill was so truncated by the plough that only her jaw remained together with a necklace of silver rings, glass beads and two gold pendants, one of them set with crystal (**colour plate 30**). One bed burial was probably in a mound yet had barely any grave pit, but the other was deeply buried. Inside was a young woman of 17-25 who suffered from leprosy. She wore two silver rings by her chin, a buckle, two knives, and a purse containing a comb, iron rods and plates, a fossil sea urchin, a sheep ankle bone and a glass bead. By her side was a sword cut down to make a weaving batten and a key, and there was a bucket at her feet (**colour plate 31**).

# 8  The later Anglo-Saxons

The earthly part, the shattered dwelling of bone within the abode
rests on its deathbed, and the heavenly part has left the body vessel
to seek the reward of victory in the light of God.
*Guthlac B.*

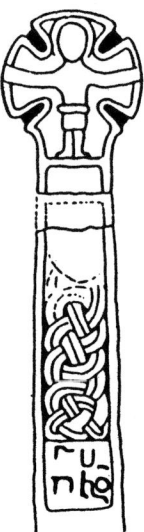

# The later Anglo-Saxons

Only in a very few cases is evidence found for early Anglo-Saxon cemeteries in parish churchyards, the move away from the old sites being complete. The cases where this does occur are mostly in Kent, where the Frankish custom of continuing to use old pagan cemeteries was more popular than elsewhere, and there are a couple of examples in Norfolk. These rare cases tend to have higher-status artefacts, such as crystal balls and glass. There are also a few sites with mounds in or near churchyards. In general however we are looking at decisive changes that come about in a series of jumps (pagan — Final Phase/home burial — fully Christian cemetery — parish church). Not all the stages were followed everywhere and the staging of sequences was uneven, affected in part by royal interests and missionary activity, for clerics from Ireland, France, Italy and Tarsus in Turkey arrived with different views of burial practice as of so many aspects of Christianity.

In the eighth century a few pagan cemeteries were still used in Kent, where grave goods such as coins occur, and there may be more than we think hidden as 'poor' graves in older cemeteries. This practice was acceptable in Ireland, for example, for Irish canons from this phase rule that monks, nuns and church tenants should be buried at their churches but others could be buried in their ancestral cemeteries. The upkeep of these cemeteries was still a community responsibility even though 'a greater gift' should be made to the church's graveyard. Elsewhere, the new seventh-century cemeteries often carry on into this century before they make another change, and, for a while at least before the new institutions caught up with them, one option was home burial near the farms. Churches were still few and far between (Bede describes Cuthbert travelling around remote villages, where people gathered to hear him preach but mentions no churches). Nor was there yet any automatic connection between churches and graveyards, and many 'field' churches were never granted rights of burial. However, there is increasing archaeological evidence for cemeteries with small timber churches which never developed into parish churches. In Cambridgeshire two such sites, Gamlingay and Cherry Hinton, have been found in the last three years (**70**). Outside England, this is a pattern that can be seen clearly on the Isle of Man, where numerous early Christian *Keills* and their graveyards were not replaced by the parochial system until the twelfth century.

Further afield we have one vivid picture of how systems of burial might develop when there were few priests or accepted traditions but many competing superstitions. The saga of Eirik the Red, set in Greenland in the tenth century,

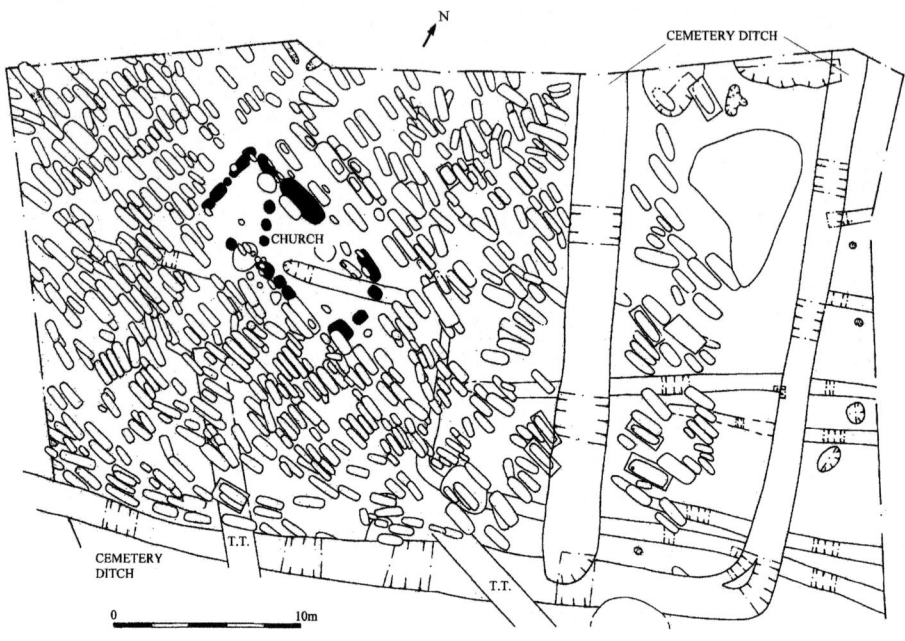

*70 Plan of the church and churchyard at Cherry Hinton, Cambs.*
  © Hertfordshire Archaeological Trust

tells how it was the custom in the very early days of Christianity there to bury people in unconsecrated ground on the farms where they lived. A stake was put up over their breast, to be pulled up when a priest next visited. He would then pour holy oil down the hole and sing a service over them. This was not considered good enough to stop the hauntings that were troubling one settlement and the dying hero, Thorstein Eiriksson, asked to be carried to a church for burial. He also ordered cremation for the man he thought responsible for the hosts of dead that were seen walking, demonstrating a splendid confusion of rites even amongst one family. This pattern of home burial without significant grave goods is another custom that may be very under-reported. It could be seen for example at Hinxton, Cambs, where a woman with a knife at her waist lay close to a mid-Saxon farm (**71**). Many small groups of bodies near settlements in Oxfordshire have a west-east alignment and only occasional knives as grave goods, and similar west-east graves at Carlton Colville, Suffolk, have just been excavated within the settlement. A simple home burial of this kind was also the first instinct of the unassuming St Cuthbert, who asked to be buried in his hermit's hut on Farne, though his followers persuaded him on his deathbed that he should be taken to a church because of his unusual sanctity.

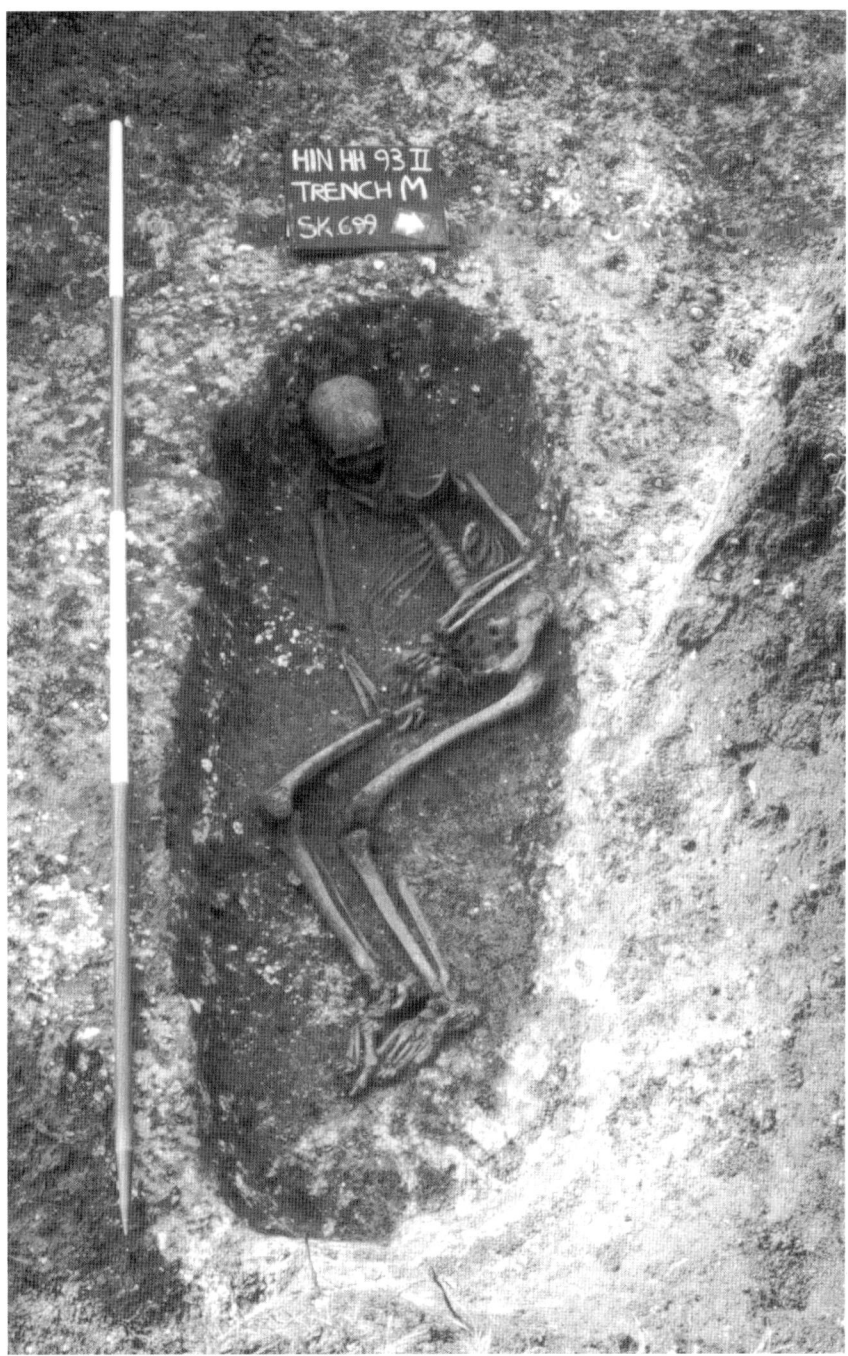

71 *'Home burial'. A single grave of a woman with a knife (therefore clothed) just outside a middle Saxon farm at Hinxton, Cambs.* © Cambridgeshire County Council Archaeological Field Unit

Eighth-century burials might therefore be in various locations, especially as one significant taboo had been broken, for now it was acceptable to bury the dead near to habitation: a break with the past that would have a lasting effect on the development of England's medieval landscape. A Canterbury tradition (recorded in a chronicle that was seen in the seventeenth but lost in the eighteenth century) credits this change to Archbishop Cuthbert who, in the mid-eighth century, received papal permission to have cemeteries *intra civitates*, and was himself buried inside Canterbury. Already, as seen in chapter 7, some cemeteries had relocated, and in Kent in particular there seem to be Roman mausolea that became churches which then attracted settlement. Thus the distribution of population, religious sites and cemeteries converged, a process contributing to the nucleation of villages in the next few centuries. As the Church gained a permanent hold and trained more priests this trend was decisive if not necessarily popular. The story of one old chieftain in the Heidarviga Saga who caused serious trouble when he was being carried a long distance to a churchyard, his corpse killing one girl and repeatedly falling off a horse, reminds us of the confusions these changes in tradition involved. The burial party of this tale had to give up and temporarily bury him in a cairn, though the new forces won in the end and they got him to a church the next year.

On the Continent Charlemagne's ordinances of parish rights expressly forbidding the use of heathen cemeteries, followed by a change to central burial places supervised by parish churches, were issued in 786 and 810/3. The formality of this ruling may have confirmed official attitudes in England, for the ruling families' and the Church's ties with the Continent were close. However, the change to church (though not necessarily *parish* church) burial, like the almost uniform use of shrouds, was already commonplace. However, the ninth century saw the disruption of many institutions due to Viking raids and conquests and the Church lost power over much of England for a while. The pattern of change in these poorly recorded years does not appear smooth. There are obvious variations, for example, between the patterns followed at Castledyke South (Barton on Humber), which had burials from the sixth century, with one area for seventh-century Christians, before moving to St Peter's church in the ninth century; Yarnton, Oxfordshire, with ordinary burials near the settlement in the ninth century before a later shift to the parish church, and Raunds, Northants, where there was a small thegn's church but no churchyard at this time.

Up to the tenth century pastoral care was centred on minsters, where communities of clerics lived and took care of groups of villages. Yet with the reconquest of the Danelaw after 920, a revival of religious life and the administrative reforms of the energetic and devout Wessex kings, parishes and parish churches took on pivotal roles in many aspects of life. The development of a churchyard consecration rite after 900 was part of this growth in status. The laws of Athelstan, 925-39, started by insisting on payments to churches and upheld the importance of the parish church by ensuring dues were paid in their proper place and that priests attended to their duties. Burial in one's own parish church became obligatory although, with some churches not having rights to bury, this could still mean travel to a mother-church for some people. The only restrictions seem to be unrepentant perjurers and suicides that were not mad, though priests could evidently make allowances in even these circumstances. The enclosure of churchyards was a feature of this tenth-/eleventh-century phase. Churchmen now had an increasing financial interest in their churches becoming the place of burial, for fees were paid both for burial and the provision of masses.

The development of parish burial can be seen at Raunds where, in the late seventh century, enclosed buildings became a manor which by about 900 had a small church. Only in the mid-tenth century was a graveyard added. The acquisition of burial rights promoted the church to more than a field church though, like quite a number now being discovered, it never became the parish church (**72**).

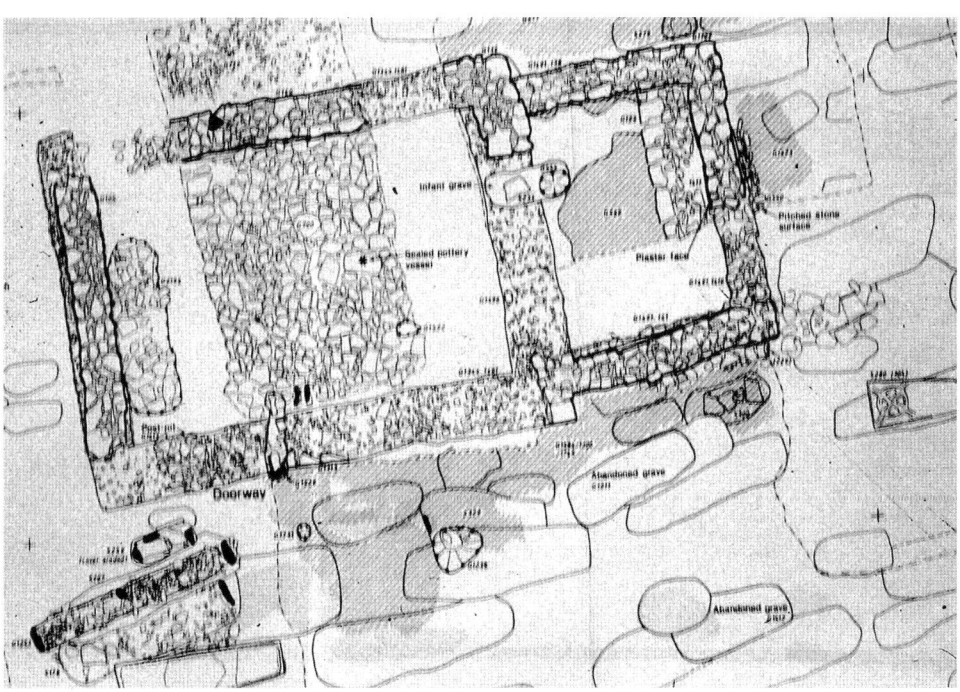

*72 Raunds, Northants. The graveyard only came into use when the chancel was added to the church in the mid-tenth century.* © English Heritage

*73 Heaven, from the* Liber Vitae, Winchester. *Drycthelm's account, recorded by Bede, of his tour of the afterlife describes the place where the righteous wait for Judgement as a pleasant meadow surrounded by a high wall within which men sat around in white robes.* © By permission of the British Library (Stowe 944, ff.6v, 7r)

## Religious beliefs

Complete belief both in an eternal afterlife and judgement there for behaviour on earth (baptism, faith, good works and intercessory prayer being required) were basic tenets of Christian teaching. There were also firm convictions about heaven and hell, though there were contradictory views on whether judgement was immediate or waited until a universal judgement day. Bede writes of one man, Drycthelm, who returned from the dead and recounted how he had been taken on a tour of the immediate afterlife. He told how the extreme anguish in burning flames and bitter cold and the bliss in flowery meadows were only a prelude to Judgement Day, the truly good having gone straight to heaven and the most evil fallen into the fiery pit of hell. *The Blickling Homilies*, 971, describe a Last Judgement when St Michael commands the blowing of trumpets, causing all bodies, whether buried, drowned or eaten by beasts, to rise and be judged 'in such form as they previously adorned themselves; but not with gold nor with purple garments but with good and holy deeds'. King Alfred's translation of St Augustine's

*74 Hell. Drycthelm's description of the afterlife for those who had done wrong and had not repented included wicked spirits dragging human souls into burning chasms, and the alternating torments of bitter snow and terrible heat.* © By permission of the British Library (Stowe 944, ff.6v, 7r)

Soliloquies includes the conviction that people would arise on the Day of Judgement and bodies thereafter would not age or decay; even if the body had decayed the soul was still alive. In other cases (and descriptions of the hereafter are a constant theme in the literature of the time, nearly all written by monks) the next life began immediately, some saintly souls being drawn up to heaven by golden cords or escorted by angels, and Bede on his deathbed talked of being called to God (**73**). Guthlac's soul was taken to heaven in the arms of angels, and 'lovingly they led him before the face of the eternal judge'. Views of hell (**74**) were drawn from Roman and other ancient views of the most damned, but heaven was rather more cerebral than the Norse, Celtic and classical versions, stressing bliss in the presence of God and with little in the way of activity. Alfred translated St Augustine's elaborate views of particular gradations of heaven and hell, with everyone having torment or glory on merit, but generally there seems little in between the extremes, and concepts of Purgatory were not yet developed. It was also taught, as in earlier periods, that the dead were not separate from the living and they could help each other. Prayers for the dead became a major function of monasteries, and St Augustine's teaching that the dead visited the living in their sleep, not for macabre reasons but to give them comfort or, as in Bede's accounts, instructions, was widely accepted, as was terror of the ghosts of the unquiet dead.

75 *One of five stone coffins from Raunds, and a slot to hold a grave marker.*
© English Heritage

76 *Gravestone from Raunds, engraved with a crucifix.* © English Heritage

## Memorials

There was a tradition of marking important graves, especially ecclesiastical ones, and a considerable number and variety of stones decorated in different regional styles have survived. Excavations of the church and churchyard at Raunds have produced useful evidence for the ways in which (in an area where good stone was plentiful) several burials had covers, slots or posts to mark the graves (**75**, **76**). In Cornwall, lack of Saxon disruption meant there was continued literacy, so actual inscriptions occasionally survive, if of poorer quality than the earlier dedications (**77**). Eastern England saw Scandinavian in-fluence, resulting in distinctive interlace or plaitwork carvings on memorials. Such memorials took two forms: slabs flat over the grave, and free-standing crosses, often with wheel-headed crosses on the top. These occasionally still stand in churchyards (**colour plate 32**).

77 *Tenth-century carved crosses in the churchyard at Sancreed, Cornwall.*
    © Cornwall Archaeological Unit

Grave slabs, often found in fragmentary form built into the later fabric of churches, seem to have been laid at ground level so they were visible, two being found in their original position outside Peterborough Cathedral. Nearly 50 somewhat similar gravestones were found under York Minster, where Anglian ones of the eighth century were succeeded by Scandinavian style ones, with plaitwork decoration, vines and birds. The grave of a child can still be seen in the Crypt beneath the Minster, a flat slab above the grave carved with a cross, with upright stones at either end. In areas of Viking settlement in north-east England elaborately carved hogback tombs are found. These incorporate Anglo-Saxon plaitwork decoration with the effect of roof shingles of a miniature house, which they resemble, and have biting bears at either end. The learned monks of Northumbria had Latin and runic inscriptions at Monkwearmouth, Lindisfarne and other churches in the area. Memorials in churches could serve gruesome but useful purposes. When Chad, bishop of Mercia, was moved inside a new church his burial was covered with a wooden tomb in the form of a little house with an opening into which people could reach for dust which, mixed with water, was drunk by the sick.

A late reintroduction from Scandinavia of the ancient barrow building tradition is seen at Ingleby, Derbys. Swords, cremated animals and iron nails were found here. One cremation had taken place on site, but some of the other mounds were empty cenotaphs. There was another mound at Repton, where the Viking army wintered in 874. Here a Saxon building was used as a burial chamber, with a possible central grave and bones of about 250 bodies, 80 per cent of them males of fighting age, and coins dating the burials to 873-4. The chamber was covered by a mound and a stone cairn and surrounded by a stone kerb, a typical high-status Viking grave ritual. Four young people seem to have been sacrificed in association with these presumed war graves.

## Treatment of the body

In popular belief though not in theological teaching the body was due to rise again and so ought to be preserved in a pure and complete form. By the eighth century clothed burial had virtually disappeared for everyone except clerics, and burial in a shroud in the style of the Mediterranean and Near Eastern world was the almost universal style, based on the gospel description of Christ's burial. This consisted of a white sheet wrapped tightly around the body, apparently without fastenings (two shroud pins were found at Winchester but generally they are unknown until post-Conquest times) (**78**). Etheldreda's shroud is described as of fresh new linen cloths which enfolded the body, and Guthlac had a linen shroud sent for his use by an East Anglian princess. In the description of Columba's burial in Ireland in 597 there were three days and nights of funeral ceremonies before he was buried in this shroud, with no mention of any coffin or other grave furniture. A similar three days prayer preceded Guthlac's burial.

Orderly parallel rows of west-east graves with no intercutting until the cemetery was full enough to start the sequence again was the normal pattern throughout this period (**colour plate 33**), though sometimes there was zoning of important graves around founder burials. One good example of an ordinary tenth-century cemetery is Raunds, where corpses were often protected, sometimes with coffins, covers or elaborate arrangements of stones used in

*78 A shrouded body is carried to its grave*

particular for propping up the head. Five children were in complete cists but usually only part of the body and especially the head were covered. Some were tightly wrapped in shrouds and preserved their parallel shape, others were tumbled about and were thought by the excavators to be in clothing. Somewhat earlier at Gamlingay there were nearly 120 tightly bound burials in a mix of coffins and shrouds in a fenced enclosure connected with a small timber church. This site had evolved from an earlier settlement of sunken-floored huts and preceded a shift to the present village in the tenth century. At Cherry Hinton there was a rather similar arrangement, this time of nearly 700 west-east burials around a small (9.5 x 3.5m) church, babies clustering beneath its presumed eaves. Pillow-stones here included some large stone blocks decorated with interlace ornament. Burials continued into the eleventh century (leading to intercutting as many as five deep), after which the parish church, some 400m away, was used. At Sedgeford too the eighth-century cemetery had burials spaced in rows where there was room. In the area of greater use there was intercutting but the layout of the shrouded bodies was the same. One regularly-observed feature is that children were buried under the eaves, a clustering that has been noted for example at Raunds, Whithorn, Jarrow, Winchester, Hartlepool, Ely and Cherry Hinton. This is sometimes said to be due to ensuring constant baptism from water dripping off the church roof, particularly desirable if a child died before baptism, though sometimes (as at Ely) children were too old for this to be case.

Coffins played a practical part when bodies were transported long distances, a frequent necessity and in the case of important clerics and royalty often involving several days travel. At Raunds it was noted that some coffins had unusual bone tumble, as if there had been some delay before burial, which the excavators suggested could be due to their being brought from some distance. It seems that wooden coffins, like those of stone or lead thoughtfully sent in good time by well-wishers, were unsentimentally prepared before death, and when Bishop John of Beverley went to visit a sick boy the coffin in which he expected to be buried lay beside him. Wooden coffins were probably in use from the beginning of burial at Winchester Old Minster, starting around AD 675, with occasional nailed coffins by about 700 and becoming progressively more common thereafter. Iron fittings appear at Winchester in the ninth century, and several used stones and tiles in various positions, often as a pillow or to hold the head facing upwards. Such 'ear muffs' are quite often found at this time and are symptomatic of the care given to proper positioning of the body. York Minster too had coffins with metal fittings and locks. Some, possibly all, of these were originally large domestic chests. One grave in this cemetery was on a different alignment to the rest and generally seemed alien, probably Viking. He was in a small boat, a ninth-century example of the tradition seen much earlier in East Anglia. At Barton on Humber there were 40 timber coffins, single nails generally only being used to fasten the lids. Waterlogged conditions here meant that actual coffins with dowelled joints were found. Normally, as at Raunds, neither metal nails nor fitments were used, though at Sedgeford (Norfolk) one group had heavy iron fittings. Unusual coffins include a group at Caister on Sea which had ships' timbers used as grave covers, and Cuthbert's final coffin, which was engraved on the inside with Christ, Mary, the apostles, the evangelists and the archangels.

Stone coffins are principally referred to in connection with important clerics, and lead ones also occur in the archaeological record and in literature (Guthlac had a lead coffin sent before his death). Sometimes the reuse of Roman ones can be deduced, and there seems to have been no problem in using others of quite recent date. Etheldreda, founder of the monastery at Ely, is a well-known example, for when she was exhumed by her sister the monks sailed up the river to Roman Cambridge to find what was described as a white marble sarcophagus with close fitting lid. This is generally assumed to have been a Roman coffin, though mention of a shape cut out for the head perhaps makes this suspect. Others were being made in this period, presumably on quite a large scale for they were not always for particular customers. When Sebbi, king of Essex, dies as a monk, there is a stone coffin ready for him but it is too small, and it takes a miracle as well as chipping out a larger area to get it to fit. This story of Bede's also mentions the importance of having a pillow, and of lying straight, for bending his knees was considered only as a last resort. Occasionally there is archaeological evidence for reuse where the first body is not totally removed, as seen at Bampton, Oxfordshire (**79**). Small numbers of stone coffins also occur in village cemeteries such as Raunds, usually with a shape cut out to hold the head. Exceptional stone covers were excavated around the east apse of Winchester Old Minster (992-4). One was inscribed 'Here lies Gunni, the earl's companion'. A footstone was carved with the 'hand of God' holding a cross within an open arch. Gunni was a Scandinavian name, and he had probably come to England with the Danish king Cnut who was buried in the Minster in 1035 (**80**).

Incorruptibility of the flesh was a common sign of an Anglo-Saxon saint, with many exhumed bodies described in terms of their miraculous preservation and improbably sweet fragrance. This was the case for Guthlac, lifelike and with clothing undecayed when he was moved into a shrine above ground a year after his death. Bede ascribes a similar preservation to virtuous people such as Etheldreda of Ely, her sister Aethelburgh, Fursey (an Irish monk who led the conversion of East Anglia), and most notably to Cuthbert (below). Fragrant smells are often remarked upon after other exhumations, and coffins above ground in churches were evidently tolerated. Some cases

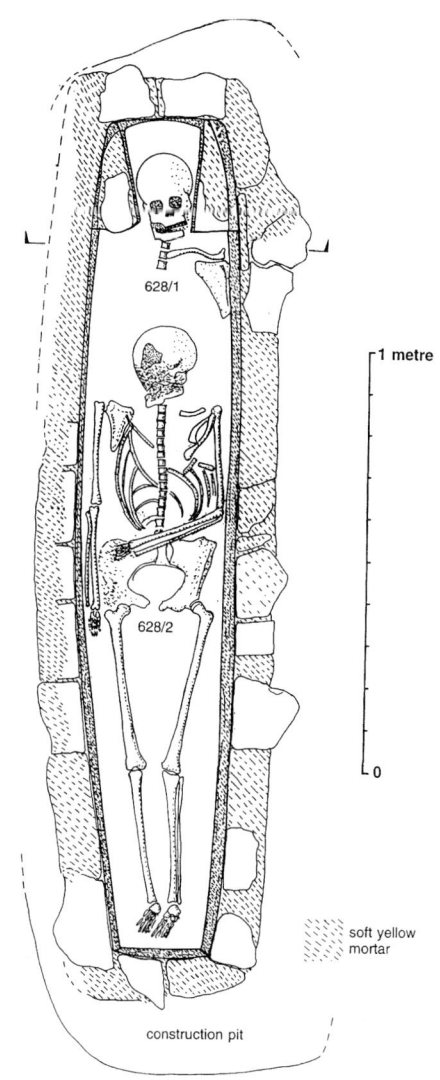

*79 A grave within the minster church of Bampton, Oxfordshire, in which a man, buried about AD 1000, has been partially displaced by an ageing woman. This unusual cist is made of mortared rubble, a style that had only just been adopted for high-status graves in France, later becoming popular in England. The bowed sides and head-niche are often found in late Saxon graves.* John Blair

*80 Stone grave cover inscribed 'Here lies Gunni, the earl's companion' from Winchester Old Minster.* © Winchester Excavation Committee

may be due to unusual decay processes but it also seems likely that the embalming techniques, perfumes and preservatives contributed. Embalming was also apparent from the exfoliated state of bones excavated at Wells, and the adventures of Cuthbert's body made such treatment vital.

Burials were more uniform now than in previous eras but there were still variations. Charcoal, perhaps in literal response to the phrase 'bed of ashes', was spread in selected graves, particularly those of distinguished churchmen, for it is common near cathedrals (notably Exeter, York, Winchester and Lincoln) between the ninth and eleventh century, mostly for adult males. Parish churches also have a few. At Raunds several graves had traces of charcoal or pieces of burnt wood. Whether there was any connection with the early Anglo-Saxon use of burnt wood in graves is hard to say.

When graveyards were full, orderly recutting was acceptable, as seen in excavations at Sedgeford. On urban sites the available space would fill more rapidly. In Hamwic, the eighth-century predecessor of Southampton, nine cemeteries have been found, in some of which there was evidence for the cavalier treatment of older graves, many bones being thrown aside when rows were reworked. Though at first surprising this is inevitably the case when parish churchyards within settlements are used for prolonged periods. Theologically it is not a problem, for the teaching had always been that life after death was not a literal raising of a skeleton from the grave, even if that was a popular conception.

The fate of those who died in battle seems to have been left to the proverbial and actual wolves and ravens unless friends or relatives retrieved them, a meritorious act and of practical help to the dead in the afterlife. One abbot found what he thought was his brother on a battlefield and took him to the abbey for honourable burial and masses which proved of benefit to the still-living brother.

## Grave goods

The Church pronounced various strictures against pagan practices such as funeral feasts, burning grain and the use of 'spells, amulets and other devilish secret arts', and its vision of the afterlife stressed the journey of the soul alone. Thus the old provisions were no longer necessary and, as the use of a shroud replaced normal clothing, even items of dress all but disappeared. However, the first Christian influences in Kent and to a lesser extent East Anglia were Frankish, and on the Continent there was no dichotomy between grave goods and Christianity. In areas of this influence grave goods were slow to die out in the seventh century and might be included in rather covert positions in later Christian burials. Those converted by the more austere Irish church moved quickly to a standard Christian grave. This also seems to have been the Roman policy, with the important exception of their own priests of whom Cuthbert, dressed after death in priestly clothes and shoes so that he would be ready to meet Christ, is the supreme example.

Instead of grave goods status was accorded to lay people by the position of the grave as well as the elaboration of the coffin. They would often leave lavish benefactions, and all church burials required payment of soulscot. Christian burial was therefore no cheaper than burial with grave goods, and few could have afforded both. Therefore, with the exceptions of some Viking burials and occasional coins, the haul of lay grave goods is remarkably small. At Winchester one man had gold braid on his head and garter hooks by the knee, at Caister on Sea there was an iron finger ring, a coin and a spear, and at Cherry Hinton a few buckles and bracelets. At Hamwic, an international port, the vast majority followed the standard burial pattern though references to glass vessels, two graves with spears and an eighth-century continental *seax* suggest foreigners in their midst could follow their own customs. No doubt more examples will come to light, but effectively the custom as a formal part of burial was dead.

## Relationship to earlier sites

Pope Gregory instructed that pagan temples be converted to Christian use. Many Roman walled towns, forts and major villas were in royal or aristocratic hands and could be given to established monastic sites; in a few cases Roman cemeteries and mausolea attracted first Christian burials and then mortuary chapels that evolved into churches. Such factors, linked to desirable ideological associations, commonly resulted in the appropriation of Roman sites for minsters and monasteries. Then, too, churches were likely to be built on nodal points (eg the *fora* of towns such as Verulamium), road junctions, the gateways out of walled Roman towns and other locations connected with Roman topography, for the road network and much of the urban landscape were still their legacy. This pattern of change is still poorly understood, though case studies such as Rivenhall, where the stages were investigated whereby a Roman villa became a sixth-century hall, then mid-Anglo-Saxon mausoleum/chapel, and finally a late Anglo-Saxon timber church, give some clues to the processes at work. The use of old pagan sites can often be seen as churches appearing on prehistoric monuments or in association with features such as standing stones. In Cornwall, where there was continuous Christianity, many prehistoric sites were reused as churches. Historical sanctity drew Guthlac to live (and to be buried) next to 'a certain great burial mound' that was presumably Bronze Age, the minster at Bampton was built over a line of three barrows and there must be many more examples of this relationship. The clearest example of an actual Iron Age/ Roman temple turning into a church is Uley, Glos.

## St Cuthbert (81)

Exceptional treatment was reserved for saintly figures. Careful descriptions that Bede gives in two different accounts provide invaluable information about St Cuthbert's successive burials, an extreme case but not untypical of those considered sanctified. Cuthbert died in 687, having been persuaded that his body should not be buried on the hermit's site where he lived, as he first wished, but in the church of the monastery at Lindisfarne. As a priest, he was buried in his vestments. After 11 years he was exhumed and buried in a new ornate coffin, this time above ground. His incorrupt body was dressed in new vestments and shroud and his old grave beneath the new coffin was reused for a bishop who died at this time. In the late ninth century Lindisfarne was subject to Viking attacks, so Cuthbert's body was removed and paraded around Northumbria for seven weeks, transportation to Ireland being considered. Finally a shrine was built for him near Durham which became a centre of pilgrimage. Among the pilgrims who came in the tenth century was King Athelstan, who donated the elaborate vestments he

*81 Cuthbert during one of his exhumations, drawn in the early twelfth century.*
© The Master and Fellows of University College, Oxford

wore when his body was excavated in 1827, including silk garments embroidered in gold thread. He also had a gold and garnet pectoral cross, a portable altar covered in silver, an ivory comb and extra fabrics. The symbolism of these artefacts is unmistakable, but none were necessarily his actual possessions and their dates are similarly misleading. A century later he was moved again, this time to Durham, where his cult was so popular that, after yet another century had passed, the Normans wanted to appropriate its glory. They built Durham cathedral in his honour, and Cuthbert was moved once again to a new shrine within this cathedral. A further building took place for Cuthbert's glorification in the late twelfth century to revitalise the cult once more. An illuminated manuscript of his life and death created at this time is sometimes treated as a contemporary record of his exhumation, though the detail is highly misleading (**colour plate 34**). His elaborate shrine was destroyed in the sixteenth century and the grave of this seventh-century saint is now marked by a nineteenth-century marble slab. Through all these translations and throughout the Middle Ages Cuthbert's grave was visited for the sake of healing miracles.

Cuthbert's was an extreme case, but the elements of his story involving exhumation and reburial, frequent handling of his remains, miraculous incorruptibility, elaborate dress and grave goods, powers of healing and other miracles, and either removal to an important church or having a new church built over the grave (in Cuthbert's case, both), are part of the status of a saint. Such exhumations were not without controversy and good reasons were expected before removals to new sites were allowed, although the advantages of acquiring suitably saintly remains meant that convenient dreams occurred with suspicious frequency. The translation of clerics to a more honourable burial inside their churches was common, with Augustine at Canterbury and St Swithun at Winchester as well-known examples. Bede had no qualms about this custom and describes many occasions, particularly involving removal to the honoured place to the right of the altar. He himself was first buried in the south porch of his monastery, then moved to the place of honour by the altar. More prosaically, bodies might be moved for practical reasons. Men and women at the nunnery at Barking were exhumed due to shortage of space and moved into a single tomb inside the church. Saints whose burial led to churches/chapels being constructed over their graves include Guthlac, who was first buried in the ground, then dug up so that he could have a more honourable place above ground, around which various buildings were constructed. St Edmund too, after a quick burial, soon had a chapel raised over his grave, and was later moved to a better church. Royal remains were also likely to be reburied when a more prestigious situation was found (for example, Alfred, his wife and his son Edward were translated to a site in front of the altar of Hyde Abbey, Winchester when the church was finished). Dismemberment, though, was not part of their fate, and in fact when Edmund, a king as well as saint, was buried there was a miracle to fix his head and body back together. Yet saints' bones, despite protests from some early church fathers, were playing an important part in mainstream religion. King Alfred always carried saintly relics with him, and his grandson Athelstan sent throughout Europe for the bones of saints to endow a monastery at Exeter, a commonplace piety in the late Saxon period when the mortal remains of many clerics were deemed capable of miracles.

The ways in which these highly respected bones were treated so differently from the normative rite takes us back in a circle to much earlier periods, to times when it is difficult to tell the saints from sinners — in the unnatural arrangements of bones in a Neolithic barrow, Iron Age rubbish pit or a particularly secure Roman or Saxon coffin. The behaviour we see in this historic period and in a religion we think we understand has many strands linking it to more remote times, just as the sites belonging to the dead are reused in successive ages. Archaeological activity will continue to add to the clues with which we reconstruct the past, but fully understanding the 'sad sepulchral relics' will be a greater test.

# Further reading

*BAR* British Archaeological Report, British Series
*CBA* Council for British Archaeology

Alcock J.P. 1980 'Classical religious belief and burial practice in Roman Britain', *Archaeol J* 137

Allen M.J. et al 1995 'Food for the living: a reassessment of a Bronze Age barrow at Buckskin, Basingstoke, Hampshire', *Proc Prehist Soc* 61

Ashbee P. 1966 'The Fussell's Lodge long barrow excavations, 1957', *Archaeologia* 100

Atkinson R.J.C. 1965 'Waylands Smithy', *Antiquity* 39

Bassett S. 1992 *Death in towns*, Leicester University Press

Black E.W. 1986 'Romano-British burial customs and religious beliefs in South East England', *Archaeol J* 143

Blair J. and Pyrah C. 1996 'Church archaeology: research directions for the future', *CBA*

Boddington A. 1996 *Raunds Furnells: the Anglo-Saxon church and churchyard*, English Heritage

Boyle A. et al 1995 *Two Oxfordshire Anglo-Saxon cemeteries: Berinsfield and Didcot*, Thames Valley Mono 8

Bristow P.H.W. 1998 *Attitudes to disposal of the dead in southern Britain 3500 BC-43 AD*, BAR 274

Carver M. (ed) 1992 *The age of Sutton Hoo*, Boydell Press, Woodbridge

Cook A.M. and Dacre M. 1985 *Excavations at Portway, Andover 1973-1975*, Oxford University Committee for Archaeology Mono 4

Charlton B. and Mitcheson M. 1984 'The Roman cemetery at Petty Knowes, Rochester, Northumberland', *Archaeologia Aeliana* 12

Crummy N. et al 1993 'Excavations of Roman and later cemeteries, churches and monastic sites in Colchester, 1971-88', *Colchester Archaeological Trust Rpt* 9

Daniell C. 1997 *Death and burial in medieval England*, Routledge

Davies J. 1999 *Death, burial and rebirth in the religions of Antiquity*, Routledge

Davies S.M. et al 1985 'Excavations at Alington Avenue, Fordington, Dorchester 1984/5: interim report', *Proc Dorset Natural History and Archaeological Soc* 107

Evison V. 1988 *An Anglo-Saxon cemetery at Alton, Hampshire*, Hampshire Field Club

Evison V. 1994 'An Anglo-Saxon cemetery at Great Chesterford, Essex', *CBA Res Rpt 91*

Farwell D.E. and Molleson T.I. 1993 'Excavations at Poundbury 1966-80 Vol II: The Cemeteries', *Proc Dorset Natural History and Archaeological Soc Mono 11*

Fitzpatrick A.P. 1996 'A 1st-century AD 'Durotrigian' inhumation burial with a decorated Iron Age mirror from Portesham, Dorset', *Proc Dorset Natural History and Archaeological Soc 118*

Fitzpatrick A.P. 1997 'Archaeological excavations on the route of the A27 Westhampnett bypass, West Sussex, 1992: the cemeteries', *Wessex Archaeology Rpt 12*

Foster J. 1986 'The Lexden Tumulus: a re-appraisal of an Iron Age burial from Colchester, Essex' *BAR 156*

Fox C. and T.C. Lethbridge 1926 'The la Tène and Romano-British cemetery, Guilden Morden, Cambs', *Proc Cambridge Antiquarian Soc 27*

French C.A.I. 1994 *Excavation of the Deeping St Nicholas barrow complex, S Lincs,* Heritage Trust of Lincolnshire

Gibson A. and Simpson D. 1998 *Prehistoric ritual and religion,* Sutton

Geake H. 1997 'The use of grave goods in Conversion-period England, *c*.600-*c*.850' *BAR 261*

Green H.J.M. 1973 'Roman Godmanchester: Part III: Emmanuel Knoll', *Proc Cambridge Antiquarian Soc 64*

Hill J.D. et al 1999 'Hinxton Rings late Iron Age cemetery, Cambridgeshire', *Proc Prehist Soc 65*

Hirst S.M. 1985 'An Anglo-Saxon cemetery at Sewerby, E. Yorks', *York University Archaeological Publications 4*

Hodder I. and Evans C. forthcoming *Haddenham project Vol I: The making of a fen-edge landscape,* Macdonald Inst Mono.

Hyslop M. 1963 'Two Anglo-Saxon cemeteries at Chamberlains Barn, Leighton Buzzard, Bedfordshire', *Archaeol J 120*

James E.O. 1960 *The Ancient Gods,* Weidenfeld and Nicolson

Jewitt L. 1870 *Grave mounds and their contents,* London

Jupp P.C. and C. Gittings 1999 *Death in England,* Manchester University Press

Kempe A.J. 1836 'Account of the collection of sepulchral vessels found in 1821 in a Roman ustrinum, Litlington', *Archaeologia 26*

Kinsley A.G. 1989 'The Anglo-Saxon cemetery at Millgate, Newark-on-Trent, Nottinghamshire' *Nottingham Arch Mono 2*

Lane Fox R. 1986 *Pagans and Christians* Penguin

Lawson A. et al 1981 *The barrows of East Anglia,* East Anglian Archaeology

Lethbridge T.C. 1931 'Recent excavations in Anglo-Saxon Cambridgeshire and Suffolk', *Proc Cambridge Antiquarian Soc Quarto Series III*

Lethbridge T.C. 1936 'Further excavations in the early Iron Age and Romano-British cemetery at Guilden Morden', *Proc Cambridge Antiquarian Soc 37*

Lethbridge T.C. 1951 'A cemetery at Lackford, Suffolk', *Cambridge Antiquarian Soc Quarto Publications 6*

Lethbridge T.C. 1953 'Burial of an Iron Age warrior at Snailwell', *Proc Cambridge Antiquarian Soc 47*

Liversidge J. 1977 'Roman burials in the Cambridge area', *Proc Cambridge Antiquarian Soc 67*

Lucian of Samosata 1905 *Works,* trans H.W. and F.G. Fowler

Lucy S. 1998 'The early Anglo-Saxon cemeteries of East Yorkshire', *BAR 272*

Malim T. and Hines J. 1998 'The Anglo-Saxon cemetery at Edix Hill (Barrington A), Cambridgeshire', *CBA Res Rpt 112*

Marner D. 2000 *St Cuthbert: his life and cult in medieval Durham,* The British Library

Martin E.A. 1977 'The excavation of two tumuli, Chippenham', *Proc Cambridge Antiquarian Soc 66*

Mays S. 1998 *The archaeology of human bones* Routledge

McWhirr A. et al 1982 *Romano-British cemeteries at Cirencester,* Cirencester Excavation Committee

Meaney A. 1964 *Gazetteer of Early Anglo-Saxon burial sites* George Allen and Unwin

Meaney A.L. 1981 'Anglo-Saxon amulets and curing stones' *BAR 96*

O'Brien E. 1999 'Post Roman Britain to Anglo-Saxon England: Burial practices reviewed' *BAR 289*

Parker-Pearson M. 1999 *The Archaeology of death and burial,* Sutton

Partridge C. 1981 *Skeleton Green: a late Iron Age and Romano-British site,* Britannia Mono Series 2

Pearce J. et al 2000 *Burial, Society and Context in the Roman world* Oxbow

Petersen F.F. Year, to come 'Early Bronze Age timber graves and coffin burials on the Yorkshire Wolds', *Yorks Arch J 42*

Phillips C.W. 1936 'A re-examination of the Therfield Heath long barrow, Royston, Herts', *Proc Prehist Soc* 1, 101-8

Philpott R. 1991 'Burial practices in Roman Britain', *BAR 219*

Price J. et al 1997 'The archaeology of the St Neots to Duxford gas pipeline' *1994 BAR 255*

Rhatz P., Dickinson T. and Watts L. (eds) 1980 'Anglo-Saxon Cemeteries' *1979 BAR 82*

Reece R. 1977 *Burial in the Roman world* CBA Research Report 22

Smith J.C. et al 1997 *Excavations along the route of the Dorchester by-pass, Dorset, 1986-8,* Salisbury

Speake G. 1989 *A Saxon bed burial on Swallowcliffe Down,* HBMC

Stead I.M. 1965 *The La Tène cultures of eastern Yorkshire,* Yorks Philosophical Soc.

Stead I.M. 1991 *Iron Age cemeteries in East Yorkshire,* British Museum Press

Stead I.M. and Rigby V. 1986 *Baldock: the excavation of a Roman and pre-Roman settlement, 1968-72,* Britannia mono 7.

Stead M. and Rigby V. 1989 *Verulamium: the King Harry Lane site,* English Heritage

Taylor A. and P.J. Woodward 1981 'Excavations at Roxton, Beds, 1972-4; The Post Bronze Age Settlement', *Beds Archaeol J* 16

Taylor A. and P.J. Woodward 1985 'A Bronze Age barrow cemetery at Roxton, Beds', *Archaeol J 142,*

Taylor A. 1993 'A Roman lead coffin with pipe clay figurines from Arrington, Cambs', *Britannia 24*

Taylor A. 1997 'A Roman child burial with animal figurines and pottery from Godmanchester, Cambs', *Britannia 28*

Taylor A., Hines J. and Duhig C. 1998 'An Anglo-Saxon cemetery at Oakington, Cambridgeshire', *Proc Cambridge Antiquarian Soc 86*

Timby J.R. 1996 *The Anglo-Saxon cemetery at Empingham II, Rutland* Oxbow Mono 70

Toynbee J.M.C. 1971 *Death and burial in the Roman world,* Thames and Hudson

Wait G.A. 1985 'Ritual and religion in Iron Age Britain' *BAR 149*

Whimster R.P. 1981 'Burial practices in Iron Age Britain: a discussion and gazetteer of the evidence 700 BC-AD 43' *BAR 90*

Williams H. 1997 'Reuse of prehistoric and Roman monuments', *Medieval Arch 41*

Woodward A.B. and Woodward P.J. 1996 'The topography of some barrow cemeteries in Bronze Age Wessex', *Proc Prehist Soc 62*, 275-291

# Index

Page numbers in **bold** denote illustrations